Steven Pfau

Say Nephew

On Boyhood, Unclehood, and Queer Mentorship

Say Nephew

This is a work of nonfiction. However, some names and identifying details of individuals have been changed to protect their privacy, correspondence has been shortened for clarity, and dialogue has been reconstructed from memory.

ISBN: 978-1-64622-291-9

Library of Congress Control Number: 2026930391

Jacket design by Victoria Maxfield
Book design by tracy danes

Catapult
New York, NY
books.catapult.co

Printed in the United States of America

1 3 5 7 9 10 8 6 4 2

For Bruce

Contents

Say Nephew

Nephew

"Nephew, stand still."

The boy looks ready for the rodeo in his fresh white T-shirt, pale blue jeans, and chestnut-brown cowboy boots. He poses with one foot before the other, preparing to strut forward, and rests an elbow on a folding table to balance himself in these unfamiliar heels. His uncle sits in the background, in a nearly identical outfit, but with only socks on his feet, as if he's bestowed his own beloved boots to his nephew, who in fact found this miniature pair among his uncle's antique collection. The nephew turns his head to show off his dapper new hairdo, side-parted and slicked with pomade, and smirks at the camera. He can't see the way his uncle grins and rests a hand on the boy's sleeve—not an effort to rein him in but a gesture of pride, a stamp of approval: *like uncle, like nephew*. Once his father clicks the shutter, the boy strips down to his briefs, ties that T-shirt around his neck as a cape or a kerchief, leaps from his uncle's patio, and flies around the house, playing a cross between Superman and the Lone Ranger, wearing nothing else but those boots. As he watches the grown-ups watch this parade, he catches between their laughter a remark from father to uncle: "I blame you for this."

—

Everybody has a gay uncle. So say many acquaintances when they hear I want to write a book about my own gay uncle. Of course, not every parent has a brother (Bruce was my father's eldest sibling), let alone a gay one (he came out as a teenager, his partner Will was already in the picture when I was an infant), and not every uncle is close enough in age or physical proximity (we were born fifty-three years apart, he and Will lived a hundred miles away from my hometown) to spend substantive time with his nephew (around his birthday every August, we would visit his and Will's home in East Haddam, Connecticut), and not every nephew's parents are open-minded enough to permit their son to bond with his gay uncle (nobody bothered to explain who Will was or why Bruce lived with him or what made the two of them "different," they were always just *there*), and not every gay uncle even likes children (he did) or wants children to like him (he did), and not every gay uncle lets his young nephew wander freely through his home (nothing was off-limits) and unmistakably signals his gayness in his décor (images of men's bodies displayed on the walls, in books under the coffee table, in magazines by the toilet), and not every gay uncle is ready or willing to help when this boy discovers his fondness for other boys (I was fourteen, he didn't hesitate).

What these acquaintances mean, I gather, is that everybody seems to know the cultural trope of the gay uncle. He's even been reduced to a trendy portmanteau, *guncle,* in which I can't unhear the word *gunk,* but perhaps that's the point: there's something undeniably cloying about the common picture-book depiction of the uncle as a benign, cardiganed Mister Rogers type, yet also something mucky about the uncle's deviation from the norms of the nuclear family (consider, for example, the noxious green fumes that erupt wherever Uncle Scar sashays on his limp-wristed paws in *The Lion King*). The gay uncle has become practically a cliché, the butt of a joke, which might be why my father has always trusted the punch line will land whenever he tells the story behind that picture of his brother and son, as if it were his way of saying, "That's when we knew."

But the boy in that photograph doesn't know a thing. At five years old, he doesn't know what his father means by "this" or why his uncle should be blamed for it. He doesn't know who decided he should dress up as Bruce's little doppelgänger, doesn't know if he's being molded in his uncle's image or deliberately mirroring his uncle. He senses beneath all the playful teasing a deeper worry that his uncle's influence will eclipse his father's, that he'll grow up to be not a respectable, decorous son but a wilder and more wayward thing: a nephew, specifically Bruce's nephew, whatever that means.

—

"Forget the Name of the Father," writes Eve Kosofsky Sedgwick in her 1990 essay "Tales of the Avunculate." "Think about your uncles and aunts." Sedgwick is referring to Jacques Lacan's concept of the patriarch as a representative of law and order—a symbolic figure at the heart of the Oedipus complex. Yet for queer writers like Oscar Wilde, parentage can be a less meaningful subject than the unorthodox authority of figures like Lady Bracknell in *The Importance of Being Earnest*. As Sedgwick notes, *aunt* and *auntie* were slang for sexual inverts in Wilde's days, while *uncle* was slang for an older and more financially secure "male protector" in an intimate relationship. Since then, *uncle* has become "common, in gradations from the literal, as a metonym for the whole range of older men who might form a relation to a younger man (as patron, friend, literal uncle, godfather, adoptive father, sugar daddy) offering a degree of initiation into gay cultures and identities—like the older man whom a friend of mine, my age, always refers to warmly as his fairy godmother."

Why should the uncle be the family member most closely associated with queer men's tutelage? Perhaps because the uncle is always already a little queer: it's not abnormal for him to be unmarried and childless, and his relation to younger generations tends to be more oblique and versatile than a parent's. Sedgwick shares this slantwise view of the uncle, whose unique position in a family tree often allows him "to have the office of representing nonconforming or nonreproductive sexualities to children. We are many, the queer women and men whose first sense of the possibility of alternative life trajectories came to us from our uncles and aunts."

Now it's easy to take for granted that I'm one of many queer boys whose life trajectories came to them from their uncles, that Bruce is just one link in a long lineage of queer uncles, literal and figurative, who've taken lost boys under their wings. So does it follow that *nephew* could be a catchall term for the offices I've held for my queer elders and ancestors, perhaps even a metonym for the whole range of younger men who might form a relation to an older man (as protégé, friend, literal nephew, godson, adoptive son, sugar baby) and receive a degree of initiation into gay cultures and identities? If so, how should a nephew be? I don't have a Grand Unified Theory on the subject, but I can try to answer that question by examining a few more snapshots of that boy who once defined his inchoate gayness in relation to his uncle, who didn't yet appreciate the rare gift of having such a fairy godmother in his own family, who didn't know just how many possible paths to queer adulthood exist within and beyond the maps he had received from Bruce. I want to follow him down those paths, to study him the way he will later want to study his uncle, to introduce you to that boy as if he were my very own nephew.

—

Where to begin? Well, this nephew doesn't have much of a Coming Out Story. One morning I began to ask Bruce, "When did you tell your parents . . ." and he immediately caught my drift. (Then again, I wasn't fooling anyone at the time.) Instead, the Gay Nephew Origin Story I prefer to tell begins a year earlier:

Bruce and I were celebrating his sixty-sixth birthday

at Lee's Lunch, a greasy-spoon diner in a strip mall a few miles from his home. He'd just begun weight lifting, and to show off his newly voracious appetite, he ordered a second plate of biscuits and gravy. When the waitress asked if she'd heard him correctly, Bruce leaned forward on the red gingham tablecloth and pushed back his shoulders to flaunt the pecs bulging through his T-shirt; stroked his thick Freddie Mercury mustache; raised an arm in a benedictory fashion, jangling his silver bracelets to make sure all could see and hear him; and hammed up his Southern drawl and fire-and-brimstone flair as he intoned, “It takes a lot of gas to run this Cadillac!” The dish arrived at once, and Bruce dug in, glowing with triumph. Across the table, my slack jaw hung open. I had no idea what Bruce's turn of phrase meant or where it came from. (Why a Cadillac and not, I don't know, his and Will's old pickup truck?) But I was spellbound by the way he summoned these words, recited them in perfectly iambic rhythm, inflected them with so many tones at once—both flirtatious and menacing, both bombastic and self-mocking. At thirteen, I was so self-conscious about my changing body that I'd almost gone mute; I seldom raised my voice above a murmur, and I certainly couldn't imagine holding court for the mere pleasure of the performance. After lunch, I wrote my uncle's words on a yellow legal pad, in case I should ever decide to put them in a book, and I listened to Bruce riff on this incantation throughout the day, whether pouring an extra glug of vodka in his Pepsi or excusing himself for a longer-than-usual afternoon nap in the bathtub: “It takes a lot of gas!” *Someday*, I thought, *I'll be that Cadillac.*

"So that was your ring-of-keys moment," a friend recently told me over brunch at the Cadillac Café in Portland, Oregon. Of course, I couldn't resist ordering the biscuits and gravy, which prompted me to tell my friend about Bruce, which then prompted her to recall the famous scene from Alison Bechdel's *Fun Home* in which young Alison witnesses a "truck-driving bulldyke" at a luncheonette: "like a traveler in a foreign country who runs into someone from home—someone they've never spoken to but know by sight—I recognized her with a surge of joy." My friend was onto something, but it's an imperfect analogy, since my uncle and I were never really strangers to each other, and recognizing our shared queerness was a more gradual process. To explain my own luncheonette anecdote, I wanted to say something about the relationship between desire and language, the way a single utterance can open a door to another, more colorful, more enchanting version of reality. I wanted to cite Wayne Koestenbaum: "Sexuality, whether homo or hetero, does not arrive only once, in that moment of revelation and proclamation that we call 'coming out.' Our body is always coming out. Every time is the first time. Every performance is a debut." But what did I have to show for years and years of thinking about this formative scene? My friend watched me expectantly as the waiter approached and asked if I needed anything else. "No, thank you."

—

A fan of reading by candlelight in the tub, Bruce once stayed up so late with Hermione Lee's *Edith Wharton* that he fell asleep and dropped all nine hundred pages in the bathwater, startling himself awake. As a child, I failed to understand my uncle's zeal for life studies, and I politely declined whenever Bruce tried to foist on me a weighty volume on Janet Flanner or Katherine Anne Porter. Whenever I asked why a boy like me would want to read a tome of minutiae about these dead people I hardly knew, Bruce's answer never changed: "The gossip!"

He wasn't wrong: the more biographies I read, the more I appreciate the art of the dishy anecdote. But for someone so fond of gossip, Bruce never wrote down much of his own, only sprinkling it in certain letters. (*Was I at the Piers? O yes. Did I cruise porno shops, porno theaters. O yes. Did I know 1970s Times Square? Yep. OK. Used to go at midnight to watch peepshows, the people. Mugged twice, etc. And yes, I gave good audience at the GAYITY theater . . .*) My father once gifted his elder brother a ream of blank paper and a book titled *How to Sell Your Memoir*, and Bruce threw up his hands. "I can't write because I don't know who I'm talking to," he told me. "I wonder: Why would you want to know *that*?" He much preferred extemporaneous storytelling, and in his nephew, his most eager listener, Bruce found his amanuensis.

Take notes! he wrote in my thirteenth birthday card. *You'll be glad you did!* At every subsequent family meal, he would pause in the middle of a tall tale, turn to me, widen his eyes like a stern headmaster, and swivel his wrist in the air with an imaginary pencil, asking sometimes aloud but more often tacitly, "You're writing this down, aren't you?"

I tried to log as many notes as possible in my journals,

but they never added up to a unified narrative, and Bruce shied away from my attempts to sort out how he got from there to here. My parents have asked what secrets I'm keeping in those journals and whether I ever recorded a proper interview with my uncle, but to me it always seemed that my whole relationship with Bruce was an interview.

—

Bruce could be less forthcoming than he let on, selective about the adventures he chose to share from his life, and protective of his own manner of narration. If anyone ever dared to tell their own version in his presence, even a verbatim rendition, he would likely rejoin, "It's not true! But it's a good story!"

He especially liked to recall his time in boot camp during the Vietnam War. He was based somewhere near Seattle, and on weekends his Marlboro Man boyfriend would pull up on his Harley and whisk Bruce away to the city. Years later, my uncle Will relayed one of his first conversations with this Marlboro Man, which elicited a sigh and a long, dramatic pause. "Well," the boyfriend said, "it was really more like a Vespa . . ."

—

"It's hard being employee of the month," Bruce said. "You have to sing, dance, light up the room—it's *terrible*!"

I was tagging along to his part-time job as a minder at an adult day care, where Bruce led seated aerobic workouts and karaoke sing-alongs of Rodgers and Hart standards. He was older than many of the clients but too restless to retire, and he looked right at home. One woman gaped at Bruce, stunned silent.

"You looking at me?" he asked, extending his palm to her. "That'll be a dollar." He gave her a roguish low-five, and she blushed and beamed.

I decided to try out this line a few days later, hoping to elicit a similar response from a handsome boy I spotted on the sidelines of my high school's soccer field. "You looking at me?" I asked, straining to arch my eyebrows seductively and lower my voice to Bruce's sultry register. "That'll be a dollar."

The handsome stranger turned away from the game and scowled. "What the fuck is your problem?"

I shrugged off my failed come-on as a prank and ran away. Some kinds of charisma can't be learned by imitation.

—

"Light blue, right pocket!" That's all Bruce said when I first asked about hanky-flagging; it was hard to tell from his delivery whether he intended this response as a command or a confession. Years later, this is how I sometimes wear a bandanna in the back of my jeans, even though no one my age seems to pay much attention to these codes anymore: most of us initiate our sexual encounters via some kind of textual medium, and "what are you into" tends to be among the first questions on the table. Nonetheless, I still cathect this outdated piece of fabric and what it signals. Did Bruce foresee that his pubescent nephew would someday relish sucking cock? Was this inchoate predilection written on my face? Was he projecting his own desires onto me? Have I cultivated my tastes based on my uncle's unwittingly prescient remark? Or has my wishful thinking made too much of this coincidence?

I never caught Bruce flagging, but I recently discovered a gray bandanna in his sock drawer. I then raided his closet for whatever bondage gear would confirm his adherence to the code, but I found only a bag of dildos, unused for so long that they had melted and fused into a shapeless mass of silicone.

—

Whenever he and Will prepared to drive somewhere, Bruce would wait by the car and start reading. Ten pages later, Bruce would shout, "*Will!*" to which his copilot would holler back, "*I'm putting on my boots.*" This exchange would repeat itself for ten or fifteen minutes until, finally, they managed to get on the road. A sensitive artist at heart but a rough woodsman in his vesture, Will has always worn high lace-up Caterpillar boots, so his excuse for dawdling was usually the literal truth, but the phrase *putting on my boots* ended up becoming a figurative shorthand for his many digressions and diversions. During one particularly meandering drive—we pulled over in a graveyard so he could discreetly relieve himself in the grass, stopped at the supermarket for a case of Steel Reserve and three varieties of blue cheese, and took a "scenic route" through woods too dark to see after the early winter sunset—Will confessed, "I seem not to share most people's sense of time or navigation." Whenever my internal clock seems off-kilter, maybe even a little queer, I think of Will and tell myself that I'm just putting on my boots.

Cowboy boots were Bruce's go-to footwear, and they suited his Burt Reynolds–esque persona. He collected them in assorted styles and colors and wore them on every occasion, claiming they were incredibly comfortable, though he quickly switched to chunky New Balance sneakers as soon as he developed arthritis. When I was fourteen, he handed down to me his own caramel-brown boots, which were two sizes too big; even in the thickest socks, my feet rattled inside them. But I insisted on wearing them every day to school, where the *clip-clop* sound of the heels turned heads in every classroom I passed. I swayed my hips, trying to exude Bruce's magnetic swagger, but the more I played up the machismo, the more awkwardly I swayed and wobbled—less John Wayne than Nathan Lane's charade of John Wayne in *The Birdcage*. I wanted to believe my nebulous boyhood could be, as theorist Gayle Salamon says, "a realm characterized by a kind of magical thinking to which Merleau-Ponty refers when he describes the ultra-thing," to believe that a pair of cowboy boots could "have the power to confer gender." Instead, these boots only widened the gap between who I was and who I aspired to be. No matter how hard I tried to impress every boy who crossed my path, most of them looked either confused or indifferent; though they never said so, I could tell they knew I was too soft and swishy to be a real cowboy.

I didn't wear these boots for another dozen years, until a recent rodeo-themed queer dance party in Moscow, Idaho. Having spent most of my life in the Northeast, I felt even more cognitive dissonance trying on cowboy drag in a region where Western wear isn't necessarily a kitschy statement. After seeing a video of me strutting to Lil Nas X and Orville Peck, Will offered to mail me some more of Bruce's cowboy boots; I assured him I wouldn't know what to do with them, but my uncle insisted. When it arrived at my apartment door, I heaved the surprisingly weighty box onto my kitchen table, and I heard something shatter when I put it down. Inside was a set of broken ceramic statuettes, formerly boot-shaped knickknacks. I keep the fragments among my altar of avuncular mementos, relics of my nephewhood.

—

"Have you memorized *All About Eve* yet?" Bruce asked, apropos of nothing. "It's on your final exam!" Of all the classic texts in the canon of camp cinema, why did he assign this one to his adolescent nephew? Having since watched the film at least a dozen times, I've been known to announce "fasten your seatbelts" to a gaggle of friends as we march to Nowhere or The Boiler Room, but I'm still not sure what other wisdom my uncle aimed to impart through this required viewing. Perhaps he intended this fable of intergenerational rivalry and betrayal as a cautionary tale, but that seems unlikely, since Bruce and I were never terribly competitive, and he seemed too confident in his own star power to worry about being upstaged. Bruce never explained what else was on my "final exam," and despite the lengthy syllabus of art and pop culture he compiled for me, he showed little interest in developing any kind of encyclopedic connoisseurship; rather, he seemed to revel in playing up his own ignorance and forgetfulness. Whenever he struggled to recall Glenn Close's name—surprisingly often—Bruce would ask me, "Meryl Streep and *who else*?" Or he might punctuate a tale of his derring-do by misquoting, with his best Ethel Merman impression, one of Rose's numbers from *Gypsy*: "I've *lived,* Mrs. Goldstein!" Perhaps he was indirectly preparing me for my own dotage, but I like to believe he was demonstrating how to transcend the anxieties of one-upmanship by maintaining an air of indifference to exhaustive expertise.

—

Yet for a time I desperately wanted to embody the knowingness I associated with Bruce. One day, strolling home from school in those cowboy boots—and keeping my head down, lest my heels trip on the sidewalk—I heard a driver pull up beside me and roll down the window to ask, "Those boots aren't made for walking, are they?" I recognized the voice, squinted at his tightly curled hair and owllike features, and saw it was an older boy I'd noticed serenading crowds of starstruck girls at the piano in the choir room. "Want a ride?" Why not?

I watched his long, agile fingers tap the steering wheel and imagined them guiding my hands upon a keyboard as I practiced scales beside him. He kept turning away from the road to smile at me, and I wasn't sure how he knew where to go or what he saw in me, a lowly ninth grader. During our first wordless minutes together, I listened to the woman belting on the stereo and tried to break the silence by showing off the musical chops I'd gleaned from my worldly uncle: "Is this Ethel Merman?" My driver laughed and told me the singer was Idina Menzel, praising her voice so effusively that I didn't want to butt in when he sped past my street. As he described all the songs I ought to hear and shows I ought to see, I dreamt that we'd meet again at his home, probably a mansion equipped with surround-sound speakers, and we'd listen all day to his favorite CDs, and his seven or eight siblings would beg me to stay for dinner and save me the seat of honor, and my table manners would be impeccable, and his mother would hug me and thank me for bringing flowers, and his father would shake my hand and welcome me to come back anytime, and then maybe after dinner my new friend—well, now he parked near the woods behind my elementary school, unzipped his fly, and reached for my hair with those graceful fingers. I asked what he was doing, his face blanched and hand lurched as if I'd woken him from his own dream, and he instantly started the engine and chauffeured me home.

"I thought you might be more experienced," he said, "considering . . . *you know*." He nodded at my boots as I stepped out of the car and dashed up the driveway. I didn't turn around when I heard him roll down the window again and stage-whisper, "What's with that hanky in your pocket?"

Why did I think those boots and that bandanna would protect me, or at least help me flag down fellow wanderers who were just as disoriented as I was? I began to hide out in section HQ76 of the library, gradually filling the gaps in the imperfect education my uncle had given me. As for that boy in the car, I didn't speak to him again until my early twenties, when I saw him on a subway platform and asked if he remembered picking me up several years earlier—what was on his mind that afternoon, I wondered? He shrugged and said, "You were so hard to read." I wanted to bark back, *"Then you should have tried harder,"* but figured I couldn't accuse him of interpretive laziness when I hardly knew how to make myself more legible.

—

One of my college roommates was a nephew of the notorious queer theorist Lee Edelman. An opponent of "the Child in whose name we're collectively terrorized," Edelman isn't a hater of children per se but an objector to neoliberal sloganeers who insist "the children are our future." Yet I'm still tickled by the discrepancy between Edelman's critiques of reproductive futurism and my roommate's warm and fuzzy tales of Uncle Lee. I once emailed Professor Edelman to solicit his thoughts on the subject of uncles. I wanted to know if there might be something uniquely liberatory about the queer uncle's relation to his younger kin, something that might exempt the uncle from the heteronormative logic of compulsory reproductive biopolitics. Edelman replied that he could "imagine no more fully satisfying familial relation than the avuncular" but admitted he wasn't sure how to help me. Maybe some paradoxes of queer unclehood can be untangled solely in practice, not in theory.

I think of this exchange whenever Will remarks on Bruce's paternal instincts with me, since our relationship was the closest my uncle came to child-rearing. Will should know, since he has a son of his own, plus a grandson around my age. Upon first meeting these two "cousins"—neither of them queer, as far as I could tell—I speculated how my relationship with Bruce would have differed if he had been my stepfather, or even my birth father. How would our expectations have changed? Would our responsibilities to each other have been restricted by the pressures of the nuclear family structure? Would I have elected Bruce as my honorary "uncle" if we weren't already offshoots of the same tree? Does anyone choose to become an uncle, or is he typically called upon to assume that role? I know these questions are no more answerable than the one I posed to Edelman, but I imagine Uncle Lee might have been mulling over similar dilemmas when he wrote "a special word of thanks" to his nieces and nephews at the start of *No Future*: "However much they might wish it otherwise, they are part of this book as well."

—

On my uncles' mantel, I saw a new photograph of a tall, broad-shouldered model wearing a red ball gown and matching stilettos, twirling a parasol. Their friend Julia had taken this self-portrait to document "her transition," which Bruce explained with overemphatic air quotes, in case I didn't catch his drift or understand why he kept fumbling her name and pronouns.

"At first I didn't get it," Bruce said, kicking up his feet on the coffee table, "but then I realized: We *all* perform! We *all* play a role!"

He grinned, widening his eyes like a sophomore who's just discovered Judith Butler, and I—who had been such a wide-eyed sophomore just a couple of years earlier—couldn't tell whether I was supposed to believe that my uncle had never before reached this epiphany. How had Bruce spent most of his adult life wearing a uniform of leather jackets, Levi's, and cowboy boots and *not* considered himself playing a role, and what made him think his performances were any more authentic than Julia's?

I didn't tell this story to my then partner, who was beginning her own transition to womanhood. Our relationship was falling apart largely because of my failures to offer the support she needed, and to her these failures seemed to be symptoms of an unhealthy investment in reactionary ideals of gay masculinity. "Just look at your relationship with Bruce," she said, citing my attachment to my uncle as undeniable evidence that I wanted "a real man," whereas it seemed to me that we had grown apart and fallen out of love for more situationally specific reasons, not because of my general desires. But I still wonder if she was right about what I actually wanted. Was I, like Bruce and many other gay cis men I've known, simply refusing to confront the unconscious transmisogyny

I had internalized, or was I just a shitty boyfriend? Probably both.

I continue to ruminate on these questions and guiltily prefer to imagine the partner I was back then, more than a decade ago, as a different person—one whose errors I glossed over when my current partner, Tom, asked about the ways I've individuated myself from my uncle Bruce. I've tried to resist the pressure to compare myself with other gay men and to fit their mold, and yet, soon after I joined a gym and started building some muscle in my biceps, I bristled when Tom joked that I was "getting so masc." I was embarrassed to admit that I coveted a more conventionally "masc" body, fearing that this aspiration must be rooted in the ugly ideologies of toxic masculinity, though Tom assured me that truly toxic men probably don't dwell on such anxieties. When I later bleached my hair, motivated more by boredom than by any urge to make a statement, Tom teasingly called me a twink, and I once again prickled. I'm not smooth-skinned enough to join this tribe of clean-cut ectomorphs, and I remain too scarred by the bullies of my chubby childhood to enjoy an uncomplicated relationship with my leaner adult body, though I conceded that the ephebic Troye Sivan look was sort of what I was going for.

I still haven't fully accepted my not-quite-boyish, not-quite-butch gender, nor do I know if someone would refer to me or my "type" as "a real man," whatever that means. But at least I've grown to appreciate the label *otter*, which suits Tom and me both, and which I find oddly gratifying, since the term doesn't convey such narrow cultural expectations, and it seems to signal a more malleable and perhaps less easily cancelable identity. It also helps that nonhuman otters are pretty cute, and I'd love to be known as "slick, quick, amphibious, dexterous, [and] capable," as Maggie Nelson characterizes otters in *The Argonauts*. I often wonder what Bruce would say about the matching pink trucker hats my lutrine partner and I purchased as souvenirs at the Slippery Otter Pub in West Yellowstone, Montana. They remind me that our bond endures even when we elude each other, even when I try to let myself off the hook.

—

I was getting an HIV test at a New York City clinic named after AIDS activist Michael Callen and poet Audre Lorde—not my first test, but I was still green enough to feel nervous when the nurse asked a series of increasingly intimate questions, including one about how I identify my gender and sexuality. "Cis man," I said, "and either gay or queer."

The nurse frowned and asked, "Which is it?"

Did I really have to choose, especially here, in a center that called itself "the global leader in LGBTQ healthcare"? Why couldn't I be both? *Queer* seemed to describe more accurately my political and intellectual commitments at the time ("not gay as in happy but queer as in *fuck you*," as the millennial saying goes), but I was growing tired of vapid internet rhetoric about queering *this* and the inherent queerness of *that*, and I feared the term would misrepresent both my sexual track record (mostly but not exclusively other cis men) and the cultural history

Bruce had transmitted to me (very gay). Would *queer* even signify anything in my case? Would calling myself gay disqualify me from entering the radical queer socialist utopia of my dreams? Would Bruce have cared about this distinction? Why did I care whether he would have cared? I caught the nurse staring at my freshly trimmed quiff haircut, my floral Zara shirt, the Keith Haring–esque design on my tote bag. "Okay, gay."

—

I never met my mother's beloved younger brother, Stephen, who was only nine when he died of a sudden bout of pneumonia. I'm glad she decided, upon naming me two decades later, to change the spelling to Steven, subtly distinguishing her son from the ghost of his eponymous uncle. But Stephen's story still haunted me throughout my asthmatic childhood, when I dreaded my ninth birthday as if it were my preordained expiration date. It haunted me again when I, at sixteen, incurred my first spontaneous pneumothorax. At the time I didn't know how common this affliction is in teenage boys, so when the doctor explained that my lungs had burst open and collapsed for no apparent reason, I assumed this would be the end of me. And Stephen's story haunted me once more in 2018, when my mom showed me a new poem she'd written, titled "A Letter to My Son in Brooklyn." The speaker describes three moments when she feels powerless to protect her son: his coming-out at age fourteen; the first lung surgery he underwent at sixteen, for which he was sedated but conscious, while she sat and watched beside the operating table; and his imminent move from New York to Idaho, now that he's twenty-seven. "Would it make any difference," the poem ends, "if I said— / *My darling boy—Be careful.*"

I still haven't answered this "letter." What difference *would* it make if my mom told me, or if the speaker told her son, to be careful? What is a boy supposed to do with that warning? I'm no daredevil, so I can't do much apart from avoiding cigarettes to protect my lungs, and I can't do much to hide my queerness or prevent whatever homophobic violence I might face. The poem portrays me as little more than a source of parental anxiety, but I know my mom's concerns aren't entirely about me. I often wonder if my existence is predicated on compensating for the loss of her brother, if my uncles will steer my fate more than my parents ever will. Would Stephen have become a queer man if he had lived to reach sexual maturity, and would he have come to mean as much to me as Bruce has? I'll never know, but I still include Stephen among my pantheon of gay uncles, the one who never grew up.

—

But maybe every gay uncle is someone who can't or won't grow up—or someone who, as queer theorist Kathryn Bond Stockton would say, grows sideways. "I'm the oldest teenager I know," Bruce used to say. And at my college graduation, when I explained the spring-semester tradition of "senior scramble" (a last-ditch effort to hook up with every classmate you've ever had a crush on), Bruce just rolled his eyes and said, "Oh, *please*—you have the whole rest of your life for *that*." But no one, not even Bruce, is immune to the fear of death. While riding the Fire Island Ferry to a circuit party in 1977, on the eve of his thirty-ninth birthday, he finally admitted to himself, "This isn't a joke anymore"—*this* being his own mortality.

To inoculate myself against the sudden blow of such a midlife crisis, I sought a similar reckoning on my first trip to Fire Island. My friend and I, both twenty-two, had made no concrete itinerary, no plans to stay the night; we just showed up one afternoon at the Pines, ready to be graduated from innocence to experience. We reached the entrance of a mostly empty bar and spotted two weary, half-dressed drag queens sharing a cigarette among either the preparations for tonight's party or the wreckage of the last. I grabbed my friend's shoulder—*behold*, I thought, *our new uncles!* The queens approached the door and gave us a withering glare before gliding away, chuckling over some private joke we were still too young to get.

—

Opinionated and fond of attention, Bruce seemed like the kind of person who would love social media, but he never learned how to use the internet. Will often showed my Facebook posts to his husband, who would "comment" by printing the images and snail-mailing them with handwritten annotations—for example, these captions he suggested for a candid snapshot that caught his twenty-two-year-old nephew unintentionally smoldering at the camera:

A few remarks that caused S. Pfau to glower . . .

(1) Listen, dude, all I did was ask you to dance . . .

(2) But I only said your pants fit nice . . .

(3) Hey, I knew your uncle when he lived in the Village. You do that stuff too?

(4) You come here often?

I later found an old photograph of Bruce making the exact same face, though probably not unintentionally. I could imagine him fielding all the same remarks and, unlike me, never getting too flustered to come up with a winning comeback.

—

Then again, when he was twentyish, with a haircut and profile alarmingly similar to mine, Bruce seemed to share my penchant for avoiding eye contact—though in my earliest memories, Bruce often seemed to be watching me as intently as I watched him, each of us stealing slantwise glances to see who would be next to get in trouble.

Whenever I fail to face the person directly in front of me, I fear my evasive streak will get the best of me, but I also wonder if I'm not the only boy who often half-expects to catch his uncle winking back, egging on his nephew from the periphery.

—

For years I've continued accumulating notes in a file named uncle.doc, logging every fictional and historical uncle I encounter in my cultural consumption. I'm often tempted to share the avuncular trivia I've collected—for example, some of the uncle- and nephew-related entries in Stith Thompson's *Motif-Index of Folk-Literature*:

> P293. Uncle.
> P297. Nephew.
> N738. Accidental meeting of nephew and uncle.
> N738.1. Uncle and nephew unwittingly about to kill one another.
> S71. Cruel uncle.
> S71.1. Cruel uncle poisons nephew (king).
> S74. Cruel nephew.
> S74.1. Nephew (niece) kills uncle.
> X905.4.1. Boy to deceive his uncle: induces uncle to climb tree before deception begins: this is the deception.
> Q41.1 Ogre appeased by being called uncle (aunt, etc.).
> V232.1.1. Angels appear and help boy prince slay treacherous uncle.

But I don't want to know what I'll indirectly reveal about myself through what I've included in or omitted from my dossier. My acquisitive obsession remains a mostly private source of comfort; I've convinced myself that the more uncles I observe, the better I'll understand both the idea of the uncle and my uncles themselves, though I know amassing this evidence in a vacuum won't help me solve all the mysteries of nephewing, nor will it necessarily expand my definition of avuncularity beyond whatever reminds me of Bruce. Still, I'm pleased to have established a strong enough personal brand that my friends routinely text me whenever they spot another uncle in the wild. I've come to identify three subspecies of uncles and uncle-adjacent figures, whether explicitly queer or subtly queer-coded, represented in mainstream media:

First, there's the fabulous, garrulous trickster and troublemaker, à la Auntie Mame (yes, technically an aunt, but still the patron saint of many gay uncles I know), who teaches the children to *live*, for "life is a banquet, and most poor suckers are starving to death." This uncle risks being either disciplined or disowned once those children decide they must become decent, proper adults, as Shakespeare's Falstaff is ultimately forsaken by Prince Hal, or as the Falstaffian Bob Pigeon is rebuffed by arriviste Scott Favor at the end of *My Own Private Idaho*: "I don't know you, old man. Please leave me alone."

Then there's the charismatic villain, in the vein of Uncle Charlie from Hitchcock's *Shadow of a Doubt*, whose unmentionable degeneracy finds expression in lying and cheating and stealing and killing, and who appears to the youth as both an ungovernable tyrant and a flimsy scarecrow. As sociologists Ariel Dorfman and Armand Mattelart write in an essay on Donald Duck's Uncle Scrooge, Disney tends to rely on uncles rather than fathers to teach children about "envy, ruthlessness, cruelty, terror, blackmail, [and] exploitation of the weak," since the uncle's authority is relatively arbitrary; unlike fathers and sons, uncles and nephews are bound by "a contractual relationship masquerading as a natural relationship, a tyranny which does not even assume the responsibility of breeding. And one cannot rebel against it in the name of nature; one cannot say to an uncle 'you are a bad father.'"

Finally, there's the reclusive bachelor, isolated by misanthropy or bigotry or illness or grief or poverty, whose sad and lonely life serves as a cautionary tale for ambitious young men, who couldn't *possibly* want to end up a depressive Proust scholar like Uncle Frank in *Little Miss Sunshine* or a bitter old queen like Proust's Baron de Charlus—or, for that matter, a frail and sickly hermit like Proust himself.

Yet in most of these stories, the uncle seems to be a minor, forgettable character; we might see him bring the nephew to the threshold of adulthood, but we seldom see the lasting impression he'll leave once the nephew is on his own. Who does the nephew become once his uncle is no longer right behind him, and what stories can the nephew tell only after his uncle is gone?

My uncle sent me a copy of Terry Andrews's novel *The Story of Harold* with a letter tucked inside the yellowed, crumbling pages.

11 Feb 2017

Dear Steven—

I'm fascinated that you might write about The Story of Harold's author . . .

Years ago, I told some friend about my interest in Harold. The friend claimed to know the author . . . Well . . . Some time later I received a call at work. "I understand you're a reader," caller said. "Who's this?" "I wrote The Story of Harold." I was stunned! Gave him my number so we could talk more easily. Never called. End of story.

Was discussing Harold with another friend who worked in publishing. Seems his office had unsold copies of Harold. He sent me a box of paperback copies. Probably 12. Over the years I distributed copies to friends. (Will says I gave it to him before he moved in with me—probably over 25 years ago.) I think I was using it as a kind of Rorschach test!

Incidentally, Will was more recently able to find a copy on Amazon—and he found some info about the author on the internet. Until then I had thought the author might be Sendak . . . Wrong!

Real love,
Bruce

I remembered hearing a version of this story eight years earlier, back when I was preparing to move to New York and figure out how to become a writer, whatever that might mean. My uncle had moved to the city with the same vague ambition in the 1960s, taking a fifth-floor walk-up in Greenwich Village and a lowly copywriting job at McGraw-Hill. Based on their mutual friend's introduction, the writer who called himself Terry Andrews must have assumed my uncle was an influential editor at a literary publishing house, but he also must have meant "reader" in a more specific sense. Whoever was behind his pen name, Terry Andrews didn't end up reaching the audience he was looking for: soon after it was published by Holt, Rinehart in 1974, *The Story of Harold* went out of print.

I'll never forget the rueful smile on Bruce's face when he first told me this tale of "the one that got away," as if his missed connection with the author of *Harold* had dashed not just Terry Andrews's writing dreams but his own. I have no reason to believe that Bruce could have rescued *Harold* from publishing limbo if he had only called that number and helped out a fellow queer man with similar literary aspirations. But in my mind, Bruce's hesitation to follow through has become linked with his own writer's block—and with his resistance to my ongoing efforts to write a book about my uncle. Even though he once half-jokingly dubbed me his biographer, Bruce has repeatedly demurred whenever I've proposed recording an extended interview, so I've mostly given up and accepted that this project might never come to fruition. Instead, I've decided to take a stab at the next best thing and study the phantom author who eluded my uncle. Now I'm taking a night class on biographical writing and holding Bruce's last copy of *The Story of Harold*.

The novel's narrator, also named Terry Andrews, is the author of a successful children's book, also titled *The Story of Harold*. I can see why Bruce initially thought the ever-avuncular Maurice Sendak might be behind this project, since Andrews displays a similarly wry, macabre humor: even the dedication ("To my living friends—who will know who you are") reads like a cheeky note from beyond the grave. The plot unfolds through a series of diary entries in which Terry struggles to reconcile his respectable career with the lonely life of a closeted bisexual sadomasochist in downtown Manhattan. Terry occasionally spends his off-hours with a married surgeon who likes to be flogged and fisted and a pyromaniac who wants to be burned alive, but enduring and mutually satisfying connections elude him. By the time the novel begins, in October 1968, the tension between his public and private life has become too much to bear, and Terry has determined to end it all within six months. A book so morbid might sound like a slog, but the narrator's seductive voice—imagine Nabokov on poppers—keeps me reading.

Terry soon has "a curious experience" with his old friend Edith, who invites him to the Upper East Side to meet his "number-one fan." That would be her seven-year-old son, Bernard, "a lump of a little boy" who lurches "like a gob of underdone dough" and keeps his head lowered "like an animal overtamed." Edith explains that Bernard is struggling to cope with both her divorce from the boy's father and her recent engagement to Frank, a traveling businessman who tries in vain to win over his stepson-to-be with trips to the zoo and the Statue of Liberty. The only thing that makes Bernard happy is Terry's book *The Story of Harold*, a collection of modern fairy tales in which a twelve-inch-tall magician, the titular Harold, roams New York City and rescues his friends—humans, animals, toys, houseplants—from their everyday misfortunes. Edith asks if Terry would be willing to spend some time with her son: "Maybe just take a walk in the park [. . .] and just—oh I don't know. Do your thing. You must know how to deal with children." "In point of fact," Terry thinks, "I don't know how to deal with children. The terrible truth is—most I dislike. A lot bore me. The ones who don't bore me intimidate me. Because they still have that capacity, in the flesh, of the unrealized, the possible."

Nonetheless, Terry agrees to take a walk with Bernard,

steers him across Fifth Avenue, and finds them a bench to share in Central Park. In his “most uncley voice,” Terry improvises a new installment of his book, “Harold and the Crash-Proof Moth,” in which the hero assists a self-destructive lepidopteran who can’t stop colliding into walls. For the first time all day, Bernard looks alive, yet on the verge of dissolving “into a small chaos of flesh [. . .] drowning in everything—the world, his mother, psychoanalysis, his own persistent wretchedness—in everything he could not comprehend.” As Terry returns to Edith’s apartment building and prepares to say goodbye to Bernard, the boy admits that he dislikes his own name and asks, “What would Harold call me?” Terry guesses that Harold would call him Barney, and this answer pleases the boy. “Like a wound-up toy that was set to trudge, he stepped inside. And did not look around as the doors joined shut behind him.”

Reading this scene, imagining the sound of Terry’s “uncley voice,” I feel transported to Bruce’s porch, where he used to chip away at his young nephew’s shell with his own stories. Has my uncle seen me all along as the Barney to his Terry, his taciturn “lump of a little boy”? What uncertainties and insecurities did he recognize in my “small chaos of flesh” before I could even name them? I wonder what other parallels I might uncover in later chapters. Maybe if I can learn as much as possible about this mysterious novel that has occupied my uncle’s mind for decades, then maybe I can finally persuade Bruce to tell me the unexpurgated story of his own life.

A week after receiving the book, as I’m getting into

bed, I see a text from my uncle Will: "Bruce in hospital. It's serious. I really don't know what to do or say. Waiting for the docs to come out. If you are able to come up . . ."

In the morning I board a bus from Port Authority to Hartford, wearing one of Bruce's letterman jackets and carrying my half-finished copy of *Harold*. When I reach his room in the ICU, Bruce is unconscious and stuffed with tubes and wires. He's endured a "cardiac event," a doctor explains—an oddly festive euphemism for an aortic rupture. I offer to hold down the fort as Will steps outside to discuss the DNR with the nurses. Many years of working in a psychiatric ward have taught Will that even seemingly unresponsive patients can hear us, so he asks me to talk to Bruce—something, anything. But what can I say? I open my book and read to my uncle in the most nephewy voice I can muster.

—

Bruce made me want to be a reader. I probably first learned *how* to read thanks to a combination of *Sesame Street*, my preschool teachers, and my mother's shelves of poetry. But I didn't really appreciate reading until adolescence, around the time I started coming out, which happened to coincide with the time my uncle started assigning me a syllabus of more serious material, which I approached as if it were required for my gay education.

One year Bruce said he was about to send me something he'd received from his grandmother at my age, a gift that changed his life when he was growing up in Memphis. My mind danced with anticipation for this mysterious heirloom, but the long-awaited envelope contained no golden ticket. It was a *New Yorker* subscription. I could see how the high society chronicled in this magazine might have struck teenage Bruce as a cosmopolitan utopia, ready to greet a misfit Southern boy with open arms, and I could picture him scanning the pages for the passwords he would need to enter their doors. But for a boy in a Boston suburb where almost everyone's parents seemed to have fancy college degrees and white-collar jobs, "The Talk of the Town" didn't sound like a dispatch from a foreign land, and I sensed that even the cartoons didn't have much to teach me that I couldn't get from, say, watching *Garden State* or blasting Green Day's *American Idiot*. Still, I studied each issue as if it were an instruction manual, even though it mostly flew over my head.

Next year, Bruce sent me a set of J. D. Salinger's books. I recognized *The Catcher in the Rye* as one of those things teenage boys were supposed to love, but I didn't get Holden's sense of humor, so I turned to the story "Uncle Wiggily in Connecticut," hoping it might help me grasp my own slippery uncle in the Constitution State. At first the plot looked simple enough: a woman visits an old college classmate, and the two of them get drunk and reminisce while the host's daughter—the only character I could relate to—runs in and out of the house with her imaginary friend. But not much else seemed to happen; once again, I didn't get the point. I called up Bruce to ask what he thought the story could mean, and without hesitation, he exclaimed, "People change!" At first I thought he was being flippant, brushing off the lofty themes and motifs my teachers expected me to pick up on, but he sounded dead serious. I could hear Will in the background, complaining about a flood in the basement, cataloging the water damage they needed to fix, and growing audibly impatient as Bruce turned away from the phone to reply with a series of half-hearted *uh-huh*s and *mm-hm*s. I jumped when Bruce, suddenly alert, shouted into the receiver, "You hear that, Steve? Dialogue. *Ve-ri-si-mi-li-tude.*" He spat out the unfamiliar syllables as if his enunciation would convey his meaning, but I was more perplexed than before. I would just have to keep paying attention and hope to figure it out on my own. After all, people change.

Who knows how much I've changed since then, but at least I now appreciate that Bruce was teaching me to be the kind of reader Terry Andrews once understood him to be. Not a practitioner of "reading" in the shady sense that many kids my age learned from Dorian Corey in *Paris Is Burning*—too acerbic of an art form for Bruce, too fast-paced for me to keep up with—though that kind of reading *is* fundamental. I mean—and Terry Andrews surely meant—someone who can decipher the codes whereby queer people make themselves known to each other: a certain earring placement or hanky color or inside joke or unspoken gesture. (Asked to describe his sexuality, Michel Foucault likely had these codes in mind when he answered, "I identify as a reader.") And for many gay men, learning to know oneself often begins with the most literal type of reading. As a boy without a gay uncle of his own, Bruce told me he came out to himself when he stumbled upon a library book conveniently titled *All About Homosexuals* and realized, *That's me!*

That's not the whole story, but the way Bruce told it left

me with the naïve hope of discovering a similarly talismanic book, a personal Rosetta stone that would tell me everything I needed to know in preparation for the rest of my gay life. Of course, it didn't take me long to realize that this kind of literacy can't be totally self-taught, and remaining an armchair homosexual isn't much fun; eventually, I would have to get over my shyness and deal with all the messy trials and errors of interacting with other gay boys in the flesh. This messiness is among the subjects of playwright Neil Bartlett's book *Who Was That Man?*—part memoir, part biography of Oscar Wilde, part meta-history of queer literature. "You may find a certain man's body attractive," Bartlett says, "but that attraction will not guarantee you an understanding of the man; the erotic tension you feel standing outside the red-lit club doorway will teach you nothing about how to live with the men who go there twice a week; even when you have found a book from your own history, a book by a 'homosexual,' you have to learn how to read it." How do you do that? If you try to read between the lines and uncover the homosexuality hidden in every detail, you have to know what to look for, and you might be disappointed if you guess incorrectly; if you go with a more celebratory approach, reading to feel a sense of solidarity and recognition, then you might not know what to do with views or experiences that don't align with your own. Either way, what you read and how you learn to read it will depend on what's available to you. "Again and again," Bartlett says,

> it is only the contributions of the privileged to the formation of our lives, and the mythology of those

> lives, that are recorded. [. . .] Even as we discover the most obscure and outrageous fragments of our history, the more obvious and ordinary sources of information are lost. The codes of the past become unintelligible. I have a friend who is fifty-five, but I have never asked him to tell me what beliefs, enthusiasms, heroes or slang were current in London when he was my age. Our history is continually lost.

There's so much I want to ask Bruce about the beliefs, enthusiasms, heroes, and slang that were current when he was my age, and I'm just as curious about the artifacts he's chosen to contribute to the formation of my gay life. What a privilege it is to have an uncle willing to pass down so many fragments of his own history, even if he hasn't always given me the most obvious or ordinary sources of information, and even if I haven't always been ready to make use of them. Am I ready for *Harold*?

—

As a kid, I never imagined that I would now be asking these kinds of bookish questions. I was an easily distracted and tight-lipped boy, chronically afraid of saying the wrong thing. Whenever I tried to share what was on my mind, it seemed to elicit laughter or confusion, and I got the message that I should keep my mouth shut; I suspected that my classmates had all learned some crucial code of conduct from their wholesome families that I, an only child raised by divorced parents, had missed. In my fantasies, one day I would have a receptive audience that would applaud all my little thoughts and feelings, no matter how ridiculous they might sound, and no one would ask me to quit daydreaming and focus on my multiplication tables.

Then came fifth grade. Mr. Marino was more mischievous than any teacher I'd had before. I was delighted by his love of music, especially opera, and the effort he made to draw out that same love in me. Once I blew my nose with such a dramatic flourish that he raised his hand like an orchestra conductor and commanded, "Now give us an E-flat." He didn't mind if I hummed or whistled while practicing long division. On Friday afternoons, he'd even play some old Italian standards on the upright piano by his desk, and he'd encourage me to sing along. And opera was central to many of the books he read to us, my favorite of which was George Selden's *The Cricket in Times Square*.

The story begins on a Saturday night in Manhattan. While tending his family's newsstand on a subway platform, a young boy named Mario hears a mysterious sound, "like a quick stroke across the strings of a violin, or like a harp that has been plucked suddenly." He follows the noise to a pile of crumpled wastepaper and finds a cricket lying "perfectly still—as if he were sleeping, or frightened to death." Mario feeds the cricket a piece of chocolate and makes him a miniature bed out of a matchbox and a sheet of Kleenex. At first Mario's parents disapprove. "Bugs carry germs," his mother says; "he doesn't come in the house." But when they see how eagerly their lonely son craves a companion, they allow him to keep his new pet.

The next day, Mario introduces his cricket to Mr. Smedley, "a music teacher who came to buy *Musical America* at ten-thirty in the morning on the last Sunday of every month, on his way home from church. No matter what the weather was like, he always carried a long, neatly rolled umbrella." While chatting with Mario's father about Italian opera, Mr. Smedley overhears the cricket chirp a perfect middle C and exclaims with glee; he raises his hand like an orchestra conductor, and when he lowers it, the cricket chirps on the downbeat. Mario begs Mr. Smedley to give his cricket singing lessons, but Mr. Smedley refuses: "He's already been taught by the greatest teacher of all, Mario—Nature herself. [. . .] I prophesy great things for a creature of such ability."

I couldn't stop thinking about this scene, since my teacher couldn't stop smiling while reading it aloud. Did Mr. Marino see himself in Mr. Smedley? Why did he giggle at Selden's descriptions of this fussy dandy and his "long, neatly rolled umbrella"? Did Mr. Marino also "prophesy great things for a creature" like me? Perhaps acknowledging our shared love of music was his covert way of celebrating the other desires we had in common, though I was too young to identify those at the time. In Mr. Marino's classroom, with his discreet orchestration, I felt like I was finally learning to open my mouth. You could say he was teaching me to come out.

Here in the ICU, I feel a bit like my old teacher when Will returns and watches me reading aloud. I want to find out what he's discussed with the nurses, but Will looks eager to distract himself, so I show him my copy of *The Story of Harold* and ask what he knows about the novel. He admits he hasn't read anything else by the author who went by Terry Andrews, whose only novel for adults was *Harold*. "You probably don't know most of his children's books," Will says, "but maybe you've heard of his debut, *The Cricket in Times Square*?" Yes, I've heard of it. Published in 1960 by Farrar, Straus and Giroux, my current employer, and written by George Selden, who was born in 1929 at Hartford Hospital, where we're now sitting with Bruce.

—

I don't know why I waited so long to find these answers that have been hiding in plain sight. Maybe I filed away the story of *The Story of Harold* among my dossier of Bruce's far-fetched fables, too good to be fact-checked. Or maybe a simple Google search seemed like an anticlimactic solution to the air of mystery I've built up around Terry Andrews. In any case, as I keep reading, I grow sadder and angrier that I can't ask my uncle what he sees in this book; I'd give anything to watch him bolt up from this hospital bed and blurt out the kind of Delphic hot take he once gave me on "Uncle Wiggily." And I'd love to know how he would respond to my observations, especially of the novel's avuncular protagonist, who reluctantly agrees to spend more and more time with his number-one fan.

These two forlorn misfits form a mutual understanding. While Terry invents more stories of Harold, he sees his own hopelessness reflected in the little boy's face: "We mirror each other." And Barney sees right through these not entirely made-up fables: Terry begins to tell a tale about the Three-Legged Nothing, "a creature that haunts the dopey dark corners of my imagination," and Barney protests "with glum, angry incredulity," as if he knows firsthand the kind of despair this character represents to Terry. Eventually Barney begs to see the author's apartment, seeking "irrefutable proof that everything I've told him is absolutely true," and Terry worries what Edith will say if she finds out her son is inside the home of a sexual deviant. Yet no mishaps befall Barney, who—after checking under the bed and in the closets for signs of the Three-Legged Nothing—seems perfectly at home with Terry, who grows even fonder of his protégé.

But as Terry's depression deepens, he loses patience with playing a benign paternal figure. While babysitting this sullen boy one night, Terry tires of drawing him out from the "vacuum of childhood" and feels a sudden "impulse to crush his skull." He rashly offers Barney a handful of Harold's "magic pills," the barbiturates Terry has acquired for his own suicide, and the boy "jams them in his mouth: perhaps his first act of initiative." At first Terry wonders, "Shall I kill him [. . .] and then kill myself?" But then he panics, demands that Barney spit out the pills and drink a whole pot of coffee, and stays up all night, à la Scheherazade, spinning more stories of Harold to keep his charge alert: "You don't die if you're interested in listening to something, do you?" Once Barney drifts off, Terry records his sleepless vigil in a series of brief, mostly identical entries. I read them aloud to Bruce and recite my own versions throughout the afternoon.

January 19: One o'clock. He is still alive. I can hear him breathe, feel his breath on my cheek, as I bend above him.

February 24: One o'clock. He is still alive. I can hear him breathe, feel his breath on my cheek, as I bend above him.

January 19: Three o'clock. He is still alive. I can hear him breathe, feel his breath on my cheek, as I bend above him.

February 24: Three o'clock. He is still alive. I can hear him breathe, feel his breath on my cheek, as I bend above him.

January 19: Five o'clock. He is still alive. I can hear him breathe, feel his breath on my cheek, as I bend above him.

February 24: Five o'clock. He is still alive. I can hear him breathe, feel his breath on my cheek, as I bend above him.

January 19: Seven o'clock. I can wake him up. I have shaved and showered, put on clean clothes, and am ready to take him home . . . *I can wake him up!*

It's time for a meeting with the cardiologist, who explains to Will and me that a brain scan has shown no activity. Bruce won't be able to keep his ruptured heart beating on his own, and we'll have to start thinking about "making him more comfortable." Will has the right to make this choice, since he married my uncle as soon as he legally could, but Bruce requested that blood family be consulted first. And since neither of his siblings can be here—my aunt lives out in Michigan, my father's on vacation in Florida—I'm the only one who can give the go-ahead. Will takes my hand and, for the first time I've ever seen, starts to cry. "You were more like a son than a nephew to him," he says. I can't tell if this is supposed to make me feel better or worse about the decision I have to make. I nod to the cardiologist, return to Bruce's bed, and once more bend above him. I can't wake him up.

—

"You were like a son to him." "He saw himself as a father to you." Bruce's friends and neighbors keep saying things like this ever since Will and I left the hospital. I know they intend these comments to be consoling, but they all sound wrong, and not just because I'm still getting used to the past tense. Bruce was and still is my uncle, I was and still am his nephew—why should the sturdiness of that bond be measured against the parent–child model? Bruce clearly considered his responsibility to be ushering me out into the world, not shielding me from the dangers I might find there, and we never got stuck in the antagonisms that ensnare many fathers and sons. We were just two queers trying to learn what we could from each other, especially the kind of knowledge our parents couldn't give us—and as for the knowledge even Bruce couldn't give me, he pointed me toward the books where I could get it myself.

My mother intuited Bruce's role in my life long before I did. She separated from my father soon after I was born but still encouraged me to spend time with her ex-brother-in-law as often as possible. Yet when we finally had "the conversation"—not so much a coming-out as a confirmation of what was already evident to both of us by the time I was fourteen—she reacted more anxiously than I anticipated. "Be careful," she said. "You never know who might try to take advantage of you." I was grateful that she swiftly returned to watching *SVU* and couldn't see my eyes roll at her *obviously* excessive concern for my safety. Her tone softened when she turned back to me a few minutes later: "At least you have someone like your uncle Bruce to look after you."

Her faith in my uncle comes to mind as I continue reading *The Story of Harold*, in which Edith never hesitates to place her son in Terry's custody. "You're an angel!" she says when he agrees to make dinner for Barney. "No," Terry thinks, "I'm a sadomasochist. And if you knew that, Edith Willington, you'd fly down here on your broomstick—or send the police down on theirs." This is not a novel that would warm the heart of Anita Bryant, who in 1977 founded the Save Our Children campaign with the slogan "homosexuals cannot reproduce, so they must recruit." Nor would it win over many of Bryant's opponents, who wouldn't see Terry as a virtuous poster boy for gay assimilation. Yet Terry takes care to prove his trustworthiness to Edith, and he never dares to "recruit" her son. But he does privately speculate about his influence on the boy's future: "Will Barney become a fag, I wonder? I only hope he acquires enough self-confidence to think of himself as attractive to anyone." He continues to give Barney an education in gay culture that reminds me of the lessons I received from Bruce: modeling how to strut down the city sidewalks, introducing him to the Rembrandts and Turners at the Frick, demonstrating how to lift dumbbells at the gym. "Oh my God," Terry realizes, "I do love that little boy!"

But Edith is preparing to whisk her son away to Denver, where she plans to settle down with Frank. She calls to break the news to Terry, who asks what Barney will do about school, to which Edith replies, "Who *cares* about school? He's finally got a real father now!" Terry dodges this remark and offers to host a farewell party for Barney before he leaves the city. The two of them spend the whole night making up one last story of Harold, in which an eight-year-old boy must learn to take care of himself and fend off demons like the Three-Legged Nothing without the protection of Harold's spells. In the morning, Terry says goodbye to Barney, who "turns away—mournfully, hopefully—I don't know which." Will Barney warm up to his "real father"? Will Terry keep his lingering death wish at bay? Leaving these questions unanswered, the novel ends on a bittersweet note: "Surely better than nothing—if not a beginning—is the pain of this chaotic and belated love."

I reach the last page of *Harold* on the bus that returns

me to New York, where I'll have to confront my own Three-Legged Nothings without my uncle's help. No one on the subway from Port Authority to Flatbush looks fazed by my stricken face as I close the book and skim a copy of Bruce's will. He hasn't updated it since 1999, when I was around Barney's age in the novel, and I'm surprised to find my name among the beneficiaries: "To my nephew, I leave my antique world globe, to remind him of how small and wide and changing the world is." What did Bruce suspect about me then, and why did he want his eight-year-old nephew to see "how small and wide and changing the world is"? I think of all the books and gifts and other, intangible heirlooms he gave me throughout the following eighteen years. He couldn't have known *The Story of Harold* would be the last, but I'm sure he would have been tickled by the serendipitous timing of this gesture and the chaotic, belated love it's stirred in me—surely better than nothing, if not a beginning.

—

Lately I've spent most of my spare time wallowing in my apartment, waiting for someone or something to snap me out of my melancholy, yet I've been daunted by the idea of getting out and performing normalcy—let alone "having fun"—among other people. So I've decided a solo field trip is in order. Since I've been meaning to visit the New York Public Library's special collections, whose treasures include Virginia Woolf's walking cane and a lock of Walt Whitman's hair, I submitted an appointment request. I mentioned Terry Andrews's identity and George Selden's connection to FSG, devising some half-true professional reasons for snooping in my employer's records. An archivist replied that she didn't see any relevant catalog entries for Andrews, but she did find four boxes under Selden's name. Fortunately, she didn't ask why a publicist for grown-up literature would be doing research on a long-dead children's author, and she invited me to view his papers on this Saturday afternoon.

I bypass Patience and Fortitude, the legendary marble lions who guard the library's main entrance on Fifth Avenue, and take a side door to the security desk, where I leave my coat, my neatly rolled umbrella, and all my other belongings, except a composition book and a pencil (no pens allowed). The archivist greets me in a warmly lit, windowless reading room, assigns me a desk, brings me four accordion file boxes, and shows me how to remove, read, and replace each sheet of paper as gently as possible. There's a daunting volume of correspondence between the various agents and editors who worked with Selden, and I shudder to think how many boxes I would need to preserve hard copies of all my professional email exchanges. The letters are largely sunny, confirming how beloved *The Cricket in Times Square* once was: Selden's publicist described him as "a charming young man" in a pitch to the producers of *Captain Kangaroo*, and his editor compared the book to *Charlotte's Web* and *Winnie-the-Pooh* in a request for a blurb from Leonard Bernstein, adding that the protagonist "is the only cricket we know who can sing arias from *Aida*." (Bernstein evidently declined.) One of the only documents written by

Selden himself is his reply to a reporter's question about the nature of children's classics:

> Not that I am presumptuous enough—despite all your gratifying enthusiasm—to think that I have written one! For me a children's classic is, first of all, well-written. I do not subscribe to this fashionable theory which holds that an author has to limit himself to an itsy-bitsy vocabulary simply because he's writing for children. Similarly, I don't like kids' books that have an unnatural, artificial sweetness about them: the kind designed to avoid witches, accidents and anything which might suggest to the tender mind that it is living in a dangerous world. The world is dangerous! And I am convinced that those books which present a completely sentimental, safe version of it do their readers a great disservice.

Selden's characters may be lonely and misunderstood, but I wouldn't say his children's books "suggest to the tender mind that it is living in a dangerous world." While *Cricket* seems to depict a fairly "sentimental, safe version" of New York City life, there's far more darkness and danger to be found in *The Story of Harold,* and there was clearly much more to the "charming young man" described in these buoyant letters.

That buoyancy gradually deflates. In 1968, Selden finished drafting *Tucker's Countryside*, a long-awaited sequel to *The Cricket in Times Square*, but disagreements with the illustrator and other unspecified obstacles delayed the publication: in several letters, his editor explained that Selden was "having a hard time" and dealing with "very real problems." *The Story of Harold* opens that same year, when Terry has become overwhelmed by his own very real problems, but I can't find any other clues about Selden's personal life at the time. FSG finally published *Tucker's Countryside* in 1969 ("I think he's breathing happily for the first time in six months," his editor said), but the responses to Selden's follow-ups cooled over the coming years. In a 1977 memo to his agent, an editor referred to Selden's latest proposal as "a slight work. [. . .] George is such a good and successful author that I should hate to come in with a work that would do his reputation harm rather than good." A few months later, another editor described one of Selden's new stories as "mediocre. In fact, it's hard to understand how the author of the terrific *Cricket* books could be capable of producing something so conventional, mechanical, and strained."

I start to doubt that I'll learn anything more about Terry Andrews until, near the end of my search through the final box, I find a 1990 letter to FSG's contracts department from Selden's executor, who explains that the author's "will provides that all royalties on books other than *The Story of Harold* are given in equal shares to the decedent's nieces and nephews." The letter doesn't explain why Selden didn't want *Harold* to be part of their inheritance; maybe he always intended to keep this novel a secret from his heirs, or maybe they already knew about this side of Uncle George. I consider asking them myself, since the executor's letter includes their names, home addresses, and what appear to be phone numbers, but as I start to copy the details in my notebook and count the digits, I realize these are *social security* numbers. I can't imagine any way to contact Selden's kin without accounting for this breach of privacy or provoking suspicion of my motives. What would I even tell them I've discovered from my investigations without sounding totally unhinged? *Did you know your uncle and mine once lived on the same block of Charles Street? That your uncle was born in the same hospital where mine died just a few weeks ago? That my uncle gave me, shortly before then, a copy of your uncle's probably autobiographical novel about his secret life as a depressed sadomasochist? That its narrator and a young boy form a bond eerily reminiscent of that between my uncle and me?* Bruce used to tell me to "live the fantasy," but perhaps I've taken that advice too far, quixotically identifying with the real people behind a novel just because of its convergences with my life.

I return the boxes and thank the archivist for permitting me a few hours in the reading room. She suggests I stop by the microform department, where one of her colleagues has found a record for an interview with Terry Andrews in a 1979 issue of *The Advocate*.

I unspool the film and load it into the old-fashioned projector system, which illuminates my monitor, in perfect focus, with an enormous close-up of a man's six-pack abs—the cover of the magazine's October 18 issue. I blush, glance cautiously at the other patrons (all absorbed in their own screens), and fast-forward to the table of contents: "Intestinal Parasites and *You*: An Insides Story." "Dispatch: California Supreme Court Rules on

Solicitation—An End to Entrapment?" "Terry Andrews: The Story of *The Story of Harold*."

I squint to decipher the tiny text sandwiched between semi-pornographic ads for leather shops and lipotropic supplements. The writer, a critic named Karl Keller, describes *The Story of Harold* as "a work of sheer joy, both in style and subject matter," and deems it "the best gay novel in a decade or more." He laments the "long round of rejections" *Harold* received before it was published "rather reluctantly" and the perplexed reactions it elicited from readers: "To people over 40 it wasn't 'nice,' to straight men it was a 'challenge,' and homosexual respondents by and large said, 'We aren't this way!'" Eager to meet the novel's elusive author, Keller somehow tracks down Terry Andrews and arranges a lunch date in the West Village ("I still don't know his real name," Keller claims). Their discussion begins with publishing shoptalk, but then the questions get more personal:

KELLER: What made people most uneasy about the book?

ANDREWS: Among publishers and booksellers, and especially among gay movement people, combining sadomasochistic scenes with the presence of children—always perilous at best—made people very uneasy. It was simply too strong in all its details, not just the gay ones.

KELLER: Are such things in the book autobiographical? With S/M and children together in the book, are you hiding behind your pseudonym from the charge of being a literary child-molester?

ANDREWS: Not at all. I guess I'm a writer of a very different sort. I wanted to be as honest as possible. When a reader picks up a book, even a book by a famous author, and sees that the author's name is one thing and the narrator telling the story in the first person has a different name, the reader knows there's something fishy going on, something wholly fictional. He knows it's just a literary game and he has to work to suspend his disbelief. But indeed, I wanted the two to be the same, author and narrator. In fact, my way of writing is autobiographical, in a sense, in that I set aside a long period of time and actually *become* the narrator or main character in a book I am writing. I spent a whole year, in fact, "being" Terry Andrews: S/M homosexual, experimental bisexual, confused trisexual—whatever—obsessed with death and drugged on life at the same time.

KELLER: Then you *are* Terry Andrews?

ANDREWS: I was. While I was agonizing my way through the writing of the book. A lot of the scenes in the book were true. The characters were real people for me then. I knew them then and could have actually named them for you. I went through much of what is in the novel—sometimes physically, sometimes in my head—for the sake of the novel.

I don't know how well Selden succeeded in differentiating himself from the narrator of *Harold*—perhaps his contemporaries could deduce the author's identity from certain clues in the text, even though it doesn't perfectly line up with Selden's biography—but I imagine some readers must have suspected Terry Andrews of concealing some unmentionable behavior beneath his novel's many layers of artifice. Consider how quick Terry is to shut down concerns about his sense of propriety: the first time he proposes hosting Barney overnight for a slumber party, before we even know how the boy's mother responds, Terry immediately asks the reader, "Is *that* what you're thinking?" He doesn't say what he means by "*that*," and Edith doesn't seem to suspect any foul play, but I could imagine some readers believing, based on the swiftness of this preemptive denial, that Terry doth protest too much. By writing under a pseudonym, billing his work as autobiographical, and presenting such a defensive narrator, Selden may be trying to protect himself, yet he also seems to be playing with fire and inviting readers to question what he's up to.

Keller doesn't say so, but the uneasiness he mentions likely played a large part in driving *Harold* out of print, despite glowing praise from *The New York Times* ("An exceptional novel [. . .] about almost everything important that goes on between people") and a cover illustrated by Edward Gorey. I've found no other press, except a lukewarm review from *Kirkus* ("Appealing [. . .] Vaguely outrageous"), that would confirm or deny Keller's take on the novel's reception. Yet his remarks bring to mind the ongoing moral panic surrounding so-called groomers: these days, I could imagine getting canceled just for recommending a novel that merely jokes about a queer man imperiling an underage boy, no matter what really happens in the plot. At the same time, my employer is still reveling in the success of Garth Greenwell's debut novel, *What Belongs to You,* another work of autofiction, in which the narrator, who closely resembles Greenwell, pursues a fraught relationship with a young hustler.

Greenwell is a more elegant prose stylist than Andrews, and his narrator, a less abrasive personality than Terry, isn't putting any children in harm's way. Still, if most contemporary readers understand that Greenwell isn't endorsing his characters' peccadillos, perhaps *Harold* would fare better if it were released today. Keller dances around the challenges of reading *Harold* in his *Advocate* article, sounding optimistic about the book's future: "Writing this kind of novel, Andrews has avoided most of the pitfalls of the bad gay novel—superficial tours of the gay scene, melodrama of sexual conflicts, social tragedy, sorry ends." This seems to be a jab at late-seventies hits like Andrew Holleran's *Dancer from the Dance* and Armistead Maupin's *Tales of the City*, yet these melodramas have since become canonical gay classics, much beloved by readers of Bruce's generation. Would *Harold* have endured a little longer if Andrews had punctuated his dark night of the soul with more frothy banter on Fire Island?

I want to ask Keller himself, but he died long ago—"an early fatality of AIDS," according to one of his only other published articles. When I return to work on Monday, I talk to a colleague about passing along a copy of *Harold* to an editor at FSG, one of several gay men in the company's most senior positions. I sense this editor would understand the appeal of reissuing a "lost classic" by one of the house's own stars, though the book's content might give him pause. After months of radio silence, I get an email explaining that he came down against *Harold* "because he felt the world it depicted was a dead one, irrelevant to the present moment." This editor would have been around twenty when the novel's events take place, just before the Stonewall riots, and I'm now the same age he was when *Harold* was published. That not-so-distant world isn't exactly dead or irrelevant, but I can't think of anything else to say in defense of *Harold*, nor can I name a single friend of my age to whom I would unequivocally recommend the book, whose many pleasures are often spoiled by the narrator's dated humor, casual misogyny and racism, and unapologetic snobbery.

I thank my colleague and resume writing press releases for new books that might be even shorter-lived than *Harold*. Maybe it's a "bad gay novel" after all, another obscure and outrageous fragment of our history. Or maybe it really is a Rorschach test, and if I stare at it a little longer, I might find out what Bruce expected me to see in the ink. Whatever you call this troublesome book, I'm not ready to put it back on the shelf, though I suspect I'm starting to sound like an overzealous nephew defending my unpopular Uncle Terry. So I'll just keep waiting at my desk for the phone to ring, for a caller to say, "I understand you're a reader."

Friend

I'm wandering down the boardwalk along Brighton Beach. All the carnival's neon lights are dimmed, and the sky is so dark that I can't distinguish it from the ocean. I'm barefoot, wearing just a tank top and swimsuit, but the wind is too strong for me to venture out onto the sand. I've probably walked at least a mile by the time I reach a little umbrellaed picnic table where my uncle Bruce is waiting for me, smiling. As soon as I join him, bright red fireworks light up the sky above us, and we silently sit together and watch them burst over Coney Island. I turn to him, see his face reflecting the flashes of red, and think, with surprising clarity, *No, I don't want to miss out on this.*

That's all I remember from the dream. It came to me about six years ago, when I was a twenty-one-year-old trudging through a deep depression, and something about watching that fireworks display with Bruce snapped me out of it and gave me a reason to stay here—that is, alive. Even now that it's no longer possible to find my uncle at that picnic table in waking life, the possibility of returning there in my sleep has continued to get me through my worst days. I've been telling myself this story for so long that I realize only now, upon telling it aloud for the first time, how maudlin it sounds. It's happy hour at Julius', and I can feel my second gin and tonic going to my head, convincing me that I'm describing something important and useful to the artist across the table. But PJ's eyes look glazed, and I can tell I should have heeded the conventional wisdom: *nobody wants to hear about your dreams.*

PJ specializes in semi-surreal charcoal drawings of gay men, and about a year ago, soon after Bruce's death, Will commissioned PJ to do a portrait of his late husband. The piece was loosely based on a photograph I'd taken of Bruce at my uncles' house, which PJ embellished with peacocks roaming the yard and an enormous full moon in the background. When Will showed it to me, I wondered aloud what it would be like to sit for a portrait—not because I wanted or needed one, just because I was curious about the experience—and he asked PJ to make something for my twenty-seventh birthday. I was grateful for the generous gift but also unsure how to tell him I didn't actually know what I would do with a picture of myself, nor was I sure whether I would want to carry or ship it across the country, since I'm about to move to Idaho for grad school. Would I exhibit it on the wall of my home, a personal altarpiece for all my guests to admire, or let it collect dust in a closet? Both options seem gauche. Nonetheless, I've agreed to meet PJ and suggested not a conventional portrait but a more imaginative, less life-like scene, similar to the one he did for Will.

"Do you think," I ask, "you could illustrate that dream?"

PJ smirks. He's not the intimidating bohemian I envisioned but a scruffy boy around my age, wearing a loose work shirt and camo pants, and I feel a surge of tenderness toward him as he squirts some ketchup on his fries. I offer to send him more photos for reference, and he promises to sketch some ideas. "It sounds like a challenge," he says, "but I'll see what I can do."

—

While I wait to hear back from PJ, I revisit another favorite portrait of mine. When the Second Avenue subway extension began two years ago, the city commissioned Brazilian artist Vik Muniz to adorn the Seventy-Second Street underpass with a series of mosaics depicting "New Yorkers of all stripes," including a pair of stocky, bearded men holding hands and staring straight ahead like a twenty-first-century *American Gothic*. According to the local tabloids, some of the Upper East Side's parents were taken aback by this public display of homosexuality, but I was drawn to the ordinary queer affection between these two grizzled bears in wrinkled flannel and stained overalls; I'd never seen men so close in age and style to Bruce and Will commemorated like this. As soon as the station opened, my friend José joined me on a pilgrimage and photographed me standing in front of this mosaic, right where the couple's hands meet, as if they had put their arms around me. Within minutes of posting the photo online, I heard from Will that these two men were friends of friends of friends—how small the gay world is—and he offered to put me in touch. Bruce's death soon put these plans on hold. But the following spring, as I began counting down my final weeks in New York before moving to Idaho, I tracked down an email address for my Second Avenue uncles and invited them to meet me at the station.

I lean against the wall, scanning the crowds that emerge from every arriving train, and wave when I recognize one of my blind dates ascending the escalator. He introduces himself as Thor and assures me that, yes, it's his real name. I resist blurting out how well it suits him: his thick gray beard, formidable frame, and electric-blue eyes all give him the appearance of a Norse thunder god, even in his I ♥ NY T-shirt and faded Levi's. Thor tells me with delight that he feels like a celebrity, since I'm the first person to express interest in meeting him based solely on the mosaic. Before I can respond, he turns and shouts, "Patrick!"

His companion approaches from the other end of the platform, wearing tan cargo pants and a matching, paint-splattered Carhartt jacket, and pecks Thor on the lips. They ask me with impish glee if we should take a selfie, pleased to take part in this millennial ritual. As we arrange ourselves in front of their likenesses, they point out many details I've missed on the wall: the matching glass used for their buttons, the mother-of-pearl buckles, the barely visible glint of a silver wedding band on one of their fingers. They tell me they met Muniz through a mutual friend, and when the artist invited them to sit for a portrait, Thor and Patrick assumed they were among hundreds of candidates for this project. They still don't know why they were chosen, but they guess it must have had something to do with the way they instinctively joined hands when Muniz first asked them to pose for the camera.

Thor, clearly the bossier and more voluble half of this couple, leads us to a nearby sushi place. On the way, he asks me a series of probing questions ("So why did you want to meet us?" "Why Idaho?" "What are you planning to write about?" "Is nonfiction really creative writing?"), then gets sidetracked by something else, monologues on a different topic, and grows irritated when Patrick cuts him off to redirect the conversation.

I ask how the two of them met, and Thor says they became LiveJournal pen pals in the early aughts, when Patrick was getting his engineering degree in Minneapolis and Thor was living in New York with his then partner, David, a longtime editor, academic, and book collector. Thor explains that he spends much of his post-retirement days cleaning out the East Village apartment he once shared with David, who recently passed. He's been trying to sell most of his late ex's books at The Strand, whose buyers have eagerly accepted many obscure works of German philosophy but, to Thor's surprise and disappointment, have rejected just as many out-of-print classics of gay literature, claiming that most customers wouldn't be interested in those. As if I were one such customer, Thor rattles off capsule reviews of his favorite titles. He urges me to read Mart Crowley's play *The Boys in the Band* ("a study in the psychology of gay men who hate their own ugliness and aging—but don't see the new production"), Steven Millhauser's novel *Edwin Mullhouse* ("a sendup of the obsessively detailed biographical style"), Edmund White's travelogue *States of Desire* ("better than his early novels, which are twee and arch"), Ethan Mordden's story collection *Buddies* ("you should reach out to

Mordden if you really want to find a mentor"). He invites me to come over sometime and see for myself, but I hesitate to accept, since I'm in the middle of culling my own library and preparing to pack all my belongings in a ten-foot U-Haul.

"Well, I still hope we get together again before you go," Thor says. I tell him I hope so too, but after parting ways with him and Patrick, I wonder about his initial question. Why *do* I want to get to know them? What am I looking for in the short time I have left in the city? I didn't say much about Bruce tonight, but they could probably tell I'm still in mourning. I've been privately calling Thor and Patrick "my Second Avenue uncles" as a cheeky joke, but it's likely masking a sincere longing for something deeper. Bruce was such a strong, steady, consistent presence in my life that I never anticipated how much I would miss it and never considered seeking other kinds of gay companionship in his absence. Maybe if I hadn't taken Bruce for granted, if I had worked harder to practice mimicking his impressive affability—his knack for breaking the ice by simply shouldering up to a stranger and announcing, "I like *you*!"—this new connection would feel less complicated. I don't want to project these anxieties onto near-strangers, and I don't want to seem like the lost hatchling in P. D. Eastman's picture book, pathetically asking every other gay man who crosses my path, "Are *you* my uncle?" But maybe Thor and Patrick sense that's why I've gravitated to them now.

—

None of my friends wants to see *Portrait of Jason*. The Brooklyn Academy of Music is screening Shirley Clarke's 1967 film, a controversial classic of queer cinéma vérité that both disturbs and delights me. So I call up Thor, even though we saw each other just a few days ago, and invite him to join me for a matinee.

I arrive early at the theater, spy Thor taking a call by the entrance, and pretend to scroll through my phone while I eavesdrop. But Thor, unfooled, sneaks up on me and bellows, "Two can play that game." He was talking to his sister, whose teenage son is about to travel from DC to New York for a school trip. Thor admits he's always wanted to be a better uncle than his own was, though he worries that he's fallen short. His two young nephews seem to prefer Patrick, who tends to be less social and more of a homebody than Thor, but also more playful: he'll say yes whenever young kids ask him to get down on the floor and join them for a game. In fact, Thor says, Patrick proposed to him while their whole family was playing a round of Apples to Apples, and his young nephew interrupted the scene by exclaiming, "Is there a ring for me?"

During the previews, I ask Thor about his favorite movies, and he responds with a thorough summary of John Greyson's *Pissoir*. He doesn't hold back or lower his voice as he details Greyson's depiction of public sex in Toronto's gay underground, and some scandalized audience members pointedly turn our way when the lights dim. Only now do I realize what a strange suggestion this movie was. Shot during a single night in Clarke's living room, *Portrait* opens with a blurry close-up of the star introducing himself: "My name is Jason Holliday." As he gradually comes into sharper focus, he laughs and reintroduces himself with his government name: "My name is Aaron Payne." He remains the sole figure to appear onscreen, mugging and camping for the camera and telling the story of his life for Clarke's entertainment, as if she were an old friend. At first, Holliday seems to be having a good time with her, but soon you start to detect some uneasiness. "It gets to be a joke sometimes as to who's using who," he quips in an early monologue about his days as a "houseboy," clearly poking at the present tensions between himself (a gay, Black hustler and aspiring cabaret performer) and Clarke (a straight, white, well-established, award-winning filmmaker). The "joke" is also on me, a gay boy spellbound by Holliday's irrepressible flamboyance and, at the same time, a white viewer complicit in Clarke's increasingly cruel treatment of her star. She and the crew keep plying Holliday with drugs and liquor, and you can hear their voices heckling him with more and more hostility, eventually reducing him to tears. Every time, this moment surprises me anew and makes me question why I'm drawn to this film. I admit it's partly because Holliday's stagy persona reminds me of Bruce's—even the sound of his laughter is uncannily Brucean—and I wish I had recorded such a documentary of my uncle acting out his own one-man show with similarly dramatic flair. Filming Bruce wouldn't have involved the same racially charged power dynamic, but perhaps he would have felt similarly exploited and humiliated, forced to do his song and dance for the camera. I could imagine Bruce telling me, as Holliday tells Clarke at one point, “I think I’m losing my mind, but nevertheless it’s serving a purpose.”

I catch Thor scowling at the screen, and I wonder what he’s thinking. Does he imagine I proposed this film because I want to make my own portrait of Thor, to manipulate him into entertaining me with all his wisdom and humor? What am I projecting onto this new acquaintance through the filter of Jason, onto whom I’ve already projected so many feelings about Bruce? Now Thor is snoring, and I offer an apologetic shrug to my neighbors and receive a few good-natured smiles, perhaps having passed myself off as a patient nephew minding his aging uncle. He sleeps through the film’s emotional climax and wakes just in time to see Holliday pull himself together and deliver his ambiguous closing words: “Oh, that was beautiful. I’m happy about the whole thing.”

—

During a lunch break the following week, I receive a text from Thor: “Have you heard of THE STORY OF HAROLD? I have a nice edition to give you, if you haven’t read that. One of those books you end up recommending / sharing with smart + curious + gay friends. I have bought countless copies for young men ‘coming onto the scene.’”

I almost drop my phone on the sidewalk and reply in all caps, effusing my love for *Harold*. A few hours later, I arrive at David’s apartment, finally accepting Thor’s invitation, and find him sorting through a box of old Folsom Street Fair souvenirs. Piles of books and magazines are scattered everywhere, and Thor points me to a stack he’s set aside in a grocery bag, including a few of James Purdy's novels, a first edition of Judy Grahn's *Another Mother Tongue*, some self-help manuals with titles like *The Homosexual Handbook* and *After You're Out*, and Edward Gorey's illustrated edition of *The Story of Harold*. Thor insists that I take them all, even if I can't bring them to Idaho, since he'd rather I pass these books to friends than sell them to a store where they won't be appreciated. Just my luck: the more excited I get about moving out West, ridding myself of all the things that weigh me down, and starting over, I meet someone who gives me more and more reminders of what I'm loath to leave behind.

I don't want to reject these gifts, but I'm also reluctant to accept them, since I don't know what I could possibly offer him in return. But maybe I have the wrong idea about what's going on here. When Bruce used to give me books like these, the gesture seemed rooted in a sense of familial responsibility; when friends my age do something nice for each other, it seems impolite to assume there are any strings attached. Yet somehow I've been conditioned to imagine that any intergenerational friendship must be at least partly transactional. I'm haunted by a passage near the beginning of Sarah Schulman's book *The Gentrification of the Mind*, in which a young gay man requests an interview and then shows up at her apartment with "no urgency," no "theories or ideas or passions that he wanted to talk over. I had hoped," Schulman says, "that he would bring new ideas into my life, but instead he wanted them from me. He didn't have something that he *needed* to know. He just wanted me to give him the interview." I realize I've avoided seeking out older queer friends because I'm afraid of being skewered like that thoughtlessly acquisitive boy; I'm afraid, in other words, of being found wanting. Yet it seems rather unqueer of me to be ashamed of my wants, so I should probably quit overthinking and just relax.

Besides, I wouldn't dare to cast aside these relics, especially since many of these books are autographed with affectionate notes to David, and Thor shows me that some even have letters and postcards tucked between the pages. "Nobody writes these anymore," he says. I promise that we'll remain pen pals, and he laughs. Does he not envision a future for this strange, new bond we've formed? Or is he tickled, as I am, that this bond has solidified so swiftly despite its uncertain future?

On our way out, Thor stops in the lobby to chat with the young security guard, who sizes me up, clearly wondering what Thor has been up to with a boy thirty-five years his junior. (*You're not really his type*, the guard's face tells me.) I extend a hand to introduce myself, but Thor beats me to it. "This is my friend Steven," he says, and I can tell from his terseness that he's accustomed to fielding the question foisted on so many gay men: *So how do you two know each other?*

—

Not a question José has to ask, since he took the photograph that connected me to Thor in the first place—and that ultimately got us here, riding the A train out to Far Rockaway, where Thor has invited me to a Memorial Day cookout at an old friend's house. I've brought along José partly for the company, partly to show him why I've been spending more and more time with this man who's as old as our fathers. And because José is the kind of niche gay who reads Adorno on the beach and quotes Wittgenstein in his Instagram captions, I know he won't roll his eyes when I tell him I've been rereading "Friendship as a Way of Life," an interview with Foucault that's frequently cited by young queer boys who need, as I apparently do, a French philosopher's help to explain their friendships with older queer men.

When prompted to speak about desire and pleasure between "two men of noticeably different ages," Foucault asks, "What code would allow them to communicate? They face each other without terms or convenient words, with nothing to assure them about the meaning of the movement that carries them toward each other. They have to invent, from A to Z, a relationship that is still formless, which is friendship: that is to say, the sum of everything through which they can give each other pleasure." By "pleasure," Foucault doesn't mean the instant gratification sought by "two young men meeting in the street, seducing each other with a look, grabbing each other's asses and getting each other off in a quarter of an hour. There you have a kind of neat image of homosexuality without any possibility of generating unease." He means a "homosexual mode of life" that isn't conventionally beautiful, that isn't afraid of "everything that can be troubling in affection, tenderness, friendship, fidelity, camaraderie, and companionship, things that our rather sanitized society can't allow a place for without fearing the formation of new alliances and the tying together of unforeseen lines of force." That potential "force" is what makes gay friendship—especially when it involves a significant age gap—so disturbing to many straight people and also confounding to gays themselves. What could possibly motivate two men to be together, without any predetermined scripts or expectations—that is, "to share their time, their meals, their room, their leisure, their grief, their knowledge, their confidences [. . .] outside of institutional relations, family, profession, and obligatory camaraderie?" You just have to be willing to do the work, no matter how exposed or vulnerable you may feel: what characterizes this kind of friendship, Foucault says, is "a desire, an uneasiness, a desire-in-uneasiness that exists among a lot of people."

I sense some uneasiness in José (or is it desire-in-uneasiness?) as we approach the party and see Thor and Patrick tossing beanbags in the backyard. Matt, our host, offers José and me some beer and invites us into the kitchen, saving us from embarrassing ourselves in a game that's clearly not in our wheelhouse. As we follow him inside, he cautions us to watch our knees; he's been extra vigilant ever since his little nephew bumped his head against the sharp-edged coffee table, though the boy's mother assured him that small children are resilient against all kinds of damage. Matt introduces us to the other guests, most of whom are bearish men around Thor's age, and most of whom seem to know Thor—evidently the hub of this circle—from the BDSM and leather world. José and I, who look relatively baby-faced and buttoned-up among this crowd, are clearly outliers, so a number of folks ask how we met. One day, I tell them, a handsome, dapper college classmate approached me and said, "I like your jacket." Assuming someone so confident and elegant must be hiding something, I squinted skeptically, said a brusque "thanks," and walked away—failing to notice he was wearing the very same jacket. José was persistent in his efforts to crack my icy shell, which was defrosted by a couple of parties where we both accidentally drank too much and made out on the dance floor, and I now call him my best friend. To me this has always been a charming tale of two neurotic boys who like each other so much that their bashfulness comes across as disdain. Yet our interlocutors seem puzzled, and I wonder if I've unintentionally roasted myself.

"You're a basic white boy," Thor says. He and José laugh, and I smile to conceal that I have no idea what Thor's responding to, though he's not wrong. Then he corrects himself: "No, you're *extra*."

Thor keeps giggling, and I realize he's not deliberately negging me but rummaging through his repertoire of slang for a hip way to connect with my story. I catch a flash of vulnerability on his face, and for a moment he reminds me of the shy and sensitive teenager I was in the aughts. Meeting another gay boy was not impossible but still relatively uncommon then, and a sense of scarcity seemed to give many of us an all-or-nothing attitude toward each other; the two options seemed to be "fall in love with me" or "get out of my way, I'm looking for my soulmate." At the time, I had no strategy for making friends beyond drawing from my inventory of *Mean Girls* quotes and Bright Eyes lyrics and cryptic AIM away messages; if he gets the reference, I figured, surely he'll get *me*. I want to ask Thor, "Well, how did *you* learn to do friendship?" A ridiculous question, perhaps, but no one ever taught me, and Foucault isn't much help when you're trying, as I am now, to make small talk between bites of a hot dog.

Thor shifts the conversation to (what else?) the topic of orgies. He says he used to feel so much shame and guilt about his interest in BDSM and leather; he would repeatedly throw out all his gear and then replace it within a few weeks. Then he met a dom who made him come five times in five hours, and when Thor later confessed his ambivalence about his kinkiness, the dom asked, "Do you enjoy it?" (Yes.) "Does it hurt anyone else?" (No.) Only then did Thor begin to accept himself and meet the men who would become the most important figures in his life, present company included, and begin to cut ties with everyone who didn't accept him—even anyone who simply flaked on social plans or didn't reciprocate his efforts to reach out.

José gives me a look that says, *No pressure.* I wonder if this cookout is about to become an orgy where someone will expect me to make him come five times, but there's clearly no sexual tension in the air. What is the sum of everything through which Thor and I can give each other pleasure, and how will I know whether I've held up my end of the bargain? Maybe someday I'll learn the hard way.

—

"I don't want to make something that ends up looking amateur," PJ says. I've asked for an update on what he's been working on, and he says the original idea we discussed would be too difficult to complete before I leave the city. Instead, he's been studying some photos I sent him—especially my favorite, the one my father took on Bruce's patio, where I was wearing those little cowboy boots, looking like a five-year-old replica of the uncle sitting behind me. "What makes that image so great," he says, "are the little things. It's a very real moment."

Now I'm hesitant to look at the draft he's emailed me—for the first time, this project fills me with anxiety. I want to respect PJ's creative license and to honor Will's generosity in commissioning this artwork, but I also don't want a distorted caricature of a precious memory. I don't know if that's what PJ has ended up producing, but it occurs to me that I would rather pose in the flesh for a deeply unflattering portrait than let someone else reinterpret a formative scene that's already crystallized in my mind. It's too late to suggest an alternative, though, since I move to Idaho in just a few weeks, and PJ wants to deliver the final piece before I go. So I open the attached image, quickly close it, and reply with a thank-you for this "very real moment." It's beautiful, I tell him; I'm happy about the whole thing.

—

"Do you know the secret," Thor asks, "to finding the conductor car on a train?" I don't, even after living in this city for nearly a decade. Riding the Q from Midtown Manhattan, Thor texts me meticulous instructions on how to join him at the Church Avenue station near my apartment. "You will never notice this unless you look for it," he says after describing the zebra-striped sign where I'm supposed to wait for him on the platform, "but if you look for it you will see it every time." I'm skeptical, but as the train halts and I enter the door opening right in front of me, there he is, waving me in to the seat he's saved with his beach towel.

We're on our way to see the Brooklyn Cyclones, the borough's own minor-league baseball team. Normally I would have no interest in such an outing, but then again, none of the other unathletic queers in my life has ever presented the opportunity to infiltrate a wholesome sports game—an offer I couldn't refuse. We arrive at Brighton Beach in the early afternoon, and I dip in the ocean to escape the summer heat while Thor sits on the shore, building sandcastles. We ride the carousel, where he points out the real hair used for the wooden horses' manes; we ride the bumper cars and sing Grace Jones; we ride the Wonder Wheel in a sliding carriage that feels like a roller coaster suspended in the air, and he tells me his high school art teacher once explained that amusement park rides are all about moving your body in ways it isn't used to being moved. This same teacher inspired Thor's fondness for scrapbooking photos, which he now collects in ever-expanding albums on his phone. Thor shows me one titled "M"—all close-ups of unusual details from men's restrooms, including oddly shaped soap dispensers and hand dryers—and another called "Men Who Made Me the Way I Am."

I ask who some of those men are, and Thor tells me about the friends and lovers he met while living in San

Francisco in his twenties, many of them thirty or forty years older. One of them was famously promiscuous tattoo artist and pornographer Samuel Steward, whom Thor once tried and failed to seduce, just so he could boast of having kissed the lips that kissed the lips that kissed the lips of Oscar Wilde. Another man was the editor Donald Allen, whose name I remember from my copy of Frank O'Hara's *Collected Poems*, and who introduced Thor to many of the artists and writers in his circle. It wasn't a romantic or sexual relationship, Thor explains; Allen simply appreciated young Thor's eagerness to listen and learn, and they often met for long, meandering conversations over extravagant lunches that Allen insisted on paying for. After a while, Thor expressed frustration with the imbalance between them and asked how he could possibly sustain a friendship in which he seemed to have relatively little to contribute. Allen chafed at the question, accused Thor of ingratitude, and never called on him again.

"I didn't see those relationships as mentoring," Thor says. "That sounds like a craft-guild thing. But they gave me a kind of love I'd never received from my blood family, though few of them lasted very long."

"How did the others end?" I ask.

"I called things off with one guy because he drank too much. But I lost another one over an argument about the rules of Scrabble!"

Thor howls with laughter and leads me to the stadium, where we get even giddier and more playful. I confess I don't know anything about the rules of baseball, and neither does he, so we direct our attention to mimicking the cheerleaders who dance by the bleachers and toss souvenir T-shirts to the audience. We snap more and more ridiculous photos of each other ("look, mom, we're at the World Cup!"), and I make a note to add them to my own album of men who've moved me in ways I'm not used to being moved. Thor keeps getting up for sweet treats—popsicles and cotton candy and funnel cake—and when he asks for the third time if I want anything, I joke, "Are you trying to be my sugar daddy?"

"*No*," he barks, suddenly stern. "Always an uncle, never a daddy."

Chastened, I rise and offer to get him some ice cream myself. How will I show sufficient gratitude for our odd, asymmetrical friendship? But Thor grabs my arm before I can get very far.

"Wait," he says, urging me to sit down. "The game's about to end. You don't want to miss out on—"

And then we watch the fireworks burst over Coney Island.

Ghost

We're unfurling the so-called infinite scroll of images—6,450, to be exact—that I've "liked" on Tumblr over the past eight years, trying to decide which are worth downloading and which I can forget about. It's the last day of 2018, and my friend Thor and I are celebrating the occasion with a trip to Spa Castle, a cheap and popular destination in a far corner of Queens. As we ride the 7 train to the end of the line, we share what we've tried to rescue from "the Tumblr ban": in early December, the social media platform announced that it would be eliminating "adult content" by mid-January. This label applies to most of what I've sought on Tumblr, and now I feel an unexpectedly strong urge to preserve as much as possible before it slips away for good. Even before "the purge"—as many users call it—officially began, I would try to reopen an old post, watch it disappear from my screen without a trace, and receive an error message informing me that I was violating Tumblr's new "community guidelines." Whose community, and whose guidelines? Witnessing this purge spread in real time grieves me, but it's hard to say what exactly I'm losing, apart from my own voyeuristic pleasure. I'm not a pornographer or a sex worker whose livelihood depends on outlets like this, but I am one of many queer millennials for whom Tumblr provided a rare space for safe and accessible sexual exploration. Thor has been a longtime collector of homoerotic media for similar reasons, so he shares my indignation toward the Tumblr ban, though he's not as surprised by the news. For certain internet users, Thor reminds me, anything queer is always obscene and never "community-friendly."

As a child, before I knew about the internet, I browsed a much different space my uncle Bruce called "the dream room," his name for the main bathroom of his house. "It's where I do all my dreaming," he liked to say, and at first I gathered he meant the long afternoon naps he tended to take in the tub, surrounded by the vintage pinups framed on the walls and the beefcake magazines stacked on the floor, an impressive phalanx of athletes and bodybuilders and bikers and soldiers flexing their muscles and holding vigil over every bather. For what purpose, I wondered, would a man accumulate so many revealing pictures of other men? Bruce must have known them, I figured: he often waxed nostalgic about Hugh, his late partner, who appeared in many portraits displayed throughout the house, so I guessed the dream room might be a shrine to honor other dearly beloved and departed companions. Whenever I needed to relieve myself, I would pretend to be Bruce's shadow and greet the dream room's two-dimensional inhabitants as if they all recognized me; I would strip to mimic them in front of the shaving mirror, summoning my imaginary friends' assurance that I would someday, whenever I might grow up, be as happy and confident and handsome as they were. Only once I turned ten did it occur to me that Bruce had assembled this photo gallery not because he knew these men but because they turned him on.

This might not have been the place where my gayness took root, but it was definitely where I acquired my scopophilic tastes, which were tinged from the beginning with a melancholy, mournful flavor. When I discovered stray issues of more colorful, hardcore magazines like *Blueboy* and *Honcho*, their raunchy spreads didn't move me nearly as much as the coy, wistful shots in my uncle's copies of *Physique Pictorial* and *Tomorrow's Man*, forerunners of gay erotica that had to masquerade as men's fitness journals to avoid censorship. The more elusive and unattainably beautiful the models appeared, the more freedom to fantasize these images permitted me; I loved to ogle, but not as much as I loved to yearn. As a teenager, when I got a personal computer in the privacy of my bedroom, I continued to seek similarly soft, subtle photos that looked more like idyllic scenes from the past than explicit previews of the sexual experiences awaiting me in the future. This aesthetic sensibility might be why I was such a late bloomer, far less experienced than most of my peers assumed: I came out on the early side because I knew that I, like my uncle, enjoyed looking at men, but I was in no rush to figure out what I was supposed to do with these men, and I didn't feel too curious about the kinds of videos that would demonstrate the skills I was missing. (I'll always remember the upward glance of disbelief from the only boyfriend of my adolescence when

I asked, since it was his first time as well as mine, how he'd learned to do what he was doing with his mouth.) I was content to keep curating my Tumblr trove in solitude and constructing my own digital dream room, to which I could always return.

But now of course I can't return. When I sift through the remains of my Tumblr, I feel as if I'm scrambling to hold a séance for the men in these rapidly disintegrating photos; it pains me to realize that I never bothered to learn their stories or even their names, that I've treated them as taxidermied bodies to collect in a cabinet of curiosities. But I admit that their faces look even more bittersweetly seductive now that I might never see them again. At the same time, ever since Bruce died, I can't pretend anymore that the men on his bathroom wall recognize me as his nephew; now that my uncle is no longer around, it's harder to view the "dream room" through his eyes and insert myself into the fantasies he wanted this space to inspire. I already knew that inaccessibility is the soul of thirst, but I'm now discovering that, in its own perverse way, so is grief.

To some extent, this is the appeal of all kinds of photography, a medium that Susan Sontag once described as an "inventory of mortality," while Roland Barthes went so far as to call photographers "agents of Death." Erotic photos have been especially good at attuning me to my perishability, partly because they're liable to vanish just as irretrievably as the living, breathing bodies they memorialize. It's a distinctly slippery form for slippery content, one that promises to capture the most fleeting moments of pleasure, and one that bewitches me all the more when it fails to keep this promise. As queer theorist Tim Dean observes, porn "preserves evidence of something that is otherwise transient and ephemeral," yet porn itself is also "ephemeral and amenable to destruction, no less so by its fans than by the police."

I try not to let my favorite photos—obscene or otherwise—desensitize me to loss, but I also don't want to romanticize it. This double bind seems to ensnare many queer people, as theorist Heather Love notes in her book *Feeling Backward*, in which she takes up the myth of Orpheus and Eurydice as an allegory for queer history:

> Orpheus's relation to Eurydice [is] an impossible relation: by turning back he betrays her, losing her forever in the lower depths; but the refusal to turn back would count as a betrayal as well. Such is the relation of the queer historian to the past: we cannot help wanting to save the figures from the past, but this mission is doomed to fail. In part, this is because the dead are gone for good; in part, because the queer past is even more remote, more deeply marked by power's claw; and in part because this rescue is an emotional rescue, and in that sense, we are sure to botch it. But [. . .] not to botch it would be a betrayal. Such a rescue effort can only take place under the shadow of loss and in the name of loss; success would constitute its failure.

In other words, damned if you look back expecting to grasp the suffering of the queer ghosts in the rearview mirror, and damned if you don't look back, turning away from the loneliness and heartbreak and violence that made your queer existence possible.

Consider, for example, the many photographs documenting gay life just before the outbreak of the AIDS epidemic, such as the Polaroids that Tom Bianchi began snapping on Fire Island in the mid-1970s. I once gave Bruce a newly published monograph of these Polaroids, not because I was familiar with Bianchi's work, but because I was drawn to his golden-hued shots of young men embracing and dancing, nude or minimally swimsuited; they reminded me of the insouciant, heavily filtered beach pics that my generation of gays had begun posting on Instagram. I gather Bruce enjoyed the book as much as I did, since he prominently displayed it on his coffee table, but I regret that I never asked. When I finally got around to reading the book, I wished I could still ask my uncle about Bianchi's introduction: "I could not imagine that my Polaroids would so suddenly become a record of a lost world—my box of pictures a mausoleum, too painful to visit. When I reopened the box decades later, I found friends and lovers playing and smiling. Alive again." It's tempting to view photos like these as relics from a prelapsarian era, since I've been told so often that the deadliest years of the AIDS crisis are behind me, though this ongoing plague isn't a thing of the past. But no matter how many times I hear a doctor insist that HIV is "no longer a death sentence," it's hard to shake the feeling that death is still in the room, that there's always another catastrophe on the horizon. If I could tell Bruce that this context makes me see Bianchi's photos as both sadder and hotter, would he be scandalized by my irreverence, or might he have felt the same way?

I had a similarly ambivalent reaction to Billy Howard's 1989 book *Epitaphs for the Living*, which Thor recently gave me. Howard photographed dozens of people with AIDS and later asked them to submit their own handwritten testimonies. These photos, unlike Bianchi's Polaroids, are certainly not "sexy," and the captions don't sugarcoat how it feels to be "in the midst of illness, rejection, isolation, and probably death." If I had come across these photos in isolation, I don't know whether the images alone would have moved me, so it's strange to register how much more beautiful they appear when I consider the framing of Howard's project, or when I read a note like this: *Patrick died soon after this photograph was taken. A friend wrote this statement to accompany his portrait.*

Now Thor and I are swapping favorite photos we've rescued from the Tumblr purge, noting the poignant details that likely aren't intended to arouse: the faces that remind us of old friends and lovers, the figure one-handedly reading a copy of Barthes's *S/Z* as if it were smut, the coquettish poses that result from trying to stage a candid-looking shot, the sly cropping and lighting that hint at what lies just beyond the frame. As we approach our destination, I confess that I've never been to any spas, though I've heard many stories from Bruce, who used to frequent the Continental Baths on the Upper West Side and hear Bette Midler sing with Barry Manilow, who wore nothing but a towel wrapped around his waist as he accompanied her at the piano. Thor laughs and assures me this will be much different from the old bathhouses of gay lore, most of which closed in the eighties because of concerns about HIV. I know Thor didn't necessarily bring me here for a history lesson, but I can tell from his authoritative tone that he's proud to be giving me a first taste of this time-honored gay tradition, and I'm glad to have a wingman who's less bashful than I'll ever be. Once we enter Spa Castle, I can see why Thor tried to temper my expectations: most of the customers in the lobby are straight couples and families with young children. As I watch them part ways after passing the front desk, separately entering the men's and women's locker rooms, Thor explains that the second and third floors hold all kinds of mixed saunas and pools, but on the ground level we'll be in a segregated bath area—totally nude. He clearly finds nothing unusual about this, so I try not to look surprised: we've known each other for less than a year, and I'm not sure we're ready for the let's-get-naked-in-public stage of our friendship. Nonetheless, I don't hesitate to unlace my boots at the entrance to the lockers and stow the rest of my clothes and belongings as swiftly and casually as I can.

Thor marches ahead to the baths—I admire the handsome spots and folds on his back, a small surgical scar on his arm—and I stop to use the toilet on my way. I know I'm supposed to be naked here, and so is everyone around me, but I somehow feel more acutely embarrassed while standing at the urinal, as if I should have a fig leaf to cover my exposed behind while performing this crude function. I think of artist Tony Just, who photographed a number of abandoned "tearooms," public lavatories where men used to meet up for anonymous sex before the spaces were shut down. Scrubbed and sanitized by Just, these rooms show no trace of either their original squalor or his janitorial work in his photos, which both reenact and implicitly critique institutional efforts to erase the queer sexual cultures that have been decimated by AIDS. He also may have been playing with the double meaning of *haunting*, which used to be gay slang for cruising, while those who loitered in such spaces were called "ghosts." I wouldn't know, since I've never dared to cruise a stranger in public, though browsing Tumblr lately has left me feeling more and more like a ghost among ghosts, a lurker among the filthy remains that other horny gays have left in their wake. *How pristine*, I think as I flush the toilet and wash my hands in this spotless locker room. I check the mirror to make sure my body looks presentable but rush away when someone notices me preening. Who am I trying to impress here? I sweep the question from my mind as I open the door to the baths and read a sign announcing that any kind of inappropriate behavior, including photography, is strictly prohibited.

After a quick shower, I join Thor in one of the hot tubs at the center of the room. A few men turn their heads, sizing up what kind of twosome we are, but we ignore their scrutiny and move to the far corner of the baths, where we claim a pair of tile thrones, partly submerged in warm, roiling water and equipped with Jacuzzi jets to massage our flanks.

"I feel like a boneless chicken," Thor says. He laughs, sounding less gruff and looking more relaxed than ever, and soon he closes his eyes and drifts into a half-awake reverie.

I've never seen so many naked men, whether two- or

three-dimensional, all in one place. I try not to stare too overtly, but I can't restrain my voyeurism, and we all seem to be part-time exhibitionists here. No one appears to mind innocuously looking or being looked at, so I relish my panoramic view of the baths while heeding the no-eye-contact code tacitly enforced throughout the city. I scan the crowd and estimate that I must be the only bather between prepuberty and middle age, but soon a trio of willowy twentysomethings comes out of the locker room. Two of them head to the sauna, and the third approaches the shower, where his dark ringlets of hair fall into loose, floppy waves. He looks like a long-lost Jonas Brother; in my daydreaming mind, I decide to name him Jasper. He's facing away as he lathers up, but I still try not to let my eyes linger too long or too lewdly on his balletic legs and his dimpled bottom. He rinses off and turns around to grab his towel, and as soon as I catch a glimpse, it's impossible to ignore his disproportionately large dick. By now it's too late; Jasper has caught me peeping. I can't decipher his startled face from the opposite corner of the room, so I duck underwater until I'm pretty sure he's walked away and rejoined his friends.

When I resurface, I see the three of them enter the steam room. I consider following, but before I can make a move, they exit and step in another pool with a heavy waterfall pouring from the ceiling. I float to the other side of the Jacuzzi to get a better vantage point without giving myself away, but then of course the trio moves again. There's a moment in the film adaptation of *Call Me by Your Name* when Timothée Chalamet and Armie Hammer circle a monument in the middle of a piazza, dancing obliquely around admitting their attraction to each other—a scene that captures the tedious logistics of acting on a crush so painfully well that I cringe whenever it comes to mind, especially now that I'm playing out my own version of this furtive pursuit. I'm finally cruising; I've finally become a ghost. Can Jasper tell it's my first time? Maybe this chase is futile, but eventually I get tired of feigning disinterest and trail him into the steam room.

I can barely see through the thick vapor in the air, which immediately saturates my skin. I lean against the wall by the entrance, where several bathers—including Jasper—wait for a seat on the crowded benches lining the rest of the room. I try to play it cool, but I feel restless and clumsy just standing around and sweating, so I squat on the floor, hoping I'll look more at ease down there. Beneath the rising cloud of steam, I get a much clearer view, at least of the crotches arrayed on the benches, which are all now at eye level. I see more than one sitter's hand gently graze his neighbor's knee, and I see some of those hands gracefully slide up the thighs, and I see what all these men are waiting around for. Whenever someone else enters, the action pauses until everyone can tell the newcomer isn't a child or a spa staffer, and then it resumes apace. I watch this rhythm start and stop and restart again until a few satisfied men vacate the benches, and then Jasper claims a seat in the corner. I don't want to seem overeager, so I hold back for a minute or two before taking the spot to his right. I hold back for another minute or two before rehearsing the gesture I've just witnessed, and then Jasper leads my hand from his knee to where we both want it to go.

Reader, I am no southpaw, but my less dexterous arm rises to the occasion and gets to work. Jasper leans back with his hands behind his head, and I get a good look at the tattoo just below his right armpit, a little heart with cartoonish eyes and a smirking mouth, though in my steam-induced delirium it begins to resemble a mutant strawberry. I steal a few sidelong glances to see if anyone disapproves of what Jasper and I are up to, but my neighbors are all gazing straight ahead and keeping up their best poker faces, as if posing for a daguerreotype. I try to focus and savor this encounter, but my mind wanders in strange directions as the atmosphere shifts. The thermostat reads 114°. The steam reminds me of ectoplasm, the misty substance that supposedly veils photographs of paranormal apparitions. The door keeps opening and closing like a vortex, a hazy portal to the spirit world. I wonder if I'm dying, but then Jasper twitches, and I remember my real hand jerking off his real cock. The faces of all the men I've ever fantasized about appear in the fog and speak to me in unison.

"It's just a fucking handjob," they say. "Big deal, kid. This happens all the time, has been happening for centuries. Welcome to the party."

Yes, I'm late to the party, but it's still *my* first time touching a total stranger like this, or touching anyone like this in a semipublic space, without the help of any apps or screens, and I feel like I've graduated to the next phase of my queerness. I couldn't have dreamt of daring this just a month ago, and I wonder if the purge has unleashed the imp of the perverse in me. Or maybe I'm just animated by grief—for Tumblr, for Bruce's dream room, for the old bathhouses I never got to visit, for all the other communal sites of queer intimacy that could be shut down at any moment. Are these other men grieving? Is Jasper? He starts to whimper, and I wonder if he's weeping, but no, he gasps and pulses and bursts, wipes his torso with his towel, gently unclasps my sticky fingers, and dashes for the door without looking back. My limp hand lingers on his now-empty seat, and the vestiges of Jasper's sweat start to excite me even more than his solid body did just a moment ago. But then I see another man approach the bench and figure I should let go of this soon-to-be-overwritten assprint. Jasper and his friends have already left the baths by the time I step out, so I return to the thrones in the corner. Still right where I left him, Thor opens his eyes and asks, "Have fun?"

Amateur

The balloon is filled with his nephew's breath. It hovers just above the floor, dangling by a string tied to a long loop of burlap swinging from the ceiling. Nested in this makeshift hammock, two taxidermied fawn hooves rest upon a young boy's timeworn clothes, neatly folded and stacked. So many shades of blue: the bright cerulean balloon; the dark burlap, freshly dyed with indigo; the pale, faded denim of the boy's tiny overalls; and the verdigris hooves, discolored by cyanosis in the wild, where the fawn suffocated before birth.

My friend David made this assemblage. He's an artist, and I'm his assistant for the day, helping him document his work by posing beside it for scale. I struggle to find my bearings in front of his camera, though I know I'm not its focus point. But I try, since he wants the shots to look candid, to compose myself and play the role of a self-possessed museumgoer as I circle the installation. He begins to tell me about the artifacts he's arranged here, all of which come from his family's home and the surrounding landscape. I feel both disoriented and at home among this constellation of found objects, which I could see as either the skeleton of a Rube Goldberg machine or an enigmatic self-portrait, and I want to know more. *How old is your nephew,* for example, *and when did he inflate this balloon? Did these clothes belong to you or him? How did you get these hooves?* But I don't want to sound naïve or uninformed, since the artist is present, and I've known him for only a month.

We live in Moscow, Idaho, where David was born and raised, and where I moved a year ago for grad school. Lately we've been walking around town together, forming some kind of alliance, a coalition of two. If I were bolder, I'd ask who exactly we are to each other, but I like our nascent bond too much to risk ruining it with such a question. I like the way his gentle, playful manner puts me at ease. I like the empty wasp nest he found under a tree and gave me as a protective talisman after I received my first beesting. I like the local landmarks he appends to my personal map of the region: a ghost town, a witch cemetery, a neighborhood pub where we can share an ample plate of dino nuggets from the kids' menu. And I like that, when I first asked about his art, he simply answered, "A lot of my work is about longing," and invited me to see for myself at this gallery in downtown Lewiston.

—

"Mister Bluebird's on my shoulder . . ."

Bruce abruptly pauses his morning reveille and halts at the bottom of the stairs, feigning surprise to see me still on the couch where he wished me sweet dreams the night before. He winks, resumes zip-a-dee-doo-dah-ing in the kitchen, returns to the couch with coffee, and gives his full attention to the *Hartford Courant*, pretending again to have forgotten all about me. It's our old routine: hammy uncle and his bashful teenage nephew tacitly celebrate a rare moment when no one expects either of them to light up the room. I wonder if this make-believe will ever end, if we'll ever genuinely run out of things to say when alone together. He keeps humming, and I wonder if he'll ever quit this awful *Song of the South* number, which he finally gives a rest when Will comes home from the dump, hauling a bundle of timber in one arm, a pair of antlers and a rusted Tonka truck in the other.

Bruce calls him a hoarder, but Will prefers the term "maximal pack rat." They've lived together almost as long as I've been alive, and every time I visit, Will shows me yet another thick sketchbook he's filled with drawings, watercolors, poems, and collages, including a few clippings from smutty magazines. ("That's not for kids," he'll warn me if my dad's in the room, though he knows I'll end up flipping through the pages anyway.) Artistic talent doesn't run in our family, so Bruce and I are both in awe of Will, whose creative mind tends to leave me feeling like the opposite of an expert. Yet my uncles seem to think I don't need any expertise to appreciate the kind of art they love. Lately they've been talking about this guy Robert Rauschenberg as if he were a longtime friend, but no, they just saw a big Rauschenberg exhibition during their recent trip to New York. Rauschenberg apparently used to say he felt "sorry for people who think soap dishes or mirrors or Coke bottles are ugly, because they're surrounded by things like that all day." He used such things in his so-called combines, mash-ups of painting and sculpture made with everyday objects and even junk. Now Will has begun building similar combines with his own ever-growing collections of bric-a-brac. Above the couch, next to Bruce's favorite antique—a framed print of the American flag with the colors inverted in green, black, and orange—Will has mounted his latest experiment, a grid of interlocking planks on which he's affixed a broken clay pigeon, a Jägermeister label, a postage stamp, a disposable razor, some loose ribbon, a hair extension, and a mismatched set of tarnished silverware. Anyone could have found the materials for this piece, though I never would have considered using them in this way; the parts seem mismatched, but juxtaposed like this, all of it somehow makes sense. I worry that the whole thing will come unfastened and topple on my head when Will begins hammering away at his next creation, but Bruce just sighs and keeps reading the paper.

"Don't ever get married," he says. *"It's the truth! It's actual! Everything is satisfactual!"*

—

The balloon is almost deflated. It's been languishing here for several weeks by the time David and I visit this gallery in mid-July. We move on from his installation to the next room, adorned with photos of the Stonewall Inn—A PLACE THAT BECAME A MOVEMENT, according to a banner by the door. David tells me the fiftieth anniversary of the riots occasioned this exhibition featuring queer artists based in North Idaho. He met the curator by chance several months ago, and as soon as he introduced himself, she invited him to join the show. I wonder if she knew anything else at the time about David, who doesn't address the show's theme as directly as the other artists displayed here, many of whom draw upon familiar gay tropes: rainbow color palettes, homoerotic portraits, news clippings about same-sex marriage. I don't even know if a stranger encountering David's work in a different context would immediately classify it as "queer art" at all.

"What does Stonewall mean to you?" is a question that's begun to exhaust me after this year's unusually loud Pride Month. But as we silently read a set of placards about the history of the uprising and silently nod in shared approval when we see Marsha P. Johnson credited with throwing the first brick, I wonder what Stonewall means to David, who's never been to New York. He and I were both born in the early nineties, and we both now call ourselves queer men, but I can only speculate about the differences between our circumstances. I don't tell him that my late uncle Bruce lived near Stonewall in the sixties, though he was apparently too "scared shitless" to take part in the riots. (What kind of cachet does this loose coincidence even give me?) I don't tell him that, during the nine years I lived in New York, I visited Stonewall only once, on my twenty-second birthday, when all my friends wanted to drink overpriced palomas and dance to Robyn, while I moped because I just wanted to go home with Dennis, the handsome premed student I'd been eyeing for months. (Was that all Marsha had thrown that brick for?) I don't know how to tell David, without sounding callous or flippant, that what Stonewall represents both does and doesn't feel like it belongs to me;

I hesitate to call this history "mine," even though I don't hesitate to acknowledge how it's molded me. But I know publicly identifying as a queer artist is riskier and more complicated for David.

"Is my work queer enough?" he asks once we've finished our lap around the gallery. *Isn't it enough,* I want to ask in return, *that you call yourself queer, and this is your work?* But I know that's beside the point of David's predicament. I remember critic Ariel Goldberg's book *The Estrangement Principle,* an inquiry into "the phrase 'queer art' in all its sweaty megaphone pronouncements," which I stumbled upon a few years ago. Goldberg would probably refuse to answer David's question with a simple yes or no, since asking how much queerness is "enough" can quickly devolve into policing what counts as queer in the first place. "Questioning 'queer art' only seemed to reinstate the labeling practice," Goldberg writes. "Shouldn't it be enough to care [about] and be engaged in queer communities and histories?" I want to tell David that I can see his use of close-to-home materials as a commentary on his upbringing in this part of the country, where his queerness took shape, and which he's repeatedly departed from and returned to throughout his adulthood. And I can see what he means about longing, which I'm tempted to call a queer mood, paraphrasing one of José Esteban Muñoz's much-quoted theories about horizons and possibility. Yet I still don't know how to answer David. I can tell he's happy to be part of this exhibition but also unsure of its aims, wary of those who throw around *queer* as a politically hollow, mostly meaningless hashtag to make certain art more marketable. David admits that he asked the curator to omit any biographical notes from her press materials, and he skipped the opening reception, partly because he already knows the four other artists featured here: all five of them are white, he says, and all but one are men. What kind of community was the curator aiming to gather in this gallery, I wonder, and what kind of movement could this place become in Idaho in 2019?

David looks like he's getting restless, and the summer heat in these stuffy rooms is making me lightheaded, so I suggest we get some tacos down the street. Before we leave, he asks if I'd like to make a piece together sometime. I remind him that I'm no artist, but he assures me we'll figure something out.

—

My hands aren't steady or graceful enough for drawing, so I've signed up for photography. My high school requires two semesters of art, and I'm grateful for the excuse to meet the teacher, whom all the cool kids seem to call by her first name, Shireen. I've overheard them speak of her as both a trusted confidante and a clairvoyant force to be reckoned with, someone to tell all your troubles in hopes of receiving the balm you didn't know you need, and I want to find out what she'll prescribe for me. By now I've accepted that tenth grade will go down as my year of perpetual pining: after briefly dating my only out classmate, who unceremoniously broke up with me via LiveJournal, I keep falling in vain for sexually confused boys who persuade me to help them figure things out and then, once satisfied, never speak to me again. But maybe if I can win over Shireen, I can ask her what to do about my stupid heart.

For our first project, she explains, each of us will produce a set of images emulating one of a few famous photographers she's assigned. I'll be doing Cindy Sherman, best known for her series of "film stills," in which the artist reenacts various stock scenes of women in popular culture (the ingénue arriving in the big city, the beleaguered housewife picking up groceries spilled on the kitchen floor). I don't know what hubris or desperation drives me to masquerade as Shireen herself. I wear a turtleneck and borrow a classmate's pashmina shawl; I consider getting a brown bob wig and brick-red lipstick, but we're using black-and-white film. I pose at the darkroom entrance, swiveling back my head with a piercing gaze; I pose by the blackboard, my arms akimbo and mouth half-open, pretending to dispense one of her favorite aphorisms ("beauty begets beauty," "perfection is death"). I worry Shireen might be irritated by my drag caricatures, but once I develop the negatives and finish the prints, she at least puts on a good show of genuine delight, which I take as permission to join the flock of groupies who loiter in her classroom after school.

While I pretend to catch up on my homework, I eavesdrop on Shireen and her fan club. She tells us about her first encounters with the work of her favorite artists: Louise Bourgeois, Eva Hesse, Sophie Calle. She shows us samples of her own art, long sheets of butcher paper on which she's layered samples of dressmaker patterns and pages from old French novels and painted haunting silhouettes of swing sets and ceiling fans and honeycombs. We talk about music, and some older girls tell Shireen about the mixtapes they've been making—*yes*, they insist, *on real tapes*. The girls describe their mixes the way Shireen talks about her art, as if each piece were a love letter encoded with its own private symbolism: if the recipient doesn't return the feelings you've obliquely divulged, you can always save face by insisting, "I just thought you might like this Magnetic Fields song." For my latest crush, a cute Italian boy I met at a winter dance hosted by the Boston Alliance of GLBT Youth, I get inspired to compile my favorite love songs on a sixty-minute tape and write the track list inside a valentine from the drugstore. I furtively ask a mutual friend for my crush's address and mail him a package labeled FRAGILE. Weeks pass. Finally I feel the outline of a cassette in the mailbox, and I wonder what songs he's recorded for me as my fingers press its bubble-wrap padding, but then I see it's just the same one I sent him, resealed and returned without a valentine or even a note. Maybe he had no way to play it. (How many people even own a tape deck in 2007?) Maybe he just didn't want it. Either way, I trust Shireen will know what to do.

The next afternoon, I tell Shireen this story, solemnly unveiling the tape as if it were the body of a dead sparrow.

"What's that?" asks Sarah, a twelfth grader who chain-smokes cloves and can't wait to go to Pratt next year.

I show her the envelope and its contents, letting the evidence speak for itself.

"Oh," she says, "how *Perks of Being a Wallflower*."

Shireen ignores her and urges me to sit down. She

gathers some shreds of cardboard, a stack of *National Geographic* back issues, an X-Acto knife, and a set of oil paints (alizarin crimson, cadmium yellow, phthalo blue).

"Take it apart," she says.

"What?"

"Take it apart."

"What am I supposed to do with all this?"

"I don't know," Shireen says. "Just make something with your hands."

—

David proposes cohosting a collage party. He brings a jar of Mod Podge, a set of brushes, and some of his mom's old magazines to my apartment, where I've provided a plate of dino nuggets, a Bronski Beat playlist, and a pile of water-damaged books. I help him layer multicolored tissue paper over a photo spread from *Better Homes & Gardens*. He helps me clip warped and swollen pages out of *A Lover's Discourse* and asks what it's about; I promise to lend him another copy sometime, keeping up the queer tradition of passing Barthes's book among friends, lovers, and other fellow readers. For now, we're just two amateurs, playing with glue and scissors.

David asks if I remember the last time I tried to make a collage, which must have been in Shireen's classroom. I tell him about the one I started after some boy sent back the mixtape I'd mailed him: I tried to turn my heartbreak into a collage, but I ended up making a mess and throwing most of it away, though I still have a set of photograms I developed with the deconstructed tape. David lights up with curiosity, but I get shy and change the subject. I ask what his teachers were like, and he tells me about Lynne, his printmaking professor, for whom he once made a piece about not being out to his family. Lynne snorted, scanned him up and down, and asked half-sarcastically, "Oh, you mean *they don't know*?" David laughs uncomfortably, and I sense they still don't know, or at least they don't talk about it. Lynne later assigned a class presentation on a famous artist and tried to match each student with an aesthetically kindred spirit. "I don't know *what* to do with you," she told David, "so I guess you can do Robert Rauschenberg."

I'd love to show David a draft of the dilettantish essay I keep struggling to write about Rauschenberg. I've been thinking more and more about the artists my uncles taught me to love, but whenever I try to write about my own relationship with Rauschenberg, I have trouble articulating what he means to me. Of all the queer artists of that generation, why is he the one who fascinates me the most? I still don't have a good answer, but I'm glad I've met someone who shares this fascination. I imagine presenting my research to David, drawing from my endless document of extracts and displaying a selection on the wall, as if they were placards for an exhibition that hasn't yet been curated; I picture David filling in the blanks and translating my intended message, the way I hoped my high school crushes would interpret the subtext of my mixtapes. But in reality, all I have is an unwieldy muddle of anecdotes and observations that reveal very little about Rauschenberg himself.

"Isn't that sort of what his work is like?" David asks. I

admit he has a point: many of Rauschenberg's best-known pieces seem open to containing anything but straightforwardly biographical content. David's favorite is *Canyon*, a controversial 1959 combine that features a pillow suspended from the canvas and a taxidermied eagle that looks ready to attack the viewer. David says it exemplifies how Rauschenberg's art tends to be more embodied than representational: it's tempting to view *Canyon* as an allegory—the eagle could symbolize the state of America or refer to the ancient myth of Ganymede, who was abducted by Zeus, disguised as an eagle—but trying to read the piece metaphorically doesn't give you much. What's more interesting, at least to David, is the experience of the encounter. You can treat the art as a kind of game to play, he adds, but Rauschenberg doesn't tell you the rules or determine the outcomes for you.

I want to ask David to elaborate, to explain the rules of the game one could play with his own art, but a protective side of me would rather let him keep his secrets. Besides, we've been getting sidetracked from the work at hand. All I've pasted so far on my collage surface is Barthes's overture: *So it is a lover who speaks and who says:*

—

I wish I could peel back the quilt and crawl inside. We're standing at the foot of *Bed*, a 1955 combine for which Rauschenberg framed and mounted his own sheets, blankets, and pillow, all defaced with paint and pencil. I've asked Thor to join me for one last visit to the Museum of Modern Art before I leave New York. We're both eager to show each other our favorite pieces, but he looks unimpressed by this one.

"I respect Rauschenberg's work," Thor says, "but I've always been disappointed that he wasn't out enough."

What does "out enough" even mean? I feel uneasy about demanding artists to sacrifice their privacy and make their work more explicitly queer for my sake. When friends my age bemoan Sufjan Stevens's reticence about the gayness of his songs, I want to ask, *Hasn't he given us enough of himself in his music? What more do you need?* Likewise, I don't see the point of expecting Rauschenberg to "prove" anything in his art, but if you need evidence of his sexuality, just look at the unmistakable scribbles on this pillow—a nod to Cy Twombly, one of Rauschenberg's collaborators and old flames. Isn't publicly acknowledging your bedmate like this a pretty bold way of outing yourself? I appreciate this covertly queer move, especially in the context of McCarthy-era homophobia, but its coyness seems to frustrate Thor, who was born a year after Rauschenberg made his *Bed*, and who came of age around the time of the Stonewall riots. I try to chalk up our disagreement to generational differences and move on, but I can tell from Thor's expression that I've touched a nerve.

"When I was growing up," Thor says, "I was desperate for visible role models. By the time you were born, you could find thousands of them. Lucky you!"

True, lucky me. By the time I was eighteen, when I moved to New York and began visiting this museum, I had no shortage of queer role models, and I guess I considered myself out enough. Yet I gathered I had something more to learn from Rauschenberg when I discovered *Rebus*, the first combine I saw in person, nine years ago. Through the doorway of the adjacent gallery, I noticed a triptych of enormous canvas panels, covering almost the whole wall. The first thing to stop me in my tracks was the range of colors—a long row of swatches, the kind you might find in a hardware store, stretching across the center like a horizon, surrounded by bold blocks of goldenrod and ultramarine and splashes of white and crimson. From a distance, the canvas appeared otherwise bare and unvarnished, faded to a dirty sepia, but upon approaching I saw a collection of yellowed images flanking the horizon line: an election poster, photos of a track-and-field race, comic strips, a small reproduction of Botticelli's *Birth of Venus*. The rough, messy look of it all reminded me of refashioning my bedroom wall back in high school, when I dreamt of recklessly dispersing my favorite shades of paint around my own pantheon of pinups and mementos. And the piece's melancholy atmosphere conjured my adolescent heartsickness, echoing my earliest attempts to take apart that feeling and make something with my hands.

At least that's how I remember the encounter. I didn't know much about Rauschenberg, who had died a year earlier, and whose name I recognized only because he had inspired my uncle Will's eccentric bricolages. The placard attributed the coinage of *combine* to Rauschenberg's "friend" Jasper Johns, whose name I recalled from Bruce's beloved print of the inverted American flag. And I knew the title, *Rebus*, referred to the kind of clever visual riddle my mom used to leave in my lunchbox (in third grade I once found a Post-it on which she'd written, *Hope today's history lesson isn't,* and then sketched the numeral 2, a knotted ribbon, and a wedding band—that is, "too boring"). Rauschenberg seemed to have encrypted some private message in a similarly tricky way, and maybe he was just trying to remain "closeted enough" to protect his career, as were so many other queer artists of his generation. But *Rebus* has always given me the impression that Rauschenberg was daring me to decipher his coded yearning. I often think about what he once told composer John Cage in a discussion of artistic technique: "What do you want, a declaration of love? I take responsibility for competence and hope to have made something hazardous with which we may try ourselves." It *is* hazardous for a queer artist like Rauschenberg to put himself out there, but his work also puts viewers in a dicey position, making us not passive bystanders but active participants in solving the puzzle he's presented; I'd much rather join Rauschenberg in the discomfort of that uncertainty than watch him make a straightforward declaration of love that leaves nothing to the imagination. Wouldn't that be 2️⃣🎀💍?

But I don't manage to explain all this to Thor, who's already marched ahead to the Warhols and Ruschas in the next room. Once I catch up, he asks if I want to walk over to Third Avenue and visit his favorite bagel shop. "Bet you won't find anything like it in Idaho," he says. "Or art like this, for that matter." I'm not so sure about that, but I wouldn't mind a toasted everything.

—

Early on a Saturday morning, I wake to a text from David: "Hey! I'm going to the junkyard—want to come?"

I'm still half-asleep, and I should get back downtown in an hour or so for the Pride festivities, which Moscow holds in late August, once all the university's students and faculty return from summer break. But I'd hate to decline such an invitation, so I say yes, throw on the thin tank top and short shorts I plan to wear to the parade, and meet David outside my apartment building in Friendship Square.

On our way to the outskirts of town, he pulls off the highway to stop at a drive-through coffee stand in an empty lot. Somehow we've never before noticed this spot, where we feel like we've passed through a portal to another dimension. We read a menu decorated with paintings of leprechauns and fairies and try to shout over the barista's Irish jig music to order our beverages, which she hands us in two baby-blue cups with frosting-pink lids. I feel a little ridiculous sipping out of this thing, but David insists the fairies must have endowed it with magic powers, so I carry it with me once we reach our destination.

Wasankari Construction advertises itself as a "building recycler," but to me it looks like the end of the world. We roam the grounds among heaps of abandoned home equipment: rusted shovels and hoes, upturned stoves and sinks, lopsided cement mixers and wheelbarrows, run-down tractors and cranes, even the skeleton of a whole prefab house. We spelunk in a trio of huts designated as ART DEPT #1, ART DEPT #2, and ART DEPT #3, lined with shelves full of old pulleys, gears, coil springs, Polaroid cameras, toasters, and alarm clocks. David tells me Wasankari became important to him in his adolescence, when he was coming to understand his queerness, and I ask if he thinks there's something queer about junk, recalling both Rauschenberg's and my uncle Will's fondness for scavenging "trash." David says he doesn't know about that; what mattered to him was learning to make his own imaginative space with whatever scraps he could find and to appreciate how intimate that process can be. That toaster warmed someone else's bread, for example, and this sink washed someone else's hands.

"I want to know where a person ends and their surroundings begin," David says. He points to a wrought-iron bed frame outside ART DEPT #3, noting that you can view such an object as an extension of the body if you think about all the iron in our blood. "I want to know," he adds, "where does a body stop?"

Today David is seeking supplies for his latest sculpture. He wants to get some wire to coat in wet clay until it rusts, but he's not interested in getting it from a chain store; he wants something with a story embedded in it, something emotionally charged by its connection to *this* particular landscape. "I'm where I'm longing for," he says, explaining that he finds himself in a double bind. On one hand, so much of his art is about having grown up in Moscow, and continuing to live here gives him access to site-specific props and backdrops; on the other, he thinks he's made his best art elsewhere, in the throes of homesickness, and he feels more calculated and less spontaneous while working in such close proximity to his birthplace. Of course it doesn't help, he says, that he's living with his parents for the time being, with only a cramped corner of their garage to use as a makeshift art studio. Selfishly, I want him to stay here in Moscow, though we've known each other for such a short time, and I don't know how to define what I'm afraid of losing. But I don't tell him this, since I know he wants—and probably needs—to leave this town for good.

David gives up his quest for wire and opts for a bundle of frayed twine. We flag down a clerk driving a golf cart through the rubble, and she frowns as we approach. "Is that all you want?" she asks, squinting skeptically at David's modest purchase, my skimpy outfit, and our pastel coffee cups. For the first time I realize how out of place David and I look here. Though he's more respectably dressed in jeans and a hoodie, I see the clerk sizing up what the two of us are doing together, shopping for used twine in a junkyard on a Saturday morning. David deferentially hands her a dollar, and she chuckles without softening her face. "You boys have fun at that parade now."

I catch David glower and roll his eyes as we return to his car, where he releases a deep sigh and starts the engine. I want to ask him to join me at Pride, but he says he doesn't want to get caught in any photographs that might end up on the internet, so I don't push the subject. He drops me off at the post office, where the march is about to begin. I find my friend Toby among the PFLAG contingent in the crowd, and he hands me a wand for blowing bubbles as we walk through the center of town to East City Park. Toby and I talk about poet CAConrad's somatic poetry rituals and "power sissy interventions," one of which involved standing at a busy intersection in

Asheville, North Carolina, "to bless children with bubbles that will make them queer." This isn't necessarily our mission, though we receive smiles and giggles from all the kids we consecrate with traces of soapy water, and their parents and chaperones nod approvingly as we pass. David's question echoes in my head: *Where does a body stop?*

—

Those who live in glass houses should pave the grounds with stones—or at least gay boys should, as Bruce used to warn me. When he was growing up in Memphis, the sound of his mother's car in the gravel driveway was always his cue to quit horsing around, yank off her earrings, hide her high heels, and wipe away her makeup before she came inside and caught him red-handed and red-lipped. Someone must have relayed similar advice to architect Philip Johnson, who built his own glass house in 1949 and shared it with his partner, gallerist David Whitney, for about half a century. Now it's a museum, and for a substantial fee—sometimes a hundred dollars or more, depending on the day—you can visit this house and the thirteen other buildings on Johnson's estate. My uncles had planned to go before Bruce died, so I've taken the Metro-North train from Grand Central to New Canaan, Connecticut, to accompany Will alone.

"This gravel was Johnson's doorbell," the tour guide says, referring to the crunching noise of our feet on the path. I dig in my sneakers a little deeper as we walk toward the house, which is at least far enough from the main road that its occupants had plenty of time to hear interlopers approaching. But the walls of this house—I don't know why this surprises me—are entirely transparent, so Johnson and Whitney must not have worried much about hiding in plain sight.

The building comprises a single rectangular room, bigger than most apartments I've seen in Brooklyn, though it feels smaller. Nothing separates the kitchen, dining area, parlor, or sleeping quarters, except the fireplace and bathroom, both contained in a cylindrical brick column at the center of the space. Two hipsters in our tour group snap photos of the tile work on the floor and ceiling, sketch the view of the pond behind the house. A trio of dapper silver foxes circle the mid-century modern couch and coffee table, as if they were shopping at Crate & Barrel. And Will inspects the seamless sheets of glass—all at least ten feet tall, some thirty feet long—that wall the house.

"When I moved in with your uncle," he says, "the town clerk told us she didn't care what we did in there, as long as we got curtains." He cackles, and the reverberation startles the guide, who shoots us a puzzled look and suggests that we all move on to the gallery.

Outside, she tells us John Cage and Merce Cunningham used to stage their "happenings"—the interactive performances they developed at Black Mountain College—on this lawn, which is now so impeccably mown that I'm afraid to step on it. The guide leads us down a sloping path to a daunting stone doorway burrowed beneath a mound of grass. Not until she brings us inside the space, apparently modeled on an ancient Greek tomb, do I realize this *is* the gallery, which includes work by Andy

Warhol, Jasper Johns, and Robert Rauschenberg. A former curator once told me museums are where art goes to die, and here I can see what she meant: this windowless cavern feels so cold and sterile that I barely register anything about the current exhibition. I'm reminded of a photo of a young and strapping Rauschenberg dancing on the grounds of Black Mountain, wearing just a pair of ballet tights, looking sprightly and fearless as he prepares to leap skyward. What would that Rauschenberg have thought upon seeing his work stored in this mausoleum?

The guide shepherds us to a guest annex, a drafting studio, a pavilion by the pond. As she describes each structure, I hear her repeat words like *sanctuary* and *shrine*, and I keep wanting to ask, *For whom?* Perhaps this place once felt like a utopia for securely established figures like Johnson and Whitney, but for the gay artists in their circle—especially one as discreet as Rauschenberg—this must have felt like a glass closet.

On our way back to East Haddam, Will makes his customary stop for doughnuts at the Big Y supermarket. He grabs a discounted box of day-olds from the bakery and grumbles, "What does 'artisanal bread' even mean?" It's almost evening by the time we get home, so we bring our treats across the road to the shad shack, an abandoned fishing outpost where Bruce used to swim, and watch the sun begin to set over the Connecticut River. Sitting with my uncle on the edge of this rickety dock on an overgrown riverbank, I feel at ease for the first time all day; I'm tempted to say I feel free. I sense some moisture on my chest and assume it's more sweat from the late-spring humidity, but no, it's my melting Boston cream, which is dripping custard and chocolate icing all over me. Without thinking, I peel off my soiled T-shirt and toss it in the water. Well, shit. I could just let it go—it's nothing precious, and it's starting to drift downstream—but I've already begun stripping off my shorts and sneakers. Will and I laugh, surprised by my sudden fit of impudence. He glances at the traffic on the busy road behind us and the crowd of diners at the canteen across the river, though my briefs are less revealing than the little Speedo that Bruce always wore here. I don't know what I'm doing or why, but for once I don't care who can see me. I take a breath and dive.

—

A little splash snaps me out of my reverie.

"It's full of pink crocodiles," David says. I turn away from the water and catch him suppressing a sly grin. "According to my nephew."

Standing among the tall reeds at dusk, we can't see much of this pond near his parents' house, but David can tell the wet sound was a heron, his favorite bird. He loves the way they make themselves at home in water, how they always return to the habitats they leave behind. He says he'll never again live in Moscow for longer than a month, and he'll get a heron tattoo when he migrates this time.

I change the subject back to his nephew. David tells me that cerulean balloon was already more than a year old by the time I saw it at that gallery in Lewiston. His sister's son had inflated it at his fifth birthday party and presented it as a gift to Uncle David, who kept it as a peculiar relic, an ephemeral way to locate his nephew at a fixed point in time. David then began to wonder whether a balloon can be a piece of high art. It's a symbol of celebration but also a memento mori, usually inflated with either helium, an increasingly scarce resource, or air from living lungs. It's a playful, kitschy thing, but it can also elicit fear—of loud popping noises, of clowns and circuses, or of what can happen when it floats out of reach.

David shows me the stash of orange balloons in his grocery bag, which also holds a tin of breath mints and a vial of lavender oil. Orange, he says, signifies warnings, boundaries, roadblocks—not what one typically associates with balloons. He's acquired these supplies for a new performance, which has less to do with his nephew, he explains, than with the elasticity of the body. He opens his sketchbook to a draft of the score and traces his finger along an elaborate web of lines representing the performers' movements, but to me it looks like a blind contour drawing of the road to Moscow Mountain. "It's a very simple ten-step piece," he says, not hiding his sly grin this time.

We move on from the pond and keep walking to a tattoo parlor downtown, where we're about to debut this supposedly simple piece. When I invited David to perform in a pop-up reading series I cohost around Moscow, I didn't expect him to ask me to share the stage. I don't consider myself a performer, but I agreed to try something new on the condition that he write about the experience for me; he told me he doesn't consider himself a writer, but he'd think about it. We haven't rehearsed any of the movements, but we've discussed the steps several times, and I think I'm getting the hang of it. I'll begin by inflating a balloon and passing it to David, who will deflate it by inhaling the air inside; he'll then reinflate the balloon with his own breath and pass it back to me. We'll repeat this exchange a few times, filling the balloon with a blend of David's breath and mine, and then each of us will begin moving around the space more boldly and loosely and freely, pantomiming the idea that this commingled air has some kind of inspiriting effect. We'll then pass the balloon to a few audience members and let them take part in this communal ritual. Once David decides the audience has had enough fun, he'll begin gradually moving outside the space, while I'll move more deeply inside it—to the upstairs balcony, for example, or into the back storage closet. After a few cycles of this push and pull, he'll hand me the balloon and leave the building, and he won't come back, not even when I take my seat in the audience to signal that we're finished.

I prepare to describe this piece to my friend Clare, one of the audience plants we've recruited to help us out, and I realize how bizarre it might sound. David and I have never done anything so physically intimate together, let alone in a public setting, and if any spectators were to ask me what the performance is about or what it means, I have no idea what I'd tell them. But he seems much less worried about what they'll think. "They don't need to know what balloons mean to either of us," he says, "to see a narrative embedded in the material. I don't expect their story to be the same as ours, but I hope they feel the warmth of the gestures we're offering them." I'm tempted to ask what story he considers "ours," but I get distracted by the scents of lavender oil, which he dabs on my wrists to calm my nerves, and of the mint he dispenses on my palm. "And whatever happens," he adds, "we're collaborators now."

I suppose it's true. I'm pleased that our shared fondness for Rauschenberg has led us to this creative partnership, though it feels strange to have such a definite label suddenly adhered to this nebulous bond that's been growing over the past three months. But I don't say so to David. Maybe I'll learn to appreciate this strange feeling.

"We could even make a book together!" he says. Not a bad idea, I think—maybe he can finally help me complete that dilettantish essay of mine. But before I can ask how we'd assemble the words and images, David goes on, his energy reaching a fever pitch. "We could include some mail art in the book! Or do a piece involving the post office once I move away!"

I start to chime in but stop short, suddenly winded, and watch David continue walking ahead. Soon he realizes I'm no longer beside him, and when he turns around to rejoin me, I can't bring myself to meet his eyes, embarrassed that I don't know how to explain why the thought of his departure pains me so much. I'm not even ready to think about how I'll feel later tonight, once he makes his final exit, though I know it's just a performance.

—

"How depressing life would be, if our lucky stars hadn't introduced you to me." So says a comic strip pasted in the upper right corner of *Collection* (1954), one of Robert Rauschenberg's earliest combines, which he makes soon after meeting Jasper Johns in New York. The two artists have recently moved into the same studio complex on Pearl Street, where Rauschenberg creates his most celebrated combines, including *Rebus*, *Bed*, and *Canyon*, and Johns initiates his famous series of flag paintings. During this period, their friend John Cage observes the pair growing so close that they frequently finish each other's sentences. Poet Frank O'Hara visits one day with his companion, Joe LeSueur, who later admits, "I don't think Jasper liked me," to which O'Hara replies, "What he didn't like was the way Bob kept looking at you."

Johns tries to destroy most of the pieces produced in his own studio before moving out in 1961. This is the year when he makes *In Memory of My Feelings*, a two-panel combine named after one of O'Hara's poems. On the left side, Johns has mounted a fork and spoon, bound together with wire; on the right, the two utensils, barely visible in a field of muted gray paint, are split apart.

"Rauschenberg sometimes snags his sweater between the sanctum of private reference and the littered tundra of commemorative decay," writes a reviewer for *ARTnews*, also in 1961. "A poof of incense disperses the bracing pungency of the urban miasma; the sharp punning weapons of the inscrutable ironist corrode gracefully with a lavender rust . . . We get too close to the artist in the wrong sense."

In 1964, Johns writes in his sketchbook, "An object that tells of the loss, destruction, disappearance of objects. Does not speak of itself. Tells of others. Will it include them? Deluge."

Rauschenberg has been estranged from Johns for nearly half his life by the time this conversation with art critic Paul Taylor appears in a 1990 issue of *Interview* magazine:

> TAYLOR: We have previously talked about your relationship with Jasper. How much will you go on the record about this? I think there are lots of reasons to talk, especially in the current climate of suppression of gay art and artists.
>
> RAUSCHENBERG: Well, I wouldn't go into any kind of sexuality. One of the reasons is that—is this off the record?
>
> TAYLOR: Can't you say it in a way that's on the record?
>
> RAUSCHENBERG: Well, I think I'd better just leave it alone. I'm not frightened of the affection that Jasper and I had, both personally and as working artists. I don't see any sin or conflict in those days when each of us was the most important person in each other's lives.
>
> TAYLOR: Can you tell me why you parted ways?
>
> RAUSCHENBERG: Embarrassment about being well-known.
>
> TAYLOR: Embarrassment about being famous?
>
> RAUSCHENBERG: Socially. What had been tender and sensitive became gossip. It was sort of new to the art world that the two most well-known, up-and-coming studs were affectionately involved.

Two years later, Taylor dies of AIDS. Shortly before Rauschenberg's death from heart failure in 2008, the press office at the Museum of Modern Art specifies that he and Johns "wish to be described" as friends.

A decade after Rauschenberg's death, one can still see the marks of that affectionate involvement throughout both his work and Johns's, and the latter artist would still prefer to let us connect the dots at our own risk. Rauschenberg's name does not appear in a 2018 *New York Times* profile of Johns, who "says outright that he does not have faith in the process of memory, insisting it is less likely to disclose truths than to twist them," though "he seems to enjoy the process of weighing facts and evidence, even while acknowledging their limitations." When the reporter presents him with "statements of incontestable fact," Johns frequently replies, "Interesting, if true."

—

and he inflates the balloon
light dim I step up to
meet him upon meeting
him I take the balloon
and inhale
I haven't inhaled a body before.
Feel full
inflate balloon with what feels like his
air—not—mine but
struggle won't quite go

I inflate the balloon and pass it on to him once, twice, three times
inflating pass: inhale
deflate. Feel orange tiled ground and
begin motion

away from
each other. Begin movement of right turn then three steps forward around corner back.
Rectangle. Inhale and deflate. Exhale and inflate. I wonder about eye contact.

One starts spinning. Not the eye contact one. See from periphery. And he inflates the balloon
light dim I step up to
meet him upon meeting
him I take the balloon and inhale.
Spin. And pass it eye contact. They're "really going for it" big balloon.

Deer are unable to perceive the color orange.

And begin movement of right turn then three steps forward around corner back. Rectangle. Inhale and deflate. Exhale and inflate. Inhale and begin movement of right turn three steps forward around corner open door and bathroom. Pause:
three seconds. Chuckle. Open door pass and inhale. And begin movement of right turn three steps forward and corner back. Rectangle. Inhale and deflate. I haven't inhaled another body before. Feel full. Inflate balloon with what feels like
their air—not—mine. And begin movement of right turn then three steps forward around corner open door and bathroom and
narrow on through exhale and carry their breath back.

Door's a

push not a pull. Their air—not—mine. And begin movement of right turn then three steps. They're "really going for it" big inhale and I've never inhaled another body before. Narrow on through exhale and
carry their breath
back. Narrow on through exhale and door's a push not a pull.
Back. Narrow on through exhale and door's a push their air—not—mine. And begin movement of right turn then periphery carry their
air back. Narrow on through exhale and door's a push not a pull.

Door's a

—

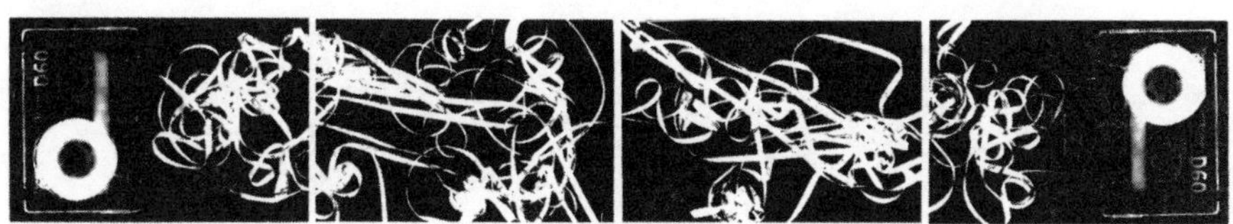

When did I become the kind of person who walks a mile along the highway at midnight to meet a stranger at a motel? This is the question I keep asking myself when cars approach on Route 8, the main road connecting Moscow, Idaho, and Pullman, Washington. Some drivers slow down as they pass, and I wonder if they're staring at my bright red jacket, which I chose because it makes me feel like James Dean in *Rebel Without a Cause*. I wonder if they can tell what I'm up to.

It's a midsummer Monday, and less than an hour ago, I received a Grindr message from a man I'd never seen before. He sent me several photos of his puckish face, enviable abs, and exceptionally beautiful ass; I assumed my own, less Instagram-worthy photos would bore him, but to my surprise, he responded enthusiastically. He's staying the night at the Super 8 by the mall and asked if I'd be down to meet there.

I hesitated, then texted my friend Cameron, a more sexually adventurous person than I'll ever be. "Am I going to get murdered?"

"No," Cameron said. "Prepare to be disappointed. But,"

he added, citing my uncle Bruce's favorite motto, "live the fantasy!"

So I said yes to the stranger with the beautiful ass, gave him my number, showered, spent a needlessly long time picking an outfit that would say *DTF but not desperately eager to please*, and tried not to get run over as I crossed Route 95.

At this hour, the traffic lights don't change colors but just flash red. The stranger sends parking directions, and I admit that I don't own a car. He falls silent for several minutes, and I wonder if he's lost patience with me as I approach the Super 8, but then he texts to apologize: he's actually at the Motel 6, another third of a mile down the road. Wary of getting catfished, or worse, I ask him to send a photo from inside the room, though I stay at motels so rarely that I can imagine making the same mistake. His reply: a shot of the bedside table's landline, its panel displaying the Motel 6 logo and the front desk number. I forward the image to Cameron: "If I die tonight, this is how you'll find my body."

I'm prepared for disappointment but not disaster; I don't have pepper spray or a knife or any other self-defense tools. (How many Grindr users take such precautions in 2019?) I'm relieved to see that the Motel 6 is near a McDonald's, and I pause by the windows, comforted by the warm glow inside. I could run here for sanctuary if something goes wrong—a ridiculous exit plan, sure, but one that soothes me all the same.

The stranger instructs me to wait by the pool, which is hidden beneath a sagging tarp. I duck under a fire escape to avoid the lampposts' glare, see a curtain quiver in one of the ground-level windows, and check my phone. "Red jacket?" he asks. I find the room number he gives me and knock tentatively, in case he's messed up that detail too. He cracks the door and invites me into a room lit by just a TV. Shirtless and gaunt, he appears to be around my age. He's wearing gray sweatpants, slung low enough that I can see the banana pattern on his briefs, and the cologne I remember my eighth-grade crush buying from Abercrombie & Fitch. On the nightstand, next to an enormous bottle of baby oil, is a white, lunchbox-shaped container emblazoned with an EMT symbol and red block letters: HUMAN ORGAN FOR TRANSPLANT. I point to it and ask if he's a doctor. At first he can't hear me over *South Park*, but then he smirks—it's a cooler full of White Claws. I laugh nervously, waiting for him to open a can for himself or hand one to me, but I can tell from his face that he's wondering why I'm still standing by the door. I sit on the tucked-in bedspread and remove my sneakers. He sits beside me, reaches for my fly, and asks, "May I?" Won over by his politeness, I slide off his sweats.

"That was fun," he says an hour later. As I fumble back into my shorts, I nod and ask what brings him to Moscow. "Business," he says, explaining that he normally stays at his parents' house here, "but sometimes I just need to get away." He doesn't ask about my situation, but he offers to let me fix my hair in the bathroom mirror before I go. I decline and joke that, since I live alone, I'll be the only one scrutinizing my appearance when I get home. He looks a little bemused, so I drop the subject and assure him I'd love to get together again when he's back in town. "Sure," he says, sounding deflated or maybe just noncommittal, and we exchange names as he shows me the door.

I remember his when I next see him on Grindr, several months later. He admits that he's forgotten mine and sends a screenshot to prove he still has my number saved under Walked From Downtown Moscow Room 111 Motel 6.

—

I don't know why I didn't invite him to my apartment from the start, nor do I know why he didn't ask. I don't consider myself a Grindr connoisseur, but even novices know its most routine question: "Can you host?"

Which is dicier: entering a stranger's home or opening your home to a stranger? Maybe this has always been the defining dilemma of hospitality, a transaction of mutual goodwill that's loaded with unsettling imbalances. The term comes from the Latin *hospes*, which could mean either *guest* or *host* but originally referred to any stranger—including a hostile enemy—who held some degree of power over another. For the ancient Greeks and Romans, the concept of hospitality encompassed both the host's duty to take in a foreigner and the guest's right to receive this refuge, regardless of the danger involved for either party. And for gays in the digital age, the practice still depends on the host's authority, which obliges you to respect certain boundaries as soon as you cross the threshold. Someone might get off on ceding this authority and pushing these boundaries, offering to leave the door unlocked and wait for you on the couch, eyes blindfolded and bare ass up; someone more cautious might prefer to meet you first at a park and determine whether you're worth bringing home—that is, if you don't end up getting down to business in a secluded spot behind a hedgerow. For some, hosting might entail the pleasure of dimming the lights, furnishing clean sheets and towels, and curating a buffet of lubes and toys and poppers; for others, it might be a less glamorous chore, requiring the labor of dealing with roommates, pets, thin walls, unlockable doors, suspicious neighbors, or a lack of any secure space to begin with. But no man I know has ever expressed any sense of duty to host a hookup or any entitlement to be hosted. Instead, our conversations dance around the specific ethics and etiquette of hospitality, though the unsexy logistics are always present in the room.

Throughout my childhood, plenty of fables taught me to expect the worst as both a host ("The Three Little Pigs," "Little Red Riding Hood") and a guest ("Hansel and Gretel," "Bluebeard"), but nothing prepared me to face the particular anxieties that arose when I, at twenty-six, first downloaded Grindr and Scruff. By the time my long-distance boyfriend persuaded me to try these apps during our time apart, I figured I had no reason to be afraid of any bloodthirsty predators, yet I struggled to shake my chronically inhospitable attitude toward most queer men my age. If they showed any interest in me, I assumed they must have wanted something I couldn't possibly give, and if they showed no interest, they must have smelled my inadequacy. My usual solution: avoid them altogether and still complain about feeling alienated. (I joked to my boyfriend that my profile should include a caveat: *not "conventionally friendly."*)

This defensive posture may have been the result of bad luck with the fuckboys of my youth, each of whom had left me newly heartbroken and increasingly distrustful of men's motives. It may have been internalized homophobia deterring me from joining any club that might accept me as a member, as if I were always already bound to be rejected. Or it may have been rooted in a much older and deeper fear of not belonging. In any case, once I pushed past these insecurities and discovered how willingly another man would invite me into his bedroom, his every additional gesture of hospitality appeared both even more extravagant and more moving. When R offered me a glass of wine on his fire escape after tenderly wiping his cum off my face, or G prepared us a naked breakfast of poached eggs and sourdough toast at two in the morning, or B performed a Reiki ritual on my back after straddling me on his couch and finding a knot of tense muscle near my tailbone, each of these efforts to put me at ease chipped away at my ingrained reluctance to get physically and emotionally intimate with near-strangers.

When I began hosting these encounters at my own home, I lived at the intersection of Ocean and Church Avenues in Flatbush, which I loved, and which was also one of the few parts of New York City I could afford on my publishing salary in 2017. I was among the few white professionals in this historically working-class West Indian community, and my role in the neighborhood's gentrification became even more conspicuous whenever I escorted a date, who was likely gentrifying some other part of Brooklyn, inside my building. My outsider status may be less overtly menacing now that I've moved to Idaho for graduate school, though renting an apartment in a converted hotel and attending a land-grant university are daily reminders that I'm an interloper in territory that doesn't belong to me. But because Moscow's queer community is relatively small, and because a far-right evangelical church is working hard to take over the town's real estate, opening our doors to each other, whether for sex or for other kinds of company, can be an overture to the kind of solidarity that many of us find lacking here. I don't know whether that stranger at the Motel 6 was trying to avoid his family's judgment or seeking a neutral, impersonal space, but either way, I remain embarrassed that I neglected to offer up my home. Maybe I would have offered him a glass of wine or a White Claw. Maybe he would have slept over, and maybe I would have made us eggs and toast and coffee in the morning. Maybe he would have taken a shower in my bathroom and fixed his hair in the mirror before returning home. Maybe we would have talked at more length before parting ways, and maybe he would have ended up remembering my name. But would I have been extending this hospitality for his benefit or mine? Maybe he didn't want or need a host in the first place.

—

I picked up most of what I know about hospitality during the first twenty-odd summers of my life, when I regularly visited Bruce and Will at the eccentrically decorated house they shared. From the two of them I learned to fix one's guests a batch of cocktails upon arrival (whiskey gingers for the grown-ups, Shirley Temples for the kids), to select just the right background music (Celia Cruz, always; Sade, maybe later), and to avoid controversial or distasteful topics of conversation (*The Real Housewives*, health-care reform). Bruce and Will were the sole committed couple in my immediate family, since my parents separated when I was an infant, so for a long time I never considered that the protocol of hosting might hold any special significance for queer people. Hospitality often seems to reinforce the codes of bourgeois respectability, but I gathered that playing host, as if it were a form of drag, provided subversive pleasures for my uncles, whose relationship with domesticity was already vexed.

Before they met, Bruce and Will were wanderers. Bruce often recalled dropping out of the University of Missouri to follow a boyfriend all over Mexico, but his favorite story to tell was about sneaking out of his parents' house as a teenager in 1950s Memphis and loitering around Graceland: one time he spotted Elvis at the gates, said hello, and somehow invited himself inside. Wearing a smug grin, Bruce would tell us that he even slept over, but he never confirmed anyone's suspicions about what happened that night, and I'll never know for sure.

Or that's what I keep telling myself. A year after Bruce's death, shortly before I move to Idaho, Will assures me, "I'm certain—I am *certain*—that if your uncle had sex with Elvis, I would've heard about it."

Let a boy dream. I ask Will if he was similarly brazen in his youth, remembering the tales he's half-told me about his first time in New York. Like me, he arrived in the city as a teenager; unlike me, he was running away from home, without any definite plans for the future. He stayed afloat by getting a job at an infamous West Village eatery named Mama's Chick'N'Rib—coincidentally, the hub for the neighborhood's chicken hawks. "The cook took me down to the basement and had his way with me," Will says. "Not that *that* was very difficult. It was about as difficult for me to be seduced as, I don't know, 'Here, have a glass of water.'" He secured lodging by cruising up Christopher Street, finding a different man to host him every night. "It was the late sixties," he explains, "after the Summer of Love but technically before the sexual revolution. Rather than go to law school, I did what a lot of people who were full of spunk and vinegar did. We weren't quite hustlers, but we were looking for sex, and there were plenty of guys hanging around who certainly loved the idea of having some young man on his arm. So that answer that?"

Yes, sort of. I still have trouble picturing how this young vagrant transformed, over half a century, into the uncle telling me this story in his living room, where we're surrounded by stacks of more coffee-table books than I can imagine ever affording. On paper, Will's life now looks relatively conventional. He's a father and a grandfather, he's worked as a patient advocate at the same hospital for nearly three decades, and for most of those years, he shared this house with Bruce. Everyone in town seems to have a story or two to tell about the "fabulous, simply fabulous" parties Bruce used to throw, and I suspect he omitted no one from the guest list. Meanwhile, on one of the several occasions when I've seen strangers invite themselves inside and ask to use the washing machine or help themselves to a Danish in the kitchen, Will told me he's earned a reputation for "taking in strays." If he has a philosophy of hospitality, it's probably what I hear him say at the end of many phone conversations: "Call on me anytime."

Bruce bought this house and moved here from New York in 1978, and he often said he would've died in the city if he'd stayed through the eighties. I used to find his survival heroic, as if fate had been on his side: *Good thing he escaped just in time!* Now this reaction embarrasses me, but I couldn't get it off my mind when I saw Matthew López's play *The Inheritance*. I expected to love *The Inheritance*, which recasts the story of E. M. Forster's *Howards End* among gay millennial New Yorkers wrestling with the legacy of the AIDS epidemic. López tackles many of the questions I ask myself about queer bonds between generations, but he stages his answers in a maudlin, didactic fashion that left me cold. Nonetheless, I was fascinated by Eric, one of the young protagonists, a softhearted, idealistic boy who lives on the Upper West Side and spends his Saturdays at the latest Whitney exhibition or Justin Peck ballet. As a softhearted, idealistic boy who once lived on the Upper West Side and spent his Saturdays at the latest Whitney exhibition or Justin Peck ballet, I squirmed watching López's spot-on caricature of my "type." Early on, Eric befriends an older, avuncular couple, Walter and Henry. One night at Eric's apartment, Walter tells the story of meeting Henry soon after arriving in New York in the early eighties:

WALTER: For five years, Henry and I clung to one another for safety, for comfort, as the city burned around us. By the summer of 1987, we had had enough of funerals and hospital visits and the sight of once vital men laid to waste. We looked for a house as far from civilization as we could find. We finally stumbled across a rambling old farmhouse on an aimless country road, three hours north of here, built in the late eighteenth century. It's set off from the road so you have the illusion of being alone in the world. And in front of the house, my favorite thing on the property: an enormous cherry tree that has been there since the time George Washington was out terrorizing them. [. . .] And—I don't know if you'll believe me but it's true—deep in the trunk of the tree are a set of pig's teeth that were put there I don't know how many generations ago. The superstition among the colonials was that if you bite the bark of the tree, it will cure all your ailments.

ERIC: Does it?

WALTER: No. Of course it doesn't. Pure superstition. And yet, there in the country, on rolling pastureland, with flowers and breezes and cherry trees with pig's teeth stuck in the bark, there was no death, there was no illness, there was no loss or danger.

After a year of this secluded pastoral life, Walter says, he grew restless and returned to New York, where he ran into an old friend who'd been ravaged by AIDS, evicted, and shunned by his family. Against the wishes of Henry, who wanted to keep the virus as far away as possible, Walter began inviting this friend and many others to their house and taking care of them as they died. "I eventually came to see," he tells Eric, "that leaving the city and our friends behind was as unforgivable an act of cowardice as I have ever performed. The answer, I realized, was not to shut the world out but rather to fling the doors open and to invite it in."

When Eric finally sees the house for himself, he hears someone inside call his name, and soon the rooms fill with the ghosts of all the former guests who died there. One by one, they shake his hand and greet him: "Welcome home, Eric." It *is* Eric's home, though he doesn't yet know that Walter has bequeathed it to him. This scene closes the first half of *The Inheritance*; by the end of the second half, Eric has turned the house into "a shelter, a refuge, a place of healing; a reminder of the pain, the fragility, and the promise of life." I initially rolled my eyes at this mawkish conclusion, but then I wondered if Bruce would have written similarly about his own home. I don't know whether he spent the worst of the AIDS years shutting out the plague or flinging the doors open to the afflicted. Nor do I know what he had in mind when he used to joke, in his morbid way, that if he outlived Will, he'd leave the house to me. Perhaps his reasoning had less to do with the property itself than with what it represented: *Someday, nephew, all the history embedded in this place will be yours*. But I'll never find out. I'm glad the house now belongs to Will, Bruce's next of kin, who will pass it down to his son and grandson. Unlike the characters in López's play, I have no idea what I'd do with such an inheritance.

At least that's something else I keep telling myself. I want to believe that if I had such a sturdy, lasting haven, and if I were as secure as someone like Eric, I'd accept the responsibilities of hosting and being hosted without any qualms. But hospitality is never so simple: no matter the circumstances, it will always require me to yield some control over my body or my space to someone else's desires, and it is always possible that I will be found wanting. This uncertainty shouldn't stop me from reaching out to welcome other people into my life, yet I get hung up on doubting whether they'll welcome me in return. Maybe someday I'll receive the invitation or the knock on my door that will quell my fears and snap me out of my self-pity, once some kind stranger finally proves me a good-enough guest or host. But I know that's not how this works.

—

When did I become the kind of person who drives eighty miles into the wilderness to meet a pair of strangers at their log cabin? Traffic has been light this afternoon, but as I ease down a steep, unpaved road at the base of the Blue Mountains, every approaching car rushes to pass me, impatient with my gawking at the endless hills and valleys adorning the horizon. The skies are clear and the snow has melted, yet I still fear slipping over the edge of these hairpin turns and tumbling into the Tucannon River.

During the blizzard a few weeks ago, in a fit of restlessness, I "woofed" at a handsome face on Scruff—a less popular app than Grindr in Moscow, which means I often see profiles from all over the region. He introduced himself as Derrick, a sculptor turned bartender, and responded enthusiastically when I told him I'd been writing about Robert Rauschenberg. After we swapped photos, he showed me the stylish website for the homestead he shares with his partner, Steven—spelled like my name, which I took as a good omen. In the summer, Derrick explained, they rent out their grounds to campers, but since winter tends to be quieter, they have more privacy to offer other kinds of visitors. And since he and Steven, a fabricator at a foundry, have opposite work schedules, he asked if I'd like to stay at their cabin over the upcoming holiday weekend, so they both could get to know me. "It'll be nice to make a new friend," he said, adding a kiss-blowing emoji.

I texted Cameron to ask if I could borrow his SUV for a few days.

"Of course," he said. "Just fill it up and get it back in better shape than your butt, which should be wrecked."

So I said yes to the strangers with the beautiful cabin, packed my most rustic-looking flannel, and accepted Cameron's challenge. But now I'm trying not to blow a tire on the rubble scattered across my hosts' mile-long driveway and wondering what I've gotten myself into.

Derrick hears me park and appears on the porch in a billowy chambray shirt, well-worn work pants, and slippers. "The nice thing about living in the middle of nowhere," he says, "is not giving a shit about dressing up." He greets me with a warm hug, carrying himself like an urbane artist roughing it in bucolic drag. Since it's still light out, he gives me a tour of the chicken coop, the fairy garden that will soon teem with irises and lilies, the forest you can hike through all the way to Oregon if you're not afraid of cougars, and their campsite on the riverbank, fractured and eroded by a recent flood—hence the bumps along the last stretch of my trip. A week earlier, he says, the whole road was submerged in water; had I arrived then, he adds with a wink, I would've been stuck here.

Derrick leads me inside the cabin and introduces me to Louisiana, a jumpy rescue mutt who seldom leaves his and Steven's bed, and Pip, the one-eyed cat who mostly hides in the loft, where I'll be sleeping. I carry up my bag, enter a wardrobe built into the wall, and slide open a door to the guest quarters—not quite Narnia, but impressive in its way. A former closet illuminated by a skylight, the room is barely wide enough for a double bed and a ladder to a cupola, which I consider climbing until I hear Derrick call my name from the kitchen. The other Steven has just come home from work, so I return downstairs to say hello. He's clearly the more reserved of my hosts, and I feel unexpectedly bashful in his presence. As I watch him unpack groceries and prepare a pot of corn chowder, we two quiet Stevens exchange furtive glances that tickle something in the small of my back.

Derrick hands me a cup of wine, refuses to let me help with dinner, and urges me to sit with him at the thick ponderosa stump they've repurposed as a dining table. He asks where and when I was born (Boston, 1991), when I began to come out (2004), whether I have any siblings (no), whether I have a partner now (it's complicated), and what I'm doing in Idaho (writing, teaching). I can tell from their reactions that he and Steven, though they're only seven and ten years my senior, view me as a different generation, at least in queer time: Steven recalls the bullying that led him to drop out of high school in Seattle, where he fell in love with Derrick, who had migrated from Houston after his mom found a copy of *XY* magazine in his bedroom.

I ask what brought them to this cabin, and Steven tells me his grandparents built it in 1978 and lived here for thirty years. When his grandfather died, his grandmother sold the place to another family, but they abandoned it amid the devastating wildfires of 2015. At the time, Steven was studying carpentry and struggling to run an antique shop, while Derrick, disillusioned with the art world after finishing his MFA, was spending more and more time in his garden and less in his studio. So they decided to leave Seattle, rehabilitate the cabin, and advertise it to travelers. Since then, they've hosted hundreds of strangers, both paying guests and casual acquaintances like me, far more than ever walked through their doors in the city. But I'm only the second Moscow boy they've met through "the apps," Steven says, shooting Derrick a look to signal that I've already made a better impression than the first.

I laugh, relieved to have outshined my predecessor, but Derrick catches me straightening my posture, senses my self-consciousness, and changes the subject to my writing. I tell him a lot of it is about my uncles, and he lifts a Bernie 2020 magnet from the fridge to show me a photo of Steven's nephew, who's just come out at eighteen. Steven smirks with pride, but before I can pry, Derrick asks what I'm working on now. I answer that I've been writing about hospitality and joke that this weekend is part of my research. To my surprise, Derrick takes me seriously.

"What's your angle?" he asks.

Do I have an angle? Perhaps I've overstepped by putting my cards on the table, but my hosts don't seem shy about sharing their life in this cabin.

"Yeah," Steven says, "how do you feel about traveling here?"

He hands me a bowl of chowder and a wedge of fresh sourdough, and I fumble between bites to find words for my excitement and my nervousness: "the apps" have never led me to such a remote location. Steven nods in understanding. He and Derrick used to worry about the isolation, but they haven't been too lonely in the country.

"We become entwined in other people's stories in a different way here," Derrick says.

"And with every new guest," Steven says, "we take a mutual leap of faith we might not otherwise risk."

I don't ask what might have inhibited them from taking such a leap with me, and I'm not sure I want to know. I can imagine feeling less anxious and breathing more easily in this rural life, but first I'd have to learn carpentry, farming, and other subsistence skills—not to mention how to make soup and bread as mouthwatering as this, which I wolf down while my hosts debate how to spend the rest of the evening. They suggest that I pick a movie from their extensive videocassette collection in the loft, and I choose *The Adventures of Priscilla, Queen of the Desert*, which I've somehow never seen. Derrick rewinds the tape and asks, "Doesn't VHS bring you back to nineties porn?" I remind him that I was a child until the twenty-first century, so most of my porn consumption has been online. He ignores this comment and summons me to join him on the love seat; Steven takes the armchair beside us and quickly dozes off. Derrick drapes my arm around his shoulder, and during the occasional lulls in the movie, I cautiously unbutton his shirt lower and lower. When I reach the bottom, he kisses me and whispers, "Take your time, why don't you," and tugs my hand to his fly.

We've shed all our clothes on the love seat and shuffled to the guest room by the time the end-of-tape static rouses Steven, who cracks open the wardrobe door to wish us good night. "Don't worry," Derrick says, "we're just frotting." Steven smiles wistfully and watches us for a moment before sliding the door shut. Once we've turned off the lights, Derrick cradles my head with one arm and points with the other up to Cassiopeia, but my eyes are too bleary to see the stars.

He's already left for his brunch shift by the time the skylight wakes me. To get a panoramic view of my surroundings, I climb up to the cupola—a drafty, unfinished roost—and suppress a yelp when I spy what must be a cougar, but no, it's just Pip prowling around the chicken coop. I briefly consider how much to cover myself before heading downstairs, where I find Steven still in bed. He invites me to join him, shoos away Louisiana to clear space for me, and removes the briefs I've needlessly retrieved from the love seat. "Mind if I put you to work today?" he asks. I shake my head, which he gently presses toward his crotch, and I notice the Cassiopeia tattoo on his left hand as it caresses my face.

After washing away his and Derrick's residues in the bathtub, I dress and rejoin Steven in the kitchen, where I help him dust and pack some knickknacks for his booth at the nearby antique mall. During the half-hour drives into town and back, after Steven tunes the radio from news of a virus outbreak in China to a local call-in show about far-fetched bucket-list items, we talk about what our lists would include. He wants to hike the Pacific Crest Trail and watch the northern lights, but most of all he wants to see the trees he's planted in his yard grow to maturity. Once home, we leash Louisiana, grab some empty jars, walk down the road to a cottonwood uprooted by the flood, and harvest the buds, which Derrick will later infuse in oil to make a healing salve. The bitterly cold wind stings my fingers, but the sweet, sticky sap makes them smell like springtime, and I never want to rinse it off.

When night falls, Steven sends me inside with some tinder, and I pretend to know how to light the hearth. He sits behind me, opens his notebook, and proposes a game of MASH. Though I haven't played since middle school, I rattle off an assortment of names, numbers, vehicles, jobs, and cities without trouble. Derrick comes home right as I finally start a fire, and Steven, having crossed off all my other options, announces that someday I'll drive a Ford F-150, work for Cirque du Soleil, and share a mansion in Albuquerque with Oscar Isaac and nine kids. They wipe away the soot smudged on my face, pour a round of whiskey, and toast to my good fortune, and I promise that Oscar and I will invite them to our lavish housewarming party. But the mood sours when

Derrick sees Steven's notebook, the source of an ongoing quarrel between them. Whenever Steven feels stuck in self-doubt, he explains, he'll write a detailed counternarrative of his own life; instead of shutting up the voices that nag him about what could have been or what still could be, he'll talk back, following the roads not taken to their logical conclusions.

"I feel so comforted by the thought of spending the rest of my life here," Derrick says, "but you're always looking for a way out."

"I'm not," Steven says, clearly bruised. "I just want to prove to myself that certain paths would be impractical or unattainable. I think you have to cauterize and mourn your life's severed branches."

They wrangle over how hard they have to work to sustain this home, how much their day jobs pull them away from both their housekeeping and their relationship, how far they feel from achieving any kind of equilibrium. Have they forgotten about me sitting at the kitchen table, or has their captive audience inspired this performance? Within a few minutes, Derrick adjourns to prepare some biscuits and gravy. While he whistles at the stove, I glimpse Steven brooding by the fire and want to ask: *What future did you long for ten years ago, at my age, or twenty, at your nephew's? What possibilities now seem out of reach? What branches have you severed to become a host of your caliber, and what do you now have to mourn?* But I can tell these are sore subjects, and it seems impolite to prod. I try to cut the tension after dinner by picking *Romy and Michele's High School Reunion* from the video shelf, but we all fade swiftly, and I wake too late to say goodbye to Steven before he heads to work in the morning.

Louisiana looks a bit put-upon as I come downstairs and approach the bed, but she gets the idea and wanders off. As I fill the spot she's warmed beside a half-awake Derrick, he turns to make me his little spoon and mutters, "Don't leave, Steven."

I can't tell whether he's sleep-talking to the one who's already gone, so I gently mention all the unread books and ungraded papers awaiting me at home. He tightens his grip on my waist and cranes his neck over mine, and I swivel my head back to face him. Like the ancient hosts who inspected each guest's station in life, testing whether the stranger's presence augured well or ill, Derrick gives me a long, intense stare. Is he calculating the debt I owe for my time here? Maybe I should invite him to visit me in Moscow, though my little apartment can't compare with this cabin. Maybe I should stick around to cook or garden or chop wood until I earn my keep. Or maybe, if this hospitality is a gift, he expects me to do something else with it. Finally, he pops the question: "You're on PrEP, right?"

Before I go, we take one last walk with Louisiana, who keeps turning around and looking askance at us, as if embarrassed by our unkempt hair and perfunctory outfits. "When you arrived here," Derrick says, "I really thought you'd be a total bottom." I ask what gave him that impression, and he shrugs, pausing to pick me another sample of the plants along the road: damiana, rose hip, sumac, yarrow. He tries to teach me their Latin names and medicinal properties, but I lose track, distracted by a Steller's jay darting among the hills. Its blue-black plumage glows against this gray-and-brown backdrop, and I have trouble believing, though Derrick keeps reminding me, that this whole landscape will be neon green in a month or two. I really need to get going, and I rehearse a little thank-you speech, promising to reciprocate his and Steven's generosity. But who am I to them now, apart from one more visitor? When will I become—well, do I need to be another kind of person? Derrick keeps talking as he beckons Louisiana and me to admire the tall ponderosas along the riverbank. Many were decimated by the wildfires and the flood, and the remnants look charred and disfigured. "But don't worry," he says, "they'll still be here whenever you come back."

Peacock

"Let's try something a little different," Jack says. I know what he means, but he says it with such a wholesome smile and courteous voice, as if he were offering me a sample of ice cream, that I second-guess myself before I start to strip. I unbutton the oxford shirt I borrowed from Tom, shimmy out of my skinny jeans, slip off the navy blue briefs I chose for the occasion, and lay them atop the stack of four other outfits I brought tonight (one was clearly more than enough). I tiptoe my bare feet back to the enormous scroll of white paper unfurled on Jack's bedroom floor, try not to wrinkle it, and wait for him to begin.

Jack is a photographer, one of the first people I met in Los Angeles. I moved here a month ago to live closer to Tom, my no-longer-long-distance boyfriend, but I didn't know anyone else in the city, so I eagerly sought new friends on the apps. Drawn to the artful photos on Jack's Scruff profile and intrigued by the risqué portraits he had posted—and tastefully censored—on Instagram, I asked to see more of his work. He mentioned wanting to build a portfolio so he could quit his day job, and I half-jokingly offered to sit for him—maybe out of vanity, maybe for lack of a better pickup line. I didn't expect him to take me seriously, but he agreed and invited me to the studio he's set up in his East Hollywood apartment. Part of me wondered if this was just a ploy to get me out of my clothes and into his bed, but by now I can tell that's not what he has in mind. Besides, we've already seen each other naked anyway.

"Stand the way you do when taking your own nudes," Jack says, smirking, now that we've gotten some warm-ups out of the way. I don't question what he means this time; we both know my go-to poses. (Like many gay millennials who first meet online, we shared the contents of our "private albums" before making introductory small talk. Why does a full-frontal reveal often seem less intimate than asking, "How are you?") I reach my left arm behind my head and rest my hand on my nape; I'm not sure what to do with my right hand, which would normally be pointing my phone's camera at a mirror—it's hard to perform for someone else the kind of artless candor I try to convey in a selfie—so I hold my hips to anchor my legs, which have already arranged themselves in contrapposto. I don't know where to look when Jack starts to click the shutter, so I stare at his feet, probably looking coy, though I'm surprised by how unbashful I feel. This isn't my first time in front of another artist's camera, and by now I'm accustomed to baring myself to new acquaintances, but I've never submitted my whole body as an object of such close, methodical study. I try to hold still but almost jump back when I see Jack lunge toward my crotch, and I instinctively turn away and clear my throat, as if this were a physical exam.

"Sorry," I say, unsure if Jack is scandalized or flattered by whatever's happening down there. He laughs and shows me his camera's preview screen. I want to admit I'm impressed, but I don't know what to say in praise of Jack's artistry when we're talking about a close-up of my penis. I remind myself that this is a technical exercise, a chance for Jack to practice directing a live model in a controlled setting. So I follow his instructions to sit on a chair, rotating positions to form different shapes, and to crouch on the floor, curling into a ball so he can zoom in on my protruding scapulae. Jack remains clothed, and I wonder if asking him to disrobe would level the field, but I like our clearly distinguished roles, and his gaze is too warm to feel voyeuristic or clinical. Still, I want Jack to reveal more of himself. I ask what other gigs he's had lately, and he tells me about doing headshots for a young West Hollywood actor. Relishing the attention after a year and a half of social distancing, the actor wistfully recalled walking down Santa Monica Boulevard and turning heads on a night out in the before times: "I miss *those eyes*."

Jack and I laugh at the actor's Norma Desmond–esque delusions of grandeur, but I also find his comment genuinely poignant: not until this pandemic did I understand the pain of being unseen. I used to hate being perceived. As a heavy child, I hated being teased about my weight; as a taller and thinner teenager, I hated comments on my awkward posture and proportions; as a chronically baby-faced young adult, I hated being infantilized by more virile men. Then, as a thirty-year-old living alone under lockdown in small-town Idaho, I developed an odd, irrational fear of becoming invisible. I tried all the popular remedies for this unfamiliar sense of disembodiment—daily neighborhood walks, virtual dance parties, *Yoga with Adriene* videos—but none of them felt, well, *gay* enough. Out of wishful thinking, I continued taking PrEP for a few months, until it became clear that sex wouldn't be on the table anytime soon. So I joined the many gays of my generation who were learning anew to appreciate the art of sending nudes, swapping NSFW self-portraits with friends and lovers and even strangers on the internet. This pastime didn't exactly sate my hunger for IRL companionship, but I wondered about the deeper emotional purpose of this titillating queer custom, which some have even called a form of mutual aid. Sure, we were bored and horny, but I suspect many of us were also undergoing an existential crisis. If a gay boy yearns in a forest, and no one is around to fall into his thirst traps, does his body still mean anything? And if I've predicated so much of my identity on the ways my body is seen and heard and tasted and smelled and touched and *read* by other boys, and if I don't give those boys evidence that I'm still here, who am I?

Yes, I'm being melodramatic, but 2020 was not exactly a banner year for calm, clear thinking. Now that the world is gradually opening up again, I probably couldn't have chosen a better place than Los Angeles to work through my complicated feelings about self-exposure. Another new friend recently told me that "LA will ground you with its ridiculousness," and I agree that this city often feels like a profoundly superficial wonderland, which has taught me to be a little more delusional and to take myself a little less seriously than I ever did in New York. But on the other hand, I don't want Hollywood life to whet an unhealthy craving for *those eyes*. After all, the real reason I moved here is Tom, who already thoroughly *sees* me, and my job tonight is to help Jack feel seen, to support his career by adding some material to his portfolio. I have no idea how these photos will turn out or what either of us will do with them, and it's possible that I'll fail to give Jack anything useful. I have no idea if this evening will deepen our nascent friendship or if he'll end up losing interest, now that I've left nothing to Jack's imagination. But for the time being I'm not worried about what will happen next or what anyone else will think about what we're doing here. I'm more interested in the thrill of this unpredictable encounter, the unexpected pleasure of ceding control over the self-image I've cultivated. And I certainly wouldn't have found the confidence to do such a thing without a model like Bruce.

"Who's Bruce?" asks Jack, and I answer by pointing to my tattoos. It's a long story.

—

I come from a family of peacocks. A bird of the genus *Pavo* is, in German, *ein Pfau*. Technically this noun refers to all kinds of peafowl, but after years and years of semantic drift, it's become nearly interchangeable with the term for the male of the species (please give the unsung peahens their flowers). I don't know how my ancestors originally got this pavonine surname, but whenever I tell acquaintances what Pfau means, most answer, "That's fitting." Is it because I seem ostentatious? One of the collective nouns for a group of peacocks is, of course, an *ostentation*. Is it because I sometimes like to wear bright jewel tones? Peacock blue does happen to be one of my favorite colors. Or is it because I'm obviously, as one character describes the pale-hued peacock who appears in the middle of Toni Morrison's *Song of Solomon*, a "white faggot"? The famously unsubtle peacock, who "comes out" again and again with his flamboyant display of gaudy plumage, has a long history as an unsubtly gay-coded animal, making heavy-handed cameos in the work of such gay writers as Oscar Wilde, Yukio Mishima, and James Merrill. No matter his pigmentation, as Morrison illustrates, there's something unmistakably swishy about the peacock, strutting like his unwieldy tail is "full of jewelry," just as so many gays are both propelled and burdened by a love of adornment. "Wanna fly," Morrison adds, "you got to give up the shit that weighs you down."

Whatever the answer may be, I've resisted identifying with my avian eponym, which I haven't found all that "fitting" for most of my life. I wouldn't otherwise have chosen the peacock as a personal mascot, and even if I share some superficial traits with that bird, I resent the expectation to be a show-off, which seems incongruous with my reserved, uncocky demeanor. Even when I do genuinely want to be seen, I avoid trying too hard to make that desire known; I would prefer that my "felt cute, might delete later" posts evince winky larking rather than malignant, incurable narcissism, but wringing my hands over optics probably doesn't help my case. I also don't want to be just another shallow gay who fixates on a "taste for the beautiful," Darwin's term for what draws other animals to the peacock's unusual appearance, which attracts mates but provides no survival advantage; there seems to be a slippery slope from uncritically accepting this theory of sexual selection to putting "just a preference" in one's hookup app profile. Whatever kind of Pfau I am, I could never—nor could anyone in our family, for that matter—out-peacock Bruce. He was no exhibitionist (no, we never saw each other in the buff), but he was not modest, and not one to keep his fan of feathers folded. "At least I was cute," he would often say to conclude his many tales of being a naïve young man who was well aware that his looks could always get him out of trouble—or sometimes into trouble, as when he beguiled a bouncer to let him cut the mile-long line at the entrance of Studio 54. There's a hint of shyness in the photos I've seen of my uncle as a boy, but by the time Bruce came into his own as a grown-up gay man, his portraits display an undeniable, Whitmanesque swagger that's prompted more than one of our relatives to remark, "He knew he was beautiful"—not as a judgment but as a simple statement of fact.

My favorite photo of Bruce was taken on the morning of his seventieth birthday. He sits on his front porch, slouched on a chair, his blue-jeaned legs propped on a footstool. There's nothing but a silver chain necklace on his broad chest, which has slackened low enough that his nipples appear almost level with his waist. He rests his right elbow on the banister to steady his drooping wrist, encumbered by five or six silver bracelets, as he lifts his hand to scratch the still-thick gray hair on his head; he faces the camera with squinted eyes and an upturned, half-open mouth as if he's either bewildered or tickled by the photographer—which would be me, age seventeen, experimenting with my first digital SLR, a Canon Rebel I'd wished for ever since taking a photography class in tenth grade. I routinely practiced by taking candid snapshots of my family, and they were all good sports about it, but Bruce was by far my most willing participant. He never said how it felt to be photographed or what exactly he saw in the boy on the other side of the camera, but I was continually stirred by the curious way my uncle looked back at me, as if he were the one trying to figure out how to capture me in the best possible light.

I may be projecting, but I think Bruce would have welcomed that projection, since he seemed to take the idea of being a role model very seriously and literally. Looking at my many portraits of my uncle, I suspect he was trying to express something to his nephew, not through the usual channel of his flair for language but through the pleasure he took in boldly asserting his bodily presence, warts and wrinkles and liver spots and varicose veins and too-tight Speedos and all. I used to think of Bruce as shameless, and I assumed he was trying to teach me, as I endured the most mortifying years of adolescence, to shrug off any shame of my own. I don't think I was entirely wrong about that, but I also think he understood that shame isn't necessarily a bad thing. As Eve Kosofsky Sedgwick writes in an essay on the subject, "shame and pride, shame and self-display, shame and exhibitionism are different interlinings of the same glove: shame, it might finally be said, transformational shame, *is performance*." How is it possible for shame to be "transformational" when that emotion can be so immobilizing, one that can stop you in your tracks, lower your head, avert your eyes, and flush your cheeks? Shame may result from a record-scratch moment of rejection or misrecognition, when the mirroring that bonds young children to their caregivers is broken and "the adult face fails or refuses to play its part in the continuation of mutual gaze." Yet even when this rupture happens without words—when no one explicitly says, "Shame on you"—shame is still a form of communication that "both derives from and aims toward sociability," that "defines the space wherein a sense of self will develop. [. . .] Shame is a bad feeling attaching to what one is: one therefore *is something*, in experiencing shame." Sedgwick observes that many queer activists and educators have championed "gay pride" as an antidote to that "bad feeling," but trying to eliminate or "heal" shame is "preposterous": "The forms taken by shame are not distinct 'toxic parts' of a group or individual identity that can be excised; they are instead integral to and residual in the processes by which identity itself is formed. They are available for the work of metamorphosis, reframing, refiguration, *trans*-figuration." For many queer artists, performers, and writers, Sedgwick concludes, shame is not just useful and healthy but powerfully creative: if you're as susceptible to this contagious sensation as I am and as Sedgwick was, you can easily be flooded by another person's "embarrassment, stigma, debility, blame or pain"—even if these feelings have nothing to do with you—in ways that redraw the "precise, individual outlines" with which you've defined who you are.

Precisely how did shame outline my individual boyhood? Well, everything seemed to be potentially humiliating then, but above all my own body—especially my misshapen trunk, which I tried to cover as often as possible, and which seemed to be the site of all my flaws and the source of all my dysphoria. There were the sharp tailbone, lordotic spine, and long, drooping neck that resulted from the extra vertebra I was born with; the fleshy pecs, persistent potbelly, and wide, stretch-marked hips around my relatively narrow waist, telltale signs of baby fat unevenly distributed during a sudden growth spurt in puberty; the constellation of surgical scars on my furry chest, which looked oddly mismatched with my smooth, boyish mug; and inside that chest, the weak, blistered, collapse-prone lungs responsible for those ugly scars, inescapable reminders that I could incur another spontaneous pneumothorax at any moment and my fragile little body could implode without warning. Maybe Bruce recognized how much I dwelled on these deficits, but he never questioned or tried to fix my insecurities. Even when he encouraged my efforts to mimic his behavior, shadow him at the gym, or commemorate him with my camera, he never framed himself as an exemplary specimen or suggested he was the kind of gay man I should aspire to become in the future. ("Let me tell you," Bruce often said, contra Dan Savage, whenever the indignities of aging made themselves known: "*It doesn't get better*.") He was just *there*, peacocking in his fashion, indirectly assuring me that I would figure out my own way to live up to our family name.

He never overtly expressed this assurance, but one time he came close after I commented on his tattoo—a blue lion rampant, standing on its hind legs, gnashing its teeth, and swiping its front claws at an unseen prey. Drawn in profile on Bruce's upper left arm and facing his chest, it looked ready to tear out and devour my uncle's heart. He had acquired it a decade or so before I was born, during a trip to Scotland, where he saw this heraldic charge on the crest of the Clan Bruce—no direct relation, as far as I know, though this royal house likely originated my uncle's given name back in the Middle Ages. By the time I first saw this tattoo, its washed-out viridian hue and faded outlines made it look much older than it was, as if it were a patch of ancient, oxidized copper gilded on my uncle's perennially suntanned skin. After I turned eighteen, old enough to get a tattoo of my own, I remarked to Bruce that his lion embodied many of his most admirable qualities: strength, charisma, fierceness, regality (he was a Leo, after all). I found these qualities mostly lacking in myself, so this lion seemed to represent everything my uncle was and I was not. I wasn't intentionally fishing for validation, but I suppose I was still hoping he would respond with some words of affirmation. Instead, Bruce just smirked and asked me, "How would you like to get matching tattoos?"

Yes, of course! But what kind of tattoo did he have in mind? Not a peacock—that would be too obvious—but another bird. Bruce described a classic sailor's tattoo he had always loved: a pair of swallows on the chest, one on either side, flying toward each other as if about to collide at the center. Bruce was never in the navy, but he knew that a sailor would customarily be marked with these swallows after traveling ten thousand nautical miles; the tattoo was a badge of honor for one's extensive seafaring but also a promise to return home, as swallows always do after their annual migration. I wasn't sure what meaning to make of this tattoo, whether Bruce intended it as a reminder of his itinerant past or an inspiration to his nephew, but I liked the idea of getting it with my uncle—partly to have the moral support, since I don't like needles and don't have much pain tolerance, but mostly to go through this significant rite of passage with Bruce, who could help me finally reclaim a part of my body that I once despised. But we never got around to it.

One of the first things I did after Bruce died was make an appointment for a tattoo. It seemed wrong and sad to get those swallows without him, so I went with a version of his lion on my left arm, both as a tribute to my uncle and as a cue to keep working on my own leonine traits. After moving from New York to Idaho a year later, I learned that the official bird of both states is the bluebird—another gay icon of the animal kingdom, known to all friends of Dorothy for flying over the rainbow, and not too different in size or shape or color from a swallow. I had driven only a couple thousand miles across the country to reach my new home—even fewer nautical miles, if I could have sailed—but all signs pointed toward following through on Bruce's proposal, with my own twist. Now my sternum is bookended by two members of the genus *Sialia*, and I think of my uncle whenever I see these bluebirds, facing each other head-on, never turning away, never lowering their feathers.

—

I don't believe in heaven, but when Jack asks me to sit on the edge of his bed and look skyward, I feel like I'm waiting for these bluebirds to carry me by the collarbone up to Bruce. Jack practices lighting me from below and from behind and through a half-open doorway, trying to emulate the dramatic chiaroscuro in George Platt Lynes's portraits of model Carlos McClendon, one of many men who posed nude for the celebrated photographer. I first encountered Lynes in one of my uncles' coffee-table books, before I was old enough to understand why these photos stirred me. You can tell from his models' vulnerable poses how trusting and uninhibited they feel with Lynes, but his use of oblique lighting in shadowy interiors gives the illusion that I'm furtively glimpsing these men through a crack in the closet door. Lynes wasn't a pornographer, but his work never fails to seduce me, perhaps because an air of mystery heightens the sensuality of these nudes, which weren't publicly displayed until the Kinsey Institute acquired them after his death in 1955. But I know I shouldn't aestheticize, from my relatively comfortable vantage point in 2021, what was at stake for Lynes, and I don't want to reduce the nature of his work to a "vibe" that Jack and I can try on like a costume.

Even when Bruce was around my age, it was dicey to do something like what Jack and I are doing now. In 1972, before becoming a punk icon in the New Wave scene, photographer Jimmy DeSana created *101 Nudes*, a portfolio documenting his queer friends in various states of undress—some situated in "respectable" domestic settings like a suburban home or garden, some captured in unvarnished, high-contrast close-ups of their genitalia.

DeSana takes a provocative, subversive approach to tackling the censorship of queer sexuality by unapologetically celebrating "deviant" behavior, like dancing on a dining table or making out with a painting of Jesus, and he plays up the pleasure of allowing one's body to be objectified on camera. DeSana also made *101 Nudes* as a cheaply reproducible set of halftone lithographs he could circulate far and wide, namely among the participants in his "invisible network" of mail artists, who sidestepped more staid institutions by collaborating on interactive projects through the postal service. Mail allowed these artists to express themselves and connect with each other in ways that didn't conform to the increasingly mainstream gay liberation movement; in another context, DeSana's photos might have appeared shocking and exploitative, but you can tell he and his subjects thoroughly enjoyed pushing the envelope of propriety within this circle of self-selected, like-minded queers.

Artists like DeSana paved the way for unorthodox zines like *Straight to Hell*, founded by editor Boyd McDonald in 1973 and much loved by my uncles. *S.T.H.* (aka *The Manhattan Review of Unnatural Acts*, *The Saturday Evening Ass-Licker*, *The New York Review of Cocksucking*, and many other X-rated subtitles spoofing higher-brow magazines) is known for the DIY aesthetic of its issues, which feature both low-budget professional porn and amateur material submitted by anonymous readers. Even the filthiest rag you could find on a newsstand can't match the level of exuberant impoliteness you'll see in *Straight to Hell*, which enthusiastically refuses to cater to middle-class, heterosexual readers. According to scholar and activist Charley Shively, *S.T.H.* aims to present those readers' "worst fears made flesh. [. . .] All the capitalist toilet training gets flushed away in many golden showers." *S.T.H.* hasn't yet folded, but a new issue hasn't been published since 2017—partly because the journal's unfiltered commentary and rejection of "political correctness" now seem to come across as more reactionary than radical to younger generations, but mostly because its anti-establishment spirit has been overshadowed by an internet culture in which anyone can be a "content creator." These days, there's not much demand for a publication like *S.T.H.* among horny, attention-hungry, digitally savvy queer boys. Why give away your spiciest photos to an underground zine when you could post them to boost your personal brand on social media—or, better yet, monetize them on OnlyFans?

I suspect Bruce may have posed for some DeSana-esque Polaroids in his youth, or perhaps he made an anonymous submission to *S.T.H.*, one I could have found among the many issues collected in his home. I never saw or heard anything to confirm this hunch, and I now feel a pang of regret that I never asked—and that I'll never get to brag to him about what his buttoned-up nephew is doing now, to prove he managed to instill some audacity in his protégé. Maybe I've grown too old to be seeking this kind of validation from my elders; maybe I should focus instead on being more generous to men of my own age, including the photographer right in front of me. But some part of me—maybe the closeted exhibitionist, maybe the obsequious nephew—still wishes my uncle were here to watch.

Throughout the night, I keep glimpsing the door to Jack's balcony, as if Bruce were out there, peeping through the window. I can imagine him stepping inside to join us, like an older version of the model in a favorite photo of mine: *In the Morning, Athens, 1936*, by Herbert List, a contemporary of George Platt Lynes. A youngish man, with a crown of tousled hair on his downcast face and no clothes on but a pair of white briefs, stands on the threshold of an archway, holding the wall on each side to steady himself as he prepares to descend from a landing. Backlit by the sun, he's mostly a silhouette, veiled by a lace curtain stitched with a leafy pattern and the outline of two swans in a lake by a Greek temple. The staging suggests he's on the balcony of a private bedroom like Jack's, but the classical embellishments on the curtain give the scene a mythological air, as if this young man were Narcissus admiring his own reflection in the lake, or perhaps Orpheus entering a portal to Hades.

In the Morning reflects much of my own ambivalence about being regarded by an older, more powerful man: the desire to be looked at while not necessarily wanting to look back, in case one of us doesn't like what he sees in the other's gaze; wanting to present myself in a casual, unassuming fashion while secretly hoping the photographer sees me as a character in a grander, more meaningful story. I first saw List's photo on the jacket of Matthew Stadler's novel *Allan Stein*, which explores similar tensions between men who look at boys and boys who display themselves to men. I hadn't heard of *Allan Stein* until a beloved professor lent me his copy, suggesting it might be relevant to my interest in the topic of nephewhood in queer literature: the titular Allan is in fact a real person, the late nephew of Gertrude Stein. Published and set in the 1990s, the novel is narrated by a disgraced teacher, on leave from his job at a Seattle high school, where he was accused of sleeping with a tenth-grade boy. "I had never imagined molesting him," the narrator admits, "until the principal suggested it by notifying me of the charges":

> In the end I succeeded in committing the crime I had been falsely accused of. The parents never found out (no one did). As it turned out, sex was exactly what the boy wanted, and he became very much the happy, satisfied child they hoped he would be, where before, during the months that I was blind to him, he had been miserable and distracted (precisely the condition, noticed by his parents, that led to their accusation). In light of this boy's satisfaction, and the handsome salary I was then receiving for a great expanse of free time in which it became that much easier to meet him, clandestinely, for sex, I must admit that I sometimes looked on the whole horrifying affair as comical and ironic. After a while he grew bored or ashamed and stopped seeing me.

The narrator goes on—"to the delight of many of you and the horror of some"—to describe in vivid detail his final tryst with this student, though not before offering squeamish readers a chance to opt out ("Those of you who can't stomach any more of this sort of thing can skip ahead to page 47, where the narrative resumes") and validating those who don't wish to turn away ("I think it's okay for you to take pleasure in these things"). Upon reading these passages, I began to wonder if my professor had other motives in passing along this book to an adoring student, but I chose to keep that wishful thinking to myself, and I found the narrator simply too endearing to question what he or Stadler or my professor were up to.

As the narrator bides his time in exile, his friend Herbert proposes an escape plan. A successful museum curator, Herbert invites the narrator to take his place on a business trip to France, where he was planning to research some long-lost drawings of Allan Stein, who may have been the model for the nude figure in Pablo Picasso's painting *Boy Leading a Horse*. Having borrowed a name and passport and alibi from his friend, "Herbert" arrives at the home of a generous host family in Paris and pretends to be an expert on the art-historical significance of Gertrude Stein's mysterious nephew. But when the narrator tries to explain his interest in studying Allan, his hosts are puzzled. Mid-conversation, the patriarch of the family asks, "Who is the nephew?"—a non sequitur that sounds at first like a philosophical inquiry on the nature of nephews. "I don't understand," he adds, "what makes this man's boyhood interesting," since Allan seems to have done nothing important in his own right. "All boys are important," his wife chimes in:

> But so few men are. [. . .] This is one of the features of the Picasso Herbert speaks of, the most erotic and moving aspect of it—that it is a boy. He has a tremendous power because he is nothing yet, no

> one, and so he has the power in him to be a god, like all children do, you see? If Picasso had painted a man leading the horse, just imagine it. This man would be someone, some man who will never be a god at all, just a man, without the limitless power this boy has.

This answer pleases the narrator, and not just because it gives him a more personally resonant rationale for this make-believe research trip ("It didn't matter if Allan was or wasn't important, he was a boy, and that was sufficient"). It also indirectly affirms the magnetism of his hosts' fifteen-year-old son, Stéphane, who right away transfixes the narrator with both his beauty and "the warmth of his regard."

At this point you might expect that *Allan Stein* is shaping up to be a modern *Death in Venice* or a gay *Lolita*, but Stadler's ephebophilic narrator isn't nearly as one-sided in his predilections as Mann's Gustav von Aschenbach or as committed to consummation as Nabokov's Humbert Humbert. What excites the narrator is the two-way duet of regarding young men and being regarded in return. While masquerading as Herbert, he eventually meets another curator who shares his "monstrous desires" for boys and who asks if there's something erotic about the narrator's interest in Allan. "Allan is erotic," the narrator answers, "but there's no scenario involved. There's no sex. [. . .] He's just standing very near and he's silent, staring at me—like in a photo, actually. The proximity is all that 'happens,' so I could touch him, though I never do. He's always poised there, but then nothing . . . proceeds."

In the boys he admires in both art and life, in both fantasy and reality, the narrator recognizes his own childhood wish both to be witnessed and to maintain a safe distance from his observers: "I think it is the same for Allan, as it is for me, or for Stéphane. It is the fate equally of the boy, the character, and the dead to blossom in the instant of our apprehension, and in the next instant to disappear. Pinned to this flickering edge where there is the possibility neither of merging nor of giving up, we are all unreachable."

"Pinned" is a nicely Nabokovian touch, a word evoking the lepidopterist who affixes butterflies within a glass display case, where they remain both protected and trapped. At first, Stéphane appears to be a similarly inaccessible object of desire, as if he were "hover[ing] behind a scrim," like the boy in that photo on the novel's cover. Yet Stéphane has far more autonomy than a figure in a photograph or a butterfly in a frame, and the narrator is increasingly beguiled by the potent "force of the boy's gaze" and "the touch of his look." The infatuated narrator projects more and more of his own memories and fantasies onto the boy, and Stéphane appears to reciprocate the older man's attraction to him, though he also asserts more and more of his own agency, maintaining as much of the upper hand as he can in their inevitably imbalanced dynamic. When the two of them finally have sex, there is nothing romantic or pretty about it. The narrator knocks Stéphane into a puddle during a rainy basketball game, probably as a deliberate ruse to get the boy out of his muddy clothes and into a shower, where Stéphane ends up furiously dominating the narrator. "It wasn't the kind of sex I had imagined," the narrator says. "If he'd been a weapon, he might have killed me. I don't think his impulse was violent, but rather the territory of our exchange was lawless and immoderate, unspeakable. Our bodies were dumb, irreversible."

This "lawless and immoderate" encounter foreshadows the novel's denouement, in which the narrator tries to run away with Stéphane, telling the family he wants to bring the boy along to visit Allan's final home in the south of France. Soon enough, Stéphane's mother uncovers the narrator's schemes and sends a scathing letter demanding that he return her son at once—and only here, in the letter's salutation, do we learn that the narrator's real name is, like the author's, Matthew. Exhausted and frustrated, Stéphane leaves him behind, and Matthew wanders to the former hotel where Allan Stein spent the remainder of his adult life, gets drunk on Allan's favorite wine, sits by the river, and reminisces about "the boy"—perhaps Stéphane, perhaps Allan, perhaps one of the many other boys who have by now blurred together in Matthew's fantasies. "I have imagined that whole worlds dwell in the body of a boy," he says, "and have pried with words to relax these meanings from their hiding place, to coax the boy into the open. He stood still for a moment, caught in the warmth of my regard, and when I reached for him he was gone."

With these closing lines, Stadler neither condemns nor redeems his ethically dubious narrator, who remains suspended in a state of interminable reaching, while "the boy"—whoever he is—continues to elude him. Yet this seemingly bleak conclusion echoes what I love most about the spirit of *Allan Stein* and what, I think, makes the novel such a successful satire. Through the interwoven stories of Allan and Matthew, Stadler interrogates the gay urge to look and be looked at in ways that defy straight sexual mores—and illustrates the consequences, both comic and tragic, of mismanaging that urge. Some adults, perceiving any queer man's gaze as a threat, may zealously defend innocent boys from prurient eyes, yet this paranoia can backfire and become a self-fulfilling prophecy—as when the parents of Matthew's student, in the inciting incident of *Allan Stein*, catalyze the very scandal they intended to defuse.

Stadler even implicates himself in his novel's complex reckoning with the looking taboo, inviting us upon closing the book to scrutinize the author photo on the back cover and wonder if this is, in fact, the narrator who has finally been identified as Matthew. A lazy reader might take *Allan Stein* as straightforward autofiction and project Matthew's "monstrous desires" onto Stadler, but I think that would be missing the point of this novel. A few years before *Allan Stein* was published, the controversial North American Man/Boy Love Association invited Stadler to "give a talk" about his previous novel, *The Sex Offender*, at their annual conference. (It's not clear whether anyone from NAMBLA actually read this dystopian novel or whether they simply took it, based on the title and jacket copy, as an apologia for pederasty.) Stadler accepted the invitation and wrote an article for *The Stranger* documenting his visit to the conference, where he found NAMBLA to be a surprisingly banal "hobby club," even though "their defining fantasy" of man–boy intimacy "is one of our greatest nightmares." He remains wary of NAMBLA, yet to his outsider perspective, its mission seems not too separate from "our culture's broader obsession with kids":

> Paradoxically, to the extent that our culture protects kids by denying their sexuality—and never socializing it—we also insure that kids remain erotic in the most profoundly disruptive way. [. . .] NAMBLA is our doppelgänger, our monstrous double, aping back to us the myth of childhood that we have constructed, and hauling out of its center the bloody heart of eros we thought we had buried deeply enough to never have to face directly.

With this context in mind, Stadler seems to be holding up a mirror to the Allan Steins who still exist today, young men who want to be seen and also want to be safe, but who are surveilled and sanctified to such an extent that they have no freedom to assert their own desires, and who are never permitted to become independent adults rather than, say, somebody's nephews. And who, after all, is a nephew?

I would love to ask Allan himself, but by the time he died sixty years ago, he was already "a lost, untraceable soul," as Stadler writes. After Allan moved to the south of France, his "only real life drifted away. His boyhood disappeared and he emerged as an inconsequential man, a man whose family preferred their amusing stories about his childhood to the stubborn, dissolute adult he had become, a man who would be eclipsed by famous paintings made of the boy he had once been." It's easy to read Allan's story as a cautionary tale, and I do count myself lucky to be living a different story and coming into my own idiosyncratic identity. But part of me still wishes I could know firsthand how it feels to take such an irreversible step across a threshold and expose oneself in such a transformative way—as Herbert List's model may have done on that morning in Athens, as Gertrude Stein's nephew did for Picasso one day in Paris, and as Matthew Stadler did in 1999 when Grove published *Allan Stein*. Whenever Jack develops these revealing photos of me, a devil on my shoulder might goad me to send one to Stadler, wherever he is, or to the professor-crush who introduced me to *Allan Stein*, now that I'm no longer his student, or even to one of my uncles—not to provoke a response or to achieve a particular goal, but just to peacock for peacocking's sake, to break a rule or two and see what happens. But that gesture may not be worth the risk, and I don't know if it would be welcome in the first place.

Jack asks if I'm getting cold, since I've been naked for two hours now, so I take that as my cue to get dressed and head home. The next day, he sends me the final images, and I love them all, though my reaction reminds me of the first time I heard the startling contrast between my perception of my own voice and the way it sounds in a recording. Jack's finesse has made me look better than I envision myself, for which I'm selfishly grateful, but from his distinctive composition, I realize my own attempts at self-portraiture will always be more curated than I want to admit. I study the shots for which Jack asked me to pose as I do in my own nudes—in which I look less like my uncle's nephew and more like the inscrutable, self-effacing figure he taught me not to be—and I try to view them through the filter of someone else's fantasy. You can see a boy with a crown of tousled hair on his downcast face, standing with one hand on the back of his neck and the other on his hip. No clothes or curtains shield him from the bright light set up somewhere off to the side, and nothing else occupies the frame. You can't see his feet, but with one leg poised before the other, he appears to be bracing himself to step downward. Judging from his severe expression and the dark shadows he casts in the background, you might think he's preparing to enter the gates of hell and staring down whoever's inside, or he could be dipping his toe in a pool of water, too deeply absorbed in his reflection on the surface to notice you. You might imagine the whole worlds of meaning that dwell in this boy's body, and you might consider coaxing him into the open. If you do, you'll see him stand still for a moment, caught in the warmth of your regard, and when you reach for him he'll be gone. But I'll be here, ready whenever you are to try something a little different.

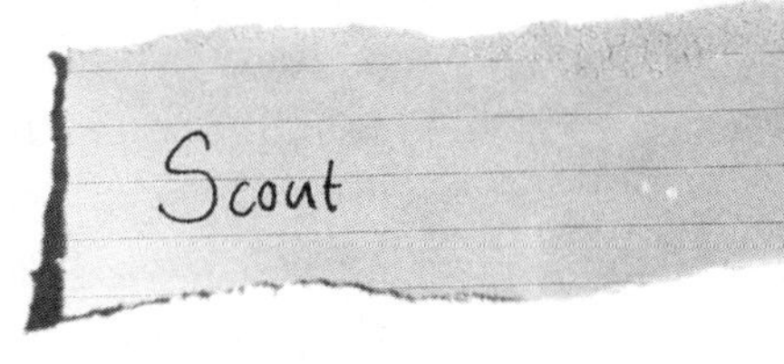

1

In the middle of my Saturn return, I found myself at the Eagle. Jack suggested stopping by after a Halloween party at Akbar, another gay bar down the street, where no one seemed to get what I was supposed to be. He had chosen the simple enough costume of a sexy axe murderer (short shorts, plastic hatchet), while I was a washed-up emo boy on the verge of a nervous breakdown (imagine Pete Wentz or Brendon Urie, still stuck in 2005, enduring a slow and painful ego death at the disco). Here, on the other hand, everyone seemed to be dressed for *some* occasion in their harnesses, chaps, and jockstraps, but Jack and I had missed this memo. We claimed a high-top on the patio, and Jack offered me one of his 27s—a guilty pleasure I couldn't resist. He wisely advised me to remove my flammable wig before lighting up, so I set it aside on a stool as we smoked and watched two bears making out on a pool table, and I must have been too enthralled to remember that asymmetrical hairpiece when we left. By the time I returned to look for it the next day, of course it was lost.

It was an apt introduction to this place, the LA outpost

of an unofficial network of leather bars around the world, all named some version of "the Eagle." When Bruce was my age, he was a regular at the original location in New York, which opened in 1931 as a longshoreman's tavern called the Eagle's Nest. "To go out was *important*," he often told me. "We'd try on T-shirts until midnight, then we'd go jiggle by the jukebox and watch all the tough guys, the bad guys, and the guys who thought they were tough and bad." Of all the stories Bruce relayed from his barhopping days, his memories of the Eagle's Nest were the most bittersweet. It was one of the bars where he first saw and fell in love with Hugh, who became Bruce's partner throughout the 1970s and '80s; it was also where he and many friends saw each other struggle with alcoholism, drug addictions, skirmishes with the police, and PTSD from military service. From the way he talked about coming to the Eagle's Nest, I gather Bruce never knew whether he'd end up having a dark night of the soul or the best time of his life.

When I started going to gay bars as a college student in New York, I imagined my outings would be similarly profound, but I didn't see what was so *important*. Before turning twenty-one, I knew I'd never get away with a fake ID, so I didn't bother trying. But my friend Adam was handsome and charming enough to get away with anything, so he often snuck me into Marie's Crisis, the legendary piano bar in the West Village. I could see why he called this place his church, and not just because he visited religiously every Friday night. There was always a spirited congregation of gays around Dexter, the bar's beloved pianist, who played along while the whole bar belted out show tunes from *Cabaret* or *Les Mis*. The crowd spanned many generations, but everyone seemed to know the words and melodies equally well, as if they had all attended the same matinees and scrapbooked the same playbills. While Adam joined the chorus, I would lean against the wall, defensively posturing as too cool for all the pageantry ("I'm not a *theater gay*"), when I really just didn't want to give away how little I knew about this world and how unprepared I was to make myself at home here. Sometimes I wished Bruce were there to clue me in, especially the handful of times one of the older men would turn to me, beckon me toward the piano, and shout, "Sing out, Louise!" Better to remain a wallflower, I figured, than to make a fool of myself and dishonor my uncle by asking, "Who's Louise?" This remained my MO well into my twenties, even as my friends and I began venturing out to other gay bars. I gravitated to the lower-key dives—Julius', The Boiler Room, Nowhere, Metropolitan, Ginger's—where my naïveté wouldn't stick out enough to get me eighty-sixed, where I could have *an experience* without drawing too much attention to my inexperience.

Little did I know that theater gays pale in comparison with leather gays in terms of specialized ceremonies and traditions, which haven't yet been as widely assimilated into mainstream straight culture as the Cole Porter songbook. By *leather* I mean not just the kinds of gays who don head-to-toe black cowhide but, as editor Mark Thompson writes in his classic anthology *Leatherfolk*, "an odd tribe within a tribe" of queer people "who share little in common other than the desire to explore taboo realms and intense erotic experience," who see wearing leather "not as stylish affectation but rather as a still daring symbol of cultural transgression and personal transformation." In the past, I've had much less firsthand contact with this "tribe" than with the Broadway queens, so I probably looked more like a tourist on that Halloween at the Eagle than I ever did at Marie's. (Bruce was one of the lucky few who could effortlessly straddle both of these circles.) Yet I could relate to Thompson's account of his first time at the Folsom Street Fair in San Francisco:

> In time, I became a Candide-like wanderer. [. . .] I thought of myself as a "nice boy"—one who doesn't admit to dark feelings—and my initial adventures were clouded with guilt and self-reproach. More than slumming on the "wild side," I thought I had gone to hell. But my yearning outweighed my inner censor, and over the years I came to accept my peculiar curiosity. Indeed, my understanding of what exactly I was exploring changed. I was no longer entertaining demons; instead I found transforming experiences beyond anything previously imagined.

I also thought of myself as a "nice boy," too demure and vanilla for the leather scene, and sensed I was straying into a forbidden underworld when I first entered the Eagle, despite the campiness of the year-round "spooky" décor, including some Guy Fieri–esque flames embellishing the walls and a giant, LED-eyed spider keeping watch atop a floor-to-ceiling web of heavy metal chains. (I later learned that the relatively open-concept LA location is one of the tamer Eagles, many of which include a discreet "dark room" for fucking invisible strangers in the shadows.) I didn't come to the Eagle aiming to confront any "demons" or work through any "dark feelings"; I just liked having an easily navigable space close to home where I could get some $7 well drinks and be gay. But surely that's not the only reason I keep wandering back here week after week.

Becoming a regular at the Eagle was never on my gay bingo card. I don't like the idea of being a regular anywhere—no, I don't want to go where everybody knows my name—so it pleases me that the surly bouncer still scrutinizes my ID as if for the first time. But ever since an astrologer told me, in early 2020, that I was about to enter a three-year transitional period of reckoning with time and age and mortality—my aforementioned Saturn return, when the planet of maturity and discipline would be back in Aquarius for the first time since I was born—I've been craving a proper rite of passage, something that will teach me what to do about these growing pains and prepare me for whatever's on the other side of this cosmic obstacle course; I've been seeking the kinds of "transforming experiences" that Thompson found at Folsom and that many others have found elsewhere in the leather scene. I don't know whether I'll find such a thing here, but the more I come to this place, the hungrier I get for whatever lessons the Eagle has in store for me.

This hunger is especially strong at Cub Scout, the popular party the Eagle hosts on the first Friday of every month. The name alludes to both the junior Scouting league, whose twee uniforms have become kitschy costumes for certain grown-ups, and the animal imagery of gay sexual taxonomy, in which "cubs" are more youthful versions of the hairy, burly men known as "bears" but generally thicker-figured and rougher around the edges than "otters" like myself. Though Cub Scout is aimed toward a younger crowd, this cheeky gathering throws into relief the Eagle's status as a surprisingly inclusive contact zone for gay Angelenos of all ages, from fresh-faced twenty-one-year-olds to seasoned veterans who've seen it all. The slightly musty, patinated atmosphere enhances the illusion that you'll discover a much broader and deeper sense of history at the Eagle than you will at the city's more polished watering holes, even though this relatively green venue opened in 2006; it's the kind of dive where you might expect to see Bruce and his crew still jiggling by the jukebox. Against this backdrop, Cub Scout makes me more aware than ever of my generational in-betweenness: in my early thirties, I'm too old to be a wide-eyed ingénue, too young to be a world-weary sage. I'm more like a literal Cub Scout, trying to prove I've earned enough merit badges to graduate to gay adulthood.

I belonged to the Scouts for a few years in my childhood and, luckily, still have my original shirt and kerchiefs. Bruce stuck with the program even longer and reached, of course, the rank of Eagle Scout. (I often look at a photo of my young uncle, around eight years old, with his kerchief wrapped like an Hermès scarf around the collar of his BSA shirt, an unusually pious-looking getup that belies his impish smirk.) But only now do I recognize the vaguely Christian ethos of self-improvement as a defining feature of Scouting. Like Bruce, I didn't have a very religious upbringing, so I never thought too hard about the meaning of either the Scout Oath ("on my honor I will do my best to do my duty to God and my country . . .") or the Scout Law, which mandates that one should be trustworthy, loyal, helpful, friendly, courteous, kind, obedient, cheerful, thrifty, brave, clean, and reverent. I probably didn't get high marks in any of these categories, and I don't know how well I'd do today. The closest I've ever come to completing such a rigorous moral education was taking a college class on the *Divine Comedy*, which often comes to mind at this bar.

Because I'm the kind of pretentious, part-Italian gay who might start rambling about Dante after a couple of gin and tonics, I'd like to tell you about one of my favorite—and one of the gayer—passages from the *Comedy*. Near the beginning of the *Purgatorio*, Dante falls asleep and dreams of being carried away by a golden eagle; he imagines he is Ganymede, the famously beautiful cupbearer, in the claws of Zeus, who assumed an aquiline disguise to snatch up the pretty boy and bring him to Mount Olympus. It's not uncommon for bigheaded Dante to compare himself to the great poets and heroes of antiquity, but it's surprising and oddly moving to see him fantasize of being this young and irresistibly beautiful boy, whose seduction by Zeus has become, for better or worse, a foundational myth for many queer men. Dante wakes at the gate of Mount Purgatory and discovers, to his disappointment, that he is still an ordinary mortal, and no adoring gods are going to fly him directly up to Paradise; instead, he'll have to take the long way and hike uphill alongside Virgil, his literary hero and avuncular mentor. The next stop on their journey is, naturally, the circle of pride, where Dante knows he'll have to spend a good chunk of time puncturing his overinflated self-regard in the afterlife.

Many nights, I sometimes feel like Bruce's ghost has swooped me up, tucked my light blue Bear Scout kerchief in my back pocket, conveyed me to the gate of the Eagle, and given me a firm pat on the rear. But I know this notion is just as far-fetched as Dante's dream. Nobody here is going to teach me how to grow up or do my homework for me; most people don't exactly come to gay bars aiming "to facilitate knowledge passing between generations," as Jeremy Atherton Lin writes in his book on the subject. ("Had I ever received wisdom on a barstool?" asks Atherton Lin. "Not really.") So I'm trying to take matters into my own hands and learn the hard way how to evolve into the kind of man who would have made my uncle proud. For starters, I'm finding my footing in Bruce's proverbial shoes—or maybe his combat boots, in this case—as I work on blending in with the Eagle's clientele. I've been experimenting with growing a thick mustache like his, leaving my shirts half-unbuttoned, and wearing a thin chain necklace; I can't tell whether I look charmingly slutty or just sleazy, like one of the 1970s porn stars you'll see on the Eagle's projector screens, but I still want to embrace this brand of effusively butch masculinity I've always idealized, even though it's never come naturally to me. I want to embody the object of my own fantasies, to resemble the kind of man that Bruce must have appeared to be at my age: confident, fun, interesting. I lean against the pool table and wait for someone to confirm this impression, for something *important* to happen. A brawny, leather-vested bear stomps my way, his stony face and peaked cap suggesting he has a mission for me.

"Got any quarters?" he asks.

I shake my head and try to look game, unsure if this man is about to flog me into oblivion or show me a good time I'll never forget. Maybe both.

"If you're not gonna play," he says, "get out of the way."

He elbows me aside to reach one of the sticks mounted on the wall, shoves some coins in the chute, and drops the cue ball on the table with a thud I want to call humbling, but it has nothing to do with me.

I hurry outside with my head down and don't want to wait around, lest someone catch me embarrassing myself again, so I decide to walk home, even if that means getting back close to one in the morning. Before I reach the end of the block, someone behind me hollers a feisty "hey!" I pause for a moment but don't look back; if I left something at the bar again, they can keep it. I keep marching ahead, and the heckler gets louder: "Yeah, you, in the maroon pants!" I turn around and almost snap back, "They're actually *burgundy jeans*," but then I see the sweet smile on my pursuer's face. As he approaches, I estimate that I have about five years and four inches on this young man. He has that air of guileless boyishness I've been struggling mightily to cast off, which I'm sure is exactly why I didn't notice him at the bar.

"I saw you had a bad interaction with that guy," he says. "You left so abruptly. Where are you going?"

"Home," I answer—more curtly than necessary, but

I'm irritated by this nosy boy's pity. (What does he mean by *bad*?)

"You're cute," he says, cocking his head and fluttering his drowsy eyes. "I was wondering if you want to connect."

"Not right now." He's drunk, I'm tired and cranky, and I'm not buying whatever he's selling, so without waiting for his reaction, I swivel back toward my destination and walk a little faster. By "connect" I assume he meant "hook up," but as I replay the conversation in my head, his words start to sound more and more philosophical, as if he were gauging my interest in the idea of connection itself, and as if by rejecting him I've renounced the possibility of kinship with any other human being.

I remember a story, possibly apocryphal, that Bruce used to tell me about the first time he saw his future partner Hugh at the Eagle. Transfixed by the sapphire-blue eyes of this elegantly coiffed adman wearing a tweed suit and bantering with a pack of gruff bikers, Bruce beelined across the room with his smuggest grin and butted in to say, "Hi!" Hugh narrowed his eyes, gave my uncle a snotty once-over, and coolly asked, "What drug are *you* on?" For all I know, Bruce may have been on *something*, but that wasn't the point of the story; the rebuff must have stung, but he was in love enough to try again and eventually wear down Hugh and leave a toothbrush at his place and remain with him for nearly two decades, the rest of Hugh's too-brief life. Now a young man has sought me out and made an effort to connect, which I've never been brave enough to do with a total stranger, and instead of accepting his invitation or even thanking him, I've shut him down even more brusquely than Hugh might have done, and I'm sure I've thereby brought a curse upon myself. I glance back, hoping that boy may be waiting to give me a second chance. But he's already returned inside the Eagle for another round.

2

"I can be your uncle, if you want."

Why the fuck did I say that? [ ] doesn't answer, and I can't tell from his blank stare if he finds my proposal ridiculous or if he simply can't hear me over the music. We've known each other for a while, but this is our first night out together: [ ] recently moved to LA, not long after I did, and to show him my idea of a fun time, I've brought him to Cub Scout. Scrambling for small-talk topics, I asked about his sister's seven-year-old son, for whom [ ] has mentioned wanting to be a gay role model. I lamented that I'll never know, since I have no siblings, how it feels to have a blood-related nephew of my own; [ ] countered that he'll never know, since there are no gay elders in his family, how it feels to have an uncle like Bruce. Whether or not [ ] wants such an uncle, it *is* ridiculous to imagine I could fill that role for him, even in the most figurative sense. I'm not even three years his senior—certainly not older or wiser enough to teach him anything he doesn't know—and besides, I'm skeptical of the notion of "chosen family." We as gay people may get to choose our families, but what if the people we choose don't choose us back, or what if they choose us with very different wishes in mind? Why should we want to claim each other as "family," a term that can sound so possessive and exclusionary and laden with unspoken obligations, as if we owe each other something we don't expect from our garden-variety friends, and as if the notion of choice somehow makes these allegiances more radically liberating than our unchosen commitments? Still, the first time [ ] referred to me as part of his family, whatever he meant by that, my heart grew three sizes, and it almost exploded when he expressed interest in joining me tonight at the Eagle.

[ ] breaks our prolonged silence and suggests we get some air. On our way to the patio, I stop by the bar to refill our gin and tonics. He insists on paying, but I refuse the cash he hands me and stick it back in the pocket of his jeans—not an intentionally lewd gesture, but I realize too late it looks like I'm tipping a go-go dancer. I turn away to hide my flushed cheeks as I carry our drinks to a high-top, though he probably catches me blushing when he offers one of his American Spirits and lights it for me, making me feel like Bette Davis in *Now, Voyager*. Neither of us is necessarily flirting, since we both tacitly understand that we share too much complicated history to risk rocking the boat. But as we chat and trade notes on our impressions of LA's gay scene, the way he looks at me sometimes leaves me wondering if we're about to make out.

I catch some knowing glances from onlookers, and I smile and nod back, assuming they must recognize me as a fellow Cub Scout regular, but their puzzled reactions suggest they were actually checking out [ ]. If someone should ask how the two of us know each other, how would I explain without drawing an elaborate diagram? *Once upon a time,* I might say, *before he started dating my ex-boyfriend's ex-boyfriend, [ ] and I were simultaneously but separately dating my other ex-boyfriend's ex-boyfriend, and I secretly coveted many of [ ]'s qualities—tall, athletic, good-humored, charismatic, able to pull off a wide range of facial hairstyles, enthusiastically beloved by all our mutual friends, graced with the kind of effortlessly earthy energy that makes me wish I were a baker or a farmer and not a writer—but of course my insecurities got in my way, and I got so caught up in wanting him to like me that I gave him no reason to believe that I like him, so now that several years have passed and we're no longer metamours and our paths have recrossed in a new context, I'm trying to atone for my past mistakes and be a good friend.* It's a common enough story among queer men, many of whom relate to one another within similarly tangled webs of nonmonogamous intimacy, and who would probably call this situation just another textbook example of the classic gay dilemma: *Do I want him, or do I want to be him?* Honestly, I want neither. What I *do* want is for this night with [ ] to culminate in something realer and truer, for our bond to crystallize in such a way that will cure me of what Edmund White once called "the bottomless gay capacity for feeling rejected and unworthy."

Edmund White happens to be the only man I know who could bring out that capacity in my uncle, who often referred to him as "the worst—I mean *the best* writer of my generation." Bruce half-jokingly resented the celebrated author for having lived through many of the same gay experiences, at the same times and places, and beaten him to the punch of telling the tale to the wider world. But otherwise, to any gay man who dared to threaten his ego or eclipse his shine, my uncle tended to puff up his chest and declare, "I'm Bruce Pfau—who are *you*?" He seemed mostly immune to envy, that ugly feeling, as critic Sianne Ngai calls it, "since it is hard to feel envy without feeling that one should *not* be feeling envy, reinforcing the negativity of the original emotion." Dante imagined that emotion as a form of schadenfreude, an inclination to rejoice more at others' woes than at one's own good fortune; Kierkegaard referred to it as "concealed admiration" and "unhappy self-assertion"; and writer Jean Garnett recently described it, in an essay on her identical twin, as "a desire that seeks to destroy" the person whose distinct successes seem to cancel out your own good-enough existence, even if that person happens to be your sibling. A nonexistent "sibling" can also factor into this equation, according to psychoanalyst Christopher Bollas, whose essay on gay cruising includes my personal favorite definition of envy. Bollas posits that a young queer man may feel he is less real than "the *internal object* held inside the mother"—that is, the idealized child that his parents wish him to be. This other "child" may become the queer man's "rival and double," and he may try to embody this "false self created by mother and child [. . .] to conceal the true self." As he grows up, this queer man realizes he

> cannot be the parent's boy, and is unsure if he can become his own person. [. . .] As he experiences this loss, he often loses the authorizing force of his true self and [. . .] projects it into an ideal boy that may later in adult life be adored back into reality.

> Love of the boy or the ideal body is a reclamatory love, an effort to unite with the divided half, to overcome one's deficiency and isolation. Needless to say, this alter being that possesses lost parts of the self is the object of intense need, the objectification of anguishing loss and, when it is acted out with the other, of a most ironic envy and hate. Perhaps the cruiser seeks his double in order to vanquish him and gain control of his destructive rival.

Is this why so many men look a little bloodthirsty in cruisy bars like the Eagle? Maybe, but I wonder if those who've had harmonious relationships with their real siblings—as Bruce did, as [ ] evidently does—are more inoculated to the anguishing loss Bollas describes, since they've already worked through such a juvenile rivalry, whereas an only child like me has to overcome his sense of deficiency and isolation on his own. This may be the reason I've treated so many queer men my age not as branches of my chosen family tree but as limbs severed from my own body, phantoms of the brother I've never had and of the "ideal boy" I'll never be. Paradoxically, by investing them with so many layers of meaning, I've reduced these men to two-dimensional objects of intense need, as if they were the missing passages from the lacunae in my own script. I probably should have learned from Bruce to shake this counterproductive habit, to let my fragile sense of self be fortified rather than splintered by the infinite variety of other men, and to ask every potential friend or foe, "I'm Steven Pfau—who are *you*?" But maybe it's not too late. Maybe tonight I'll learn to break this pattern with [ ].

"Could you hold my drink?" he asks. I take his cup, plant my feet on the patio, watch [ ] disappear into the bar, and stare at the doorway like a puppy waiting for his human to come home. Five minutes pass, and I start to worry. Did he get lost? Or did his "real" family find him, recognizing that [ ] already belongs here more than I do? A stranger approaches and compliments my aviator frames, which dumbfounds me, since I think of them as cheap imitations of [ ]'s glasses (that may not be *the* reason I chose them for the occasion, but I probably wouldn't otherwise have felt emboldened to wear them, since they're not really usual my style). I thank him, trying to be more magnanimous than I've been to other Eagle patrons, but I say no more and keep my eyes laser-focused straight ahead, not wanting to get distracted from the mission [ ] has assigned me. He returns after almost ten minutes and admits he was waiting in line for the one private toilet, since he didn't want to use the communal trough urinal in the main bathroom, and I try to hide my surprise. (How could someone so confident and self-assured be so piss-shy?) [ ] greets the stranger I ignored, who saddles up to our table, undeterred by my rudeness. He asks if [ ] and I are together, and I chuckle, amused that this man sees me as someone [ ] might want to be with, and secretly grateful that a witness at the Eagle has validated our bond as ostensibly secure. But my heart sinks a little when [ ] swiftly says no, even though we both know that's the correct answer.

The bouncer announces that the bar is closing (time flies when you're lost in your head), and I quickly run to the restroom—not too shy for the trough urinal—before we go. [ ] is still chatting with our new acquaintance when I return, and I follow them out to the sidewalk, relieved and triumphant to have accomplished something tonight, though I'm not yet sure what. [ ] and the stranger pause at the curb, smile at each other, and turn to me.

"I think I'm gonna go back to his place," [ ] says. "Is that okay with you?"

I freeze, unsure if this is a joke. I want to say, *No, it's not okay, how dare you ditch me like this, who do you think you are*. I want to scream like a version of Toni Collette in that dinner scene from *Hereditary*: "I am your *uncle*!" But I'm not his uncle; I'm just—well, who knows who I am to him. And why should I have expected a different outcome? After all, this is the Eagle, where connecting with someone you've just met is a time-honored tradition, as I should know by now. So I just shrug and nod and watch them walk away. Not until I call a car do I realize that I'm all alone on a dark, vacant stretch of Santa Monica Boulevard at two in the morning—not the worst place to be at this hour, but still unfamiliar enough to unnerve me. Suddenly frightened, I shout [ ]'s name, hoping he might think twice and turn around, wherever he's gone. But he's out of earshot, and I know I have no right to accuse him of leaving me behind. If he were my real nephew, I would want him to feel free, not burdened with all the responsibility I've projected onto him, as if I were the one in need of an uncle to come to the rescue.

3

Fri, Aug 5 at 20:56

thinking about you as the eagle plays fiona's "criminal"

Fri, Aug 5 at 23:46

this is the most erotic text i have ever received

It's true: if you want to seduce me, you should probably know that (a) sexting is this introverted writer's preferred medium of foreplay, (b) acknowledging my profound love for Fiona Apple is a major turn-on, and (c) yes, I set my phone to 24-hour time. In this case, the seducer in question is a clinical social worker I met on Scruff, so perhaps I shouldn't be surprised that he shares my fondness for this famously vulnerable singer-songwriter's psychologically complex music. We've exchanged numbers but haven't yet arranged a proper rendezvous, so I'm also pleased that he's picked up on my attachment to the Eagle and thought of me on a rare Friday night when I'm elsewhere. It strikes me as an odd setting for a DJ to play "Criminal," not because such a track seems unwelcome or unsuitable in this space—though it tickles me to imagine the Cub Scout crowd singing about being a bad, bad girl—but because no man I've met at the Eagle emotes as clearly and vividly as Apple does.

Then again, neither do I, as I've been learning the hard way, and as that astrologer reminded me. When I first sought her advice for my Saturn return, what she really wanted to talk about was Mars. I was born under Mars in Cancer, when the warrior planet was in the sign of the hard-shelled, soft-bellied, sensitive crab—a combo associated with a tendency to internalize pain and bottle up hot-blooded feelings until they erupt in impolite, inconvenient ways. “Conflict is deeply embedded in your life,” the astrologer told me, “and your natal planets are telling you to step back, close your mouth, take the high road. But you need to express, express, express. If I were you, I’d start a Mars remediation practice immediately. Take up martial arts. Wear red, Mars’s color. Make an altar with red crystals. Or donate to an organization that helps soldiers with PTSD—ideally on a Tuesday, Mars’s day.”

I thanked the astrologer, but I did not want to do any of these things. I used to dread my childhood tae kwon do lessons, I’d never loved red clothes, I didn’t know what I would do with a collection of red stones, and I didn’t want to support the military, however much I want to alleviate the suffering it produces. Tuesday might even be my least favorite day of the week. I once asked Bruce how he dealt with hurt feelings, and he recalled the one time he tried to break up with Hugh, who responded by rounding up their mutual friends and fellow barflies for a trip to Fire Island—a petty move that makes me wonder if Hugh was also born under Mars in Cancer. Bruce told me he then called up Hugh from a little phone booth in Grand Central to ask if he could come back: “I loved him, strange for me to say. I was always in love—but I was not a saint.” I asked what he meant, how he managed to stay in love without letting every heartbreak get under his skin. His answer was characteristically cryptic: “I didn’t let it be painful.” I don’t know how you just refuse to let something be painful, but I decided after speaking with that astrologer to forgo her suggestions in favor of my uncle's stoic approach. I would try to dislodge the conflicts embedded in my life through sheer force of will, hoping the ornery Mars in my birth chart would figure out how to remediate itself.

But of course it didn't. Amid the maddening isolation of lockdown, I lost my sense of scale, and every minor slight left me ruminating on all the grudges and grievances I harbored toward anyone who had ever wronged me. As social distancing frayed some already strained ties, I lost a number of friendships by gradually withdrawing instead of reaching out and clearing the air. Even after the worst of the pandemic seemed to be over, I kept snapping for no good reason; I ended up lashing out at [ ] for discarding and abandoning me at the Eagle, though I knew he had done no such thing. I could tell something needed to change, but instead of confronting the problem at hand, I kept trying to power through this turbulent period. And I listened to a lot of Fiona Apple—especially her 2020 album, *Fetch the Bolt Cutters*, which was widely celebrated for expressing righteous rage with a kind of candor and levity I was craving at that heavy, restrictive moment. I wanted to know how she'd evolved from someone who once wrote songs begging her lovers to run away and leave her alone to someone who now chooses to sing about *wanting* to be loved and heard and understood, all while imitating the squeak of a dolphin or drumming on a box of her late dog's bones or earnestly extending an olive branch to an ex-boyfriend's new girlfriend, even if this turns out to be yet another woman to whom she won't get through. Apple's answer? "I always questioned my motives," she said in an interview about the album:

> I've spent so much time writing songs like, "You did this, and you did this!" Which I still do, but I'm older now and it's boring to think that way. It doesn't do me any good. It's just going to keep me in the same place. I've got to start taking responsibility for some of the things I've done. [. . .] What angers me about so many people, many of them men, is they will not acknowledge the things they've done. There's no reason to cancel anybody as long as they can own up to the things they've done, examine them, and share their wisdom so that other people may not feel so alone in being a bit of an asshole—because everybody is sometimes.

I wanted to attain this level of clarity and confidence, to question my own motives and take responsibility for the shitty things I've done; I was also bored of dwelling on my bruises and letting them fester while pointing fingers at everyone but myself. I hoped that Apple could show me how to fetch my own bolt cutters, that her music alone could teach me how to snap out of my ego's limited perspective. But perhaps clinging to that hope makes me even more of an asshole.

I know I'm not the only gay boy who would rather outsource his unmanageable feelings to one of his beloved cultural icons than learn to communicate his own angst.

But as I meet more and more sanctimonious queers who, say, casually cite Audre Lorde's "The Uses of Anger" on a coffee date and then lambaste the barista over a minor inconvenience, I worry about how much my virtue-signaling tendencies—even my innocuous displays of fanboying—have distracted me from my own emotional labor. I worry about how little I've reckoned with the aggressive impulses I may have inherited from Bruce, who proudly declared himself a tenderhearted crybaby, and who often boasted that he never argued with Will, but who also—as I learned only after his death—got in several knock-down, drag-out fights with some of his early boyfriends, and who once advised my father to resolve some trouble with a girlfriend by hitting her. And I worry about how unprepared I am to encounter similar impulses in other men: when I finally met up with that social worker, I discovered just how wrong I was to assume—based on the delicate nature of his profession and the sweetness of his texts and our shared admiration for Fiona Apple's music—that he would be gentle with me. To be fair, when he began to grab my hair and spank my ass and fuck my throat more roughly than I would have agreed to if he had asked, I could tell he didn't intend to hurt me, and he was at least decent enough to listen when I told him to stop. Still, I realized I would need to think more carefully about the multitudes that men contain and the consequences of my hitherto laissez-faire attitude toward the Mars in us all. What kind of destructive violence could I unwittingly inflict if I don't learn to deal with my own repressed wrath?

I made a second appointment with the astrologer, who asked how my remediation practice had been going. Not well, I answered. As I elaborated, I began to ramble about becoming a regular at the Eagle, and the astrologer laughed. "That's perfect," she said. "This is the temple of Mars. Even just the aesthetics—we're wearing *leather*, there's *metal*, things have been *forged in the fire*. This is the place to work through that martial energy you're resisting." In theory, she's not wrong about the general atmosphere, and I imagine many longtime leather enthusiasts would agree, so I want to take her wisdom to heart. But in practice, telling an acquaintance that this bar is my "temple of Mars" probably won't help me de-escalate any conflicts.

For a while after my first encounter with that social worker, whenever we both happened to be at the Eagle, I pretended not to notice him through the clouds of cigar smoke on the crowded patio. Then I heard through the grapevine that he once dated an old friend of mine, who described the social worker as an "abusive partner," and I wondered what to do with that information. Would Bruce goad me to confront the guy, maybe even hit him? Or would he caution me to let go and move on? I know it's not my place to intervene on behalf of the social worker's ex-boyfriend, who happens to be one of the friends I drifted away from in the pandemic, so reconnecting might be even more fraught if he were to find out I've hooked up with his alleged abuser. What's the point of acting on my secondhand knowledge of their history when it could just make the situation worse? For now, I'll step back and keep my mouth shut, and if I ever hear a Fiona song at the Eagle, I'll try not to let it be painful. Yet another man to whom I won't get through.

4

In all the notes I took from my conversations with Bruce, I somehow recorded only one direct description of the Eagle's Nest, a parenthesis that still startles me whenever I see it in my own handwriting: *(named after Hitler's)*. I must have suppressed this offhand remark after I first heard it and scribbled it in my journal, perhaps too taken aback to verify what he was talking about. Now I see that Hitler's Kehlsteinhaus, an Alpine chalet used as a Nazi headquarters, was indeed nicknamed "Eagle's Nest," but the dates don't line up: the Kehlsteinhaus was built in 1938, so it's likely unrelated to the very different nest that some queer stevedores founded seven years earlier in New York. Still, who gave my uncle this impression, and did he question it before passing it on to me?

I don't know whether Bruce was bothered by the fascist trappings of the leather scene, if he even thought much about them at all, but he certainly wasn't the first or last man to treat them so casually. In his 1991 essay "Swastika Toys," Arnie Kantrowitz recalls noticing that loaded symbol on the cap of a fellow activist at the Spike, a now-shuttered leather bar in West Hollywood. "Oh, that doesn't mean anything," says the man in the cap. "It's just part of the look. It's nothing to make a big deal about [. . .] only an image of power. You don't think I'm a Nazi, do you?" Wary of this man's indifference to the implications of his "look," Kantrowitz situates this encounter within the widespread and ongoing tendency to reduce "the fearsome Nazi image [. . .] into a mere caricature," whether among opera queens gushing over Wagner's *Ring* cycle at the Mineshaft or art collectors displaying Tom of Finland's early drawings of the German soldiers he cruised as a young man in Helsinki. Kantrowitz posits that "the appeal of the fascist image is its sinister quality. [. . .] For most people it carries the stigma of the forbidden, a taboo that makes it all the more attractive to those who perceive themselves as sexual outlaws." He clearly doesn't believe this fetish is "nothing to make a big deal about," but Kantrowitz also hesitates to condemn it altogether, and he recognizes his own complicity in this troubling tradition. He recalls reading a pornographic story, published in a 1984 issue of *Drummer* magazine, "in which the gay male narrator is so eager to have sex with a Central American dictator that he allows himself to become a tool in the enslavement of the nation's people, knowing he will be killed in the process." Kantrowitz writes a letter to the editor, "protesting the glorification of such a fascistic sex object and the nonconsensual oppression of an entire population for the sake of an orgasm," and the editor responds that the narrator's ethically unsettling behavior is the whole point, that this story about "the fascination of fascism" is meant to challenge readers to consider the consequences of their own obsessions. "The editor's assessment is probably correct," Kantrowitz admits, "but isn't it asking a bit much of a guy with his dick about to erupt in his hand to make complex moral judgments? What stays in the memory is how hot the despot was."

I myself don't feel hot for despots, nor have I ever seen anyone wear a swastika cap. But Kantrowitz's essay comes to mind whenever I encounter the BLUF crowd—that is, the gays into "breeches and leather uniform," code for cop and soldier livery—for whom the Eagle hosts another monthly party, the week after Cub Scout. It's my least favorite night here, when I often feel like Al Pacino's character in William Friedkin's movie *Cruising*, unable to tell who's a real cop and who's just in costume—but then I remember that Pacino is playing an undercover cop posing as a gay guy to track down a serial killer in the leather scene, and I wonder if my judging the wannabe police in my midst makes *me* a prudish cop, policing everyone else's kinks. Still, my misgivings haven't yet driven me to boycott or cancel the Eagle, and it doesn't seem to have scared away the other lefties in my social circle. Maybe some are secretly ACAB in the streets and horny for BLUF in the sheets, or maybe we'd all rather turn a lazy eye to this side of a bar we love than risk killing the vibe. I know the relationship between one's outward politics and one's innermost desires is more nuanced than that, but these moments of dissonance do make me wonder, as Kantrowitz does, how much we gays are willing to slacken our moral judgment when a dick is about to erupt in someone's hand.

My own indolent brain worries me whenever I watch *Querelle*, Rainer Werner Fassbinder's film adaptation of Jean Genet's novel, which the Eagle often screens for ambiance when they're not showing vintage porn.

I'm always hypnotized by the eerie orange haze of the film's lighting and the otherworldly scenery, sometimes to such an extent that I miss the cartoonishly phallic shapes of the set. And then there are the costumes: it's easy to forget you're looking at a murderous sailor when hunky actor Brad Davis, in the titular role, shows up in his pom-pommed beret, his high-waisted white trousers, and the deep-cut tank that advertises his sweaty décolletage like a high-wattage marquee. I often walk into the bar right as Querelle, for complicated reasons that he himself may not entirely understand, agrees to be sodomized by the husband of his brother's lover, and I sometimes suspect that the bartenders play this famously steamy scene on loop and skip over the moments when, say, Querelle slits the throat of his accomplice or colludes with the police to frame another man for his own crimes.

When I finally read the novel, I wondered if Fassbinder's colorful film might have exaggerated Genet's interest in this kind of libidinous imagery, but in fact the book opens with the narrator psychoanalyzing the kind of person who might be swayed by that very imagery:

> The notion of murder often brings to mind the notion of sea and sailors. Sea and sailors do not, at first, appear as a definite image—it is rather that "murder" starts up a feeling of *waves*. [. . .] The man who dons a sailor's outfit does so not out of prudence only. His disguise relieves him from the necessity of going through all the rigamarole required in the execution of any preconceived murder.

Genet goes on, throughout the first few pages of *Querelle*, to characterize this "outfit" as if he were writing a trend piece for a fashion magazine ("It cradles the criminal, it enfolds him—in the tight fit of his sweater, in the amplitude of his bell-bottoms. It casts a sleep-spell on the already fascinated victim"), and he acknowledges that this aesthetic sensibility is particularly appealing to queer men ("We would also like to say that it addresses itself to inverts"). Based on this introduction, one could accuse Genet of writing yet another story that, as many critics have said of *Cruising*, perpetuates the stereotype of the sadistic gay villain, but then he directly addresses readers and asks us to collaborate with him in building this fictional world: "We would like these reflections, these observations, which cannot fully round out nor delineate the characters of the book, to give you permission to act not so much as onlookers as creators of these very characters, who will then slowly disengage themselves from your own preoccupations." This may be a jab at those of us who impose our own ethical standards on imaginary characters, but I imagine Genet is also drawing attention to Querelle as a product of his own preoccupations. According to critic Kadji Amin, Genet has been worshipped from the beginning of his career "as a paradigmatic figure for the romance of the alternative [who] virtually *demands* idealization as a saint or antihero":

> Eventually, however, he spoils every ideal. When we want to claim him as a precursor for today's queer and transgender prison abolition movement, he

> insists that the penal colony of Mettray was a "paradise," when we want to celebrate his transnational coalitions with the Panthers and the Palestinians, he confesses that a sexual desire for Arab and black men drew him toward these movements, and when we want to honor his queer bonds, we are confronted with their pederastic inegalitarianism. Genet has the virtue of making critics feel uneasy about the ideals we make him represent.

This is the double-edged sword Genet hands to readers of *Querelle*, in which he suggests that we too could be credulous enough to fall under the "sleep-spell" of a wolf in sailor's clothing, and the challenge that Fassbinder takes up in his adaptation, which seems to test how deeply it can lull us into this horny fever dream before we start to question our own attraction to a hot but morally hollow man such as Querelle.

Both this novel and this film remind me of a story Bruce once told me about dancing at the Eagle's Nest, looking around at the rapidly multiplying crowd, and telling Hugh, "Everybody's dressed like sailors! It's amazing!" Hugh laughed and informed him that they were, in fact, surrounded by actual sailors who had flocked to New York for Fleet Week and docked a block away at the Hudson River piers. I wonder sometimes if Bruce ever could have been the kind of "fascinated victim" Genet describes, so beguiled by the tight fit of a stranger's sweater or the amplitude of his bell-bottoms that he would end up letting a man get away with murder. I know he wasn't *that* gullible, but if he was willing enough to frequent a bar that he associated with the Führer, what else was he willing to sweep under the rug so he could keep enjoying himself?

Perhaps I'm painting my uncle as more of a lotus-eater than he actually was. I'm often haunted by this letter Bruce sent me in November 2016:

> *Here we sit, teeth clenched, waiting for the first snow, and wondering how we'll dig out. But dig we will. It's thanksgiving day and Will is banging in the kitchen, peeling potatoes, chopping pecans for the dressing. And we're thankful for the day off. I ain't reading nuthin' right now. Except the papers and their take on Trump. He won by some 200 votes here in East Haddam. Following the election a big homemade sign went up pledging kindness and tolerance which was defaced with Trump hate stuff. So we join the rest of ½ of the country, marching in protest. Our local cop is looking for the bad guys.*

I wrote a long letter in reply, expressing the "rage and despair" I also felt about the "inescapably scary and sad" news, commending the "bravery and resilience" that had gotten Bruce through many dispiriting moments in the past, and asking how he had repeatedly managed to "resist cynicism and dread" and keep going. But I never mailed it, mostly because I found the tone of earnest lamentation far too cringe, and I was already tired of hearing other gay, white, liberal millennials loudly wallowing in their own woe instead of just getting over themselves and *doing* something. Now I wish I had sent it anyway.

By the time Bruce died three months later, East Haddam had transformed from the gay bohemian utopia where he had put down roots in the 1970s to an unrecognizably conservative stronghold of pro-Trump bigots, who have since become the majority—not a sea change that Bruce could have averted, but I know he would have been a more brazen dissenter than I've ever been, and I'm sure he would still be marching in protest instead of wringing his hands over the "right" thing to do. Why should I judge any of my heroes, even Bruce, by unreasonably high standards of political engagement and ideological consistency when I often get too slothful to live up to my own ideals? I don't want to gloss over my uncle's more problematic moments, but I also don't want to take them out of context just as cavalierly as certain gays seem to divorce Genet's uglier views from Querelle's sexiness.

One night, I notice another Eagle regular sporting a version of Brad Davis's costume, including a pair of white pants with the authentic touch of a buttoned front flap and a tank with an impressively low-scooping neck that might have raised even Fassbinder's eyebrows. I ask where he got these pieces, which look like they could be vintage Gaultier. With a sheepish grimace, he whispers, "House of Bezos." I nod and wink to signal that his secret's safe with me. When he turns away, I track down everything he found on Amazon and add it to my cart.

5

But I don't want to show up at the Eagle in something I just found on the internet. I want to wear something with a real provenance; what I really want is Bruce's leather jacket. Simple and black with a zippered chest pocket and a short, banded collar, it's the only piece of leather "gear" I ever saw him wear. I don't know when or where he acquired it, but whenever he talked about trying on T-shirts until midnight before going out on the town, I couldn't imagine him worrying too much when armored in that leather jacket, which conveyed a rugged gravitas that could probably get him in just about any door.

My uncle looked a little worried, though, when he first visited me at college. He and my parents came to campus for "family weekend" at Columbia, where I had started my first semester just a month earlier. You can't tell I was an anxious eighteen-year-old in the photo my father took of Bruce and me at the library: I'm sitting in a chair, and all you can see of me at the bottom of the frame is the striped H&M scarf wrapped around my neck and the devilish smirk on my dimpled face; I look more like a dewy preteen masquerading as a caricature of an English professor. Bruce is seventy-one, standing behind me with his hands on the back of the chair; his black leather jacket blends in with the background, so at first he appears to be just a pale, disembodied head floating over mine, smiling nervously with deer-in-the-headlights eyes.

Maybe he was just spooked by the camera flash, but in retrospect, I also detect the uneasiness that academia, more than any other environment, brought out in my uncle. Though always an avid reader, a talented writer, and a profound thinker, Bruce seemed unusually shy among so-called intellectuals—perhaps because he was embarrassed to be a college dropout whose cultural education was mostly self-taught, perhaps because he was simply allergic to any whiff of cerebral snobbery. (Once my father asked if his brother had read the latest Don DeLillo novel, and Bruce scoffed and flicked his hands as if swatting away a mosquito. "Oh *no*," he said, "that's *literature*.") Meanwhile, I was trying my hardest—maybe too hard—to ingratiate myself with the ivory-tower crowd. Many of my peers had attended fancier high schools than mine and seemed to have already learned the proper rules of the game for acting smart and self-assured in the classroom. Unlike my mother, I wasn't a first-generation college student, and I hadn't grown up in a one-room farmhouse without indoor plumbing, as she had, but I still internalized some of the class shame and impostor syndrome she had carried as an academically ambitious teenager. When she later encouraged me to apply to the most competitive schools, I never imagined that someone with my middling GPA could get in, and I was unprepared for how insecure in my intelligence I would feel upon arriving at Columbia. So I tried to fake my way to fitting in by dressing the part of the erudite dandy. I stowed away the cowboy boots and Levi's that Bruce had handed down to me as part of my gay-boy starter kit, and I began thrifting wingtip brogues and houndstooth trousers and buttoned vests and paisley bowties, which I would embellish with twee accessories like that silly scarf.

Perhaps Bruce looks so unsettled in that photo because I was becoming unrecognizable to him. I was fashioning myself as someone who studies Ancient Greek and Latin and wants everyone to know it, someone unafraid to correct those who don't know the difference between purgatory and limbo—in other words, I was becoming insufferable. Now I'm haunted by that picture of my uncle and me whenever I come to the Eagle, where Bruce would surely be grinning ear to ear, unbothered and unassailable in that perfect leather jacket. But the harder I try to look like a natural here, to embody leatherman realness as effortlessly as my uncle did, the more I feel like I'm in drag.

On that note, a confession: *RuPaul's Drag Race* has played a not-so-small role in my becoming a regular at the Eagle. I wasn't a die-hard fan of the show before frequenting this bar, but I was won over watching a crowd of flinty bears absolutely losing their shit over Sasha Colby. I'm grateful that this franchise is drawing so many patrons to the Eagle, yet at the same time, I recognize that it's also partly responsible for the gentrification of gay bars, many of which have transformed from countercultural havens for disenfranchised queers into Disneyfied brunch destinations for our straight friends' bachelorette parties; it's also funding RuPaul's 60,000-acre ranch and, by extension, the fracking companies she unapologetically invites to drill her land. By supporting the Eagle's participation in the *Drag Race* industrial complex, perhaps I've joined the ranks of the "adult babies," as critic James Greig has aptly named the members of my generation who have been so brainwashed by mindless, feel-good entertainment that we've allowed the motto "no ethical consumption under capitalism" to morph into "no unethical consumption under capitalism."

But *Drag Race* is not an isolated phenomenon; in fact, it throws into relief just how draggy the Eagle can be all the time. Though rooted in the real rigging of wild outlaws like cowboys and bikers, leather is now an art form as well-established as drag, and the equipment required to compete in the International Mr. Leather contest can be just as expensive as—if not more so than—some of the fashion displayed on RuPaul's runway. Yet I've also seen many young gay influencers who seem, based on the vacation photos they share on Instagram, to have no problem affording a closetful of harnesses and chaps but who pointedly dress down at the Eagle, living a blue-collar fantasy in their couture trucker hats and work boots. These boys seem to relish performing a caricature of "rough trade"—that is, the archetype of the working-class, straight-presenting man who was fetishized by wealthy, educated gays in the early twentieth century and widely replicated in the "clone" aesthetic adopted by masc-leaning men like Bruce in the 1970s. (Rough Trade also happens to be the name of the fetish gear shop down the street, but when I first overheard the Eagle's bartenders talking about it, the bougie hipster in me thought—until more recently than I'd like to admit—they were all referring to a retailer for the indie record label.) At the Eagle, it can be hard to tell who approaches leather as a way of life or just as a matter of conspicuous consumption. But either way, each of us seems to be performing his desired social standing in more dramatic and stratified ways than I've seen at any other gay bar—partly because of the distinct image repertoire of the leather scene, and partly because we're in LA, where stylized self-curation is de rigueur.

Instead of refining my class consciousness, though,

the Eagle mostly sharpens my avarice for other men's clothes, particularly those signaling that the wearer indisputably belongs here—as if belonging were a commodity one could buy off the rack. I often catch myself mentally annotating another customer's self-presentation and determining what each component "means," as photographer Hal Fischer did in *Gay Semiotics*, his 1977 "study of visual coding among homosexual men." Fischer's photo-essays would be helpful infographics for any gay boy visiting the Eagle for the first time; he illustrates the function of various fetish paraphernalia (cat-o'-nine-tails whips, straitjackets, gag masks, poppers) and explains certain "signifiers for a male response" (i.e., where and how you should pierce your ear and attach your key ring to your belt loop and stick your hanky in your pocket, depending on your sexual inclinations). He also breaks down the trappings of the leatherman alongside several other examples of gay street fashion and archetypal media images, such as the "classical" man (an incarnation of Michelangelo's *David* with a twentieth-century haircut), the "Western" (a thick-mustached and long-sideburned buckaroo in full rodeo getup), and the "urbane" (a dead ringer for Bruce or Hugh circa 1977, sporting the kind of natty suit they both would've worn at their white-collar day jobs in advertising and PR). Whenever I try to assemble an Eagle-appropriate outfit from what I already have in my wardrobe—zippered American Apparel hoodie, flannel shirt from Urban Outfitters, Casio wristwatch, skinny Levi's, white leather Reeboks—at least no one could accuse me of putting on airs, but I end up resembling a carbon copy of what Fischer calls the "basic gay."

I must have been wearing a version of this outfit when I first met Love Connie, the legendary queen who has dubbed herself "a bayou-raised, inbred, hirsute dancing phenomenon with a love for Farrah Fawcett flips" and whom one fan has described—accurately, I think—as "an over-the-top chaos Muppet." Her most widely recognizable claim to fame may be a brief, out-of-drag cameo in the "bend and snap" scene from the original *Legally Blonde*, but to me she is the poet laureate, artist-in-residence, and grande dame of the Eagle, where she emcees the bar's screenings of *Drag Race*. One night, she passed by while I was waiting in line for the ATM and told me, "You look just like a member of INXS. Have you heard of them?" I barely started nodding my head before she said, "No, you haven't, you're too young," and walked away. I wish I'd been quick enough to come up with a clever retort, to shout back that she reminds me of a cross between Mötley Crüe and Twisted Sister—not because I wanted to rebut her assessment, which wasn't wrong, but because the arrogant undergrad in me still has a chip on his shoulder, still wants to prove that he knows exactly where he stands in the context of this storied leather bar and in his own gay lineage. I want one of my uncle's old friends from the Eagle's Nest to pass by and tell me I look just like Bruce's nephew. Have you heard of him?

At least that's what I dream of happening if I were in that leather jacket, wherever it is. After Bruce died, Will told me he wanted to get rid of his late husband's clothes as soon as possible, as if they were once-living organisms that would rapidly putrefy like their former owner's corpse. Will's grandson, Seth, was also there, and the two of us began to work on decluttering the coatrack. I was already wearing the maroon and gray letterman jacket Bruce had given me a few years earlier—not an artifact from his own school days but a secondhand item he found at a vintage store. (A gimlet-eyed antique-hunter, Bruce loved the griffin emblazoned on the back, the mascot of a boarding school for troubled boys, which we both found a little queer.) Will asked Seth to take Bruce's leather jacket, and a wave of greed overtook me. The possessive scrooge in me began to scream: *No, you can't have it, you didn't know Bruce like I did, you have no idea how much this jacket meant to my uncle and what it means to me now.* But I didn't want to be ungenerous; acting entitled to Bruce's belongings just because of our blood relation and our shared history seemed like a deeply unqueer move. So I asked to try it on, just once. It was big and boxy and much too heavy on my shoulders; I could tell from Will's and Seth's faces that, even if I were already a true-blue leatherboy, wearing this unwieldy jacket would ring hollow. I handed it over to Seth and couldn't deny how well it suited him—not weighing him down but lifting him up, just as Bruce would have wanted.

6

"Go piss, girl," Jack says, as is the custom among extremely online gay boys in the 2020s: when a friend announces his intention to visit the loo, it behooves you to cite the iconic meme remixing the title of *Gossip Girl*. Before I walk away from our table, he adds a caveat: "But beware the piss thief."

The thief in question is a man he once encountered here at the Eagle. Jack was at the trough urinal, the centerpiece of the bar's main restroom, where three users—maybe four, if you're willing to get cozy—can stand side by side and relieve themselves together in an oblong ceramic basin. Voyeurism is expected and encouraged here: there are no partitions to provide even the illusion of privacy, and there is a long mirror installed at eye level and tilted toward crotch level. Some customers prefer the private toilet in the back of the bar, others relish the open setup of this communal urinal, and others—such as Jack—seem to fall somewhere in the middle of the spectrum. As he was opening his fly at one end of the otherwise vacant trough, another customer entered the restroom and stood beside him, shoulder to shoulder. Jack tried to mind his own business and eventually, after some hesitation, opened the floodgates. Then the stranger cupped his hand, reached over to catch Jack's stream, and poured the stolen urine on his own dick. Jack soon wrapped up, zipped up, and fled. Since then, we've often speculated on what was going through the piss thief's mind. Was he into the idea of bathing his own genitalia in the discharge of someone else's, completing a perverse circle of life? Was he just turned on by this particular encounter and lubing himself up? Was he about to bring the cupped hand to his mouth and take a sip? In any case, the thief's refusal to ask permission or explain himself is what made this transgression so startling to Jack, and I can understand why he may have felt a little violated. But now, as I claim the central spot at the empty trough and watch the door in the mirror, I secretly hope to meet the thief.

I am fascinated by the psychology of watersports, as afficionados commonly refer to urolagnia—that is, the paraphilia that involves the sensation or presence of urine, whether one gives it, receives it, deliberately wets oneself, or simply observes its production. I get why many are grossed out by piss play, but I can also appreciate the kinky thrill of sharing a bodily substance that disgusts so much of polite society, and I imagine it can be especially meaningful for those who have complicated relationships with their bladders, an opportunity to transform the pain of overfullness or the shame of incontinence into a cathartic act of physical relief and emotional vulnerability. It can also be a partly spiritual practice, as Garth Greenwell argues in his essay "A Moral Education," in which he describes a scene of piss play as "a sacrament" and compares the process to kenosis, the term in Christian theology for "the self-emptying necessary before the aspirant can be filled up in divine union." I myself am an occasional practitioner, though piss hasn't yet brought me this degree of ecstasy or left me feeling anointed. Most of the time, I end up marveling at the intense preparatory work involved—namely, the volume of fluid one must imbibe to participate at length. For those who enthusiastically flag their yellow hankies at the Eagle, *watering hole* isn't just a hokey euphemism but a reminder of what this space provides in abundance. No matter what you ask the bartender to pour you, the end result is mostly the same: we're all glutting ourselves with raw material for a golden shower.

I bet my uncle would have been perfectly at home at this trough, judging from a story his neighbors love to tell. After a few martinis at one of the dinner parties he used to host for the local gays, Bruce announced, "I just got a call from this man responding to a personal ad, and he sounds just like me!" He played the message on his answering machine, and one of the guests informed him, "Bruce, that *is* you." Upon realizing what he'd done, he howled: he had anonymously submitted an ad to a gay magazine, forgetting about it by the time he saw it in print, and then somehow drunkenly called his own number to leave a voicemail in reply. As the party resumed, Bruce abruptly rose from the couch mid-conversation, kept talking as he walked to the farmhouse sink in the kitchen, and casually took a leak down the drain. "It's just men in this house," he said, turning around to gauge their reactions. Bruce wasn't showing off his cock, one eyewitness told me, but he probably was showing off some exaggerated performance of masculinity. I imagine he was also reminding everyone that he was a seasoned party boy who knew how to handle his liquor and keep his shit together, who guzzled too much to bother interrupting the action and adjourning to a discreet powder room whenever he'd thoroughly saturated himself. After all, alcohol is a diuretic, so a boozehound can't afford to be piss-shy.

I don't know if urinating for an audience was a sexual turn-on for Bruce, but I wonder if it allowed him to take pleasure in flexing his heavyweight status. Now I wish I could have asked him about the AA materials I found in his nightstand—plus a book called *Lavender Light: Daily Meditations for Gay Men in Recovery*—soon after he died, when it occurred to me for the first time that tempering his relationship with alcohol might have been more challenging than he'd let on. I wish I had asked the cardiologist about the specifics of my uncle's cause of death, which was officially an aortic rupture but which was probably catalyzed by the generous doses of ibuprofen Bruce was taking to alleviate his arthritis combined with the generous doses of vodka he was gulping to soothe the ennui of old age. I even wish I could have seen firsthand the image I will never get out of my head: the freshly filled cocktail glass by the armchair from which Bruce stood up one night in February and lost consciousness and collapsed toward the chimney, where his chin landed on the mantel and his knees slumped forward into the unlit fireplace, as if he were taking aim to douse the hearth—the improbable position in which Will, after coming home from work and starting to cook the spaghetti his husband had requested just an hour earlier and entering the living room to turn down the TV, found Bruce's already blue-faced body in soiled and piss-soaked jeans. "Sometimes," Will later told me, "Bruce thought he was cuter than he actually was when drunk, in a sweet and charming way. If I could pay anything for one more night of him to be sweet and charming and drunk."

This is what goes through my mind whenever I visit the Eagle's urinal, where I fixate on the input and output of liquid in my body and the genes I did and didn't inherit from my uncles and the number of gin and tonics I've wolfed down to mask the social anxiety I definitely didn't inherit from Bruce and the number of times this coping mechanism may have tipped my behavior from sweet and charming to piggish and mean and what I would pay for one more night with my drunk uncle and the extent to which each sip of liquor brings me closer and closer to the moment of my inevitable disintegration. The man pissing beside me clears his throat. I barely registered his arrival at the trough; I've been spaced out long enough that he could have robbed me blind, but I rule out that possibility when I catch him staring uneasily at the mirror's reflection of my half-unbuckled belt and unopened fly, and I mutter some excuse about realizing belatedly that my well is dry. I return to reassure Jack that I heeded his warning, and we clink our empty mugs. One more?

7

I arrive fashionably late. I don't pick my nails or crack my knuckles. I remember everyone's name. I get just one drink and savor it without chasing after another. I hear a Fiona Apple song without letting it get under my skin. Grudges dislodge themselves from my mind of their own accord. I am cordial and at ease among other men, to whom I harbor only goodwill, and with whom I maintain well-defined boundaries. I offer more of myself than I withdraw. I know whether to shake hands or hug. As soon as I can tell I've overstayed my welcome, I make my exit.

This is the gist of the very first poem I submitted to a workshop. I hadn't written much poetry before, and the genre daunted me, so I loosely imitated part of the *Divine Comedy*, titling the poem "*Purgatorio* XXVIII"—a reference to the canto in which Dante reaches the Earthly Paradise above the seven terraces of Mount Purgatory, but also a nod to my then-imminent twenty-eighth birthday, an age I had previously imagined as the official start of adulthood. I structured the lines in Dantean tercets and used simple present-tense verbs to make each statement a kind of magic spell—a way to practice manifesting this fantasy of shedding the bad habits of my youth, to imagine that I had already arrived at the finish line. But I'm still not there. Now I'm thirty-one, and that poem's heavy-handed bookishness embarrasses me, but it's stuck in my head as I arrive unfashionably early to meet Dylan for our night at the Eagle.

Stop me if you've heard this one before: *A boy and his therapist walk into a leather bar*. That's what I've been telling my friends all week, but it's no joke: my friend Dylan, as he's permitted me to call him tonight, is in fact the therapist I've been working with since moving to LA last fall. When I first saw his *Psychology Today* listing, which opened with an epigraph from Gloria Anzaldúa and mentioned that he's also a writer, a part-time DJ, and a "guncle," I knew he'd be the right person to get me back on track after grad school, where I'd spent three years trying and failing to fix my own mental health without any professional help. My boyfriend expressed concern that I might be expecting too much of Dylan, trying too hard to make him the new uncle figure I was craving in LA and to make myself Dylan's favorite client/nephew. Well, maybe Tom was right; maybe I was and still am falling into the predictable trap of transferring my "uncle issues" onto my therapist—who even has the salt-and-pepper hair, well-groomed mustache, twinkling eyes, and sly smile that the word *avuncular* always brings to my mind—and maybe Dylan is countertransferring some issues of his own onto me. But that might be the whole point: before we get to know someone, Dylan says, all we can do is make that person what we want them to represent, and while this kind of unconscious projection tends to spoil most relationships, it's often what makes a therapist–client bond work. And however Dylan feels about our particular bond, the one we've formed now seems pretty secure.

Lately we've been working on what we call my "exposures." Dylan tasked me with completing my own version of the "subjective units of distress scale," which ranges from 0 (*deep sleep*) to 100 (*unbearable anguish*). Quantifying my emotional life isn't my strong suit, but I found something oddly pleasurable in ranking the relative intensity of various anxiety-inducing experiences, as if I were mapping the circles of hell. (70: *quitting a job*. 75: *disappointing someone I care about*.) Since then, my therapy "homework" has involved playing out each scenario on my scale until it ceases to distress me. I've already gone through all the low-stakes items on the list—*getting a haircut* (10), *swimming* (20), *making small talk with a coworker* (30), *hosting a dinner party* (40)—and now Dylan is coaching me through the middle. *Flirting with a stranger at a bar* is a 50 on my scale, as I recently decided after doing a terrible job of introducing myself to a cute friend of a friend. When I mentioned this to Dylan, he offered to be my undercover wingman; I thought he was joking, but he explained that he'd chaperoned a few clients on exposure therapy "field trips." I assumed *this* kind of trip would be unethical, but apparently his supervisor had proposed the idea, and Dylan posited that it could be a way of "queering therapy," whatever that means. Skeptical but intrigued, I invited him to join me for Cub Scout night at the Eagle, which is conveniently located between his place and mine, and where no one would bat an eye at the sight of us hanging out. But we're not here to hang out, of course; we're here for the exposure.

I've saved Dylan a table outside the market down the street, where we've agreed to get some food and discuss our game plan before heading to the bar. In our last session, I warned him that I might be dressed a little sluttier than usual tonight. "Don't worry," he joked, "I won't wear a harness." But when he sits down, I can tell that he can tell that I can tell that each of us made an effort to choose a relatively modest outfit: he's in a sleeveless Fire Island tee and skater shorts and Doc Martens, I'm in a plain A-shirt and cutoffs and sneakers. "How should we say we met?" he asks. I shrug and suggest "the internet," and he agrees that sounds honest enough. Between bites of greasy pizza, we plot what we're about to do as if we're choreographing a piece of performance art. Neither of us seems to know how it should begin or end, but he promises, whatever happens, not to leave me behind.

I wonder if the bouncer will recognize either of us at the entrance, but he hasn't yet started his shift. I proposed beginning this "field trip" at eight o'clock, when the Eagle wouldn't yet be too loud or crowded to insert oneself in a conversation. Dylan asks how I typically do that, and I don't have a good answer. "I struggle with it too," he admits, "so we'll both be fighting through something tonight." I assure him we can fight together, though now I'm not sure which of us is more nervous. I offer to get us a round of gin and tonics, and he hesitates for a moment, debating whether he should drink; technically, he's on the clock for the next hour. But we figure it's probably fine, since we're at a gay bar anyway.

We grab a pair of corner seats and look around, pretending to see the Eagle for the first time. Dylan gestures toward the hardcore porn on all the TV screens and smirks at me as if to say, *Welcome to my office*. When we hear the opening sample of Beyoncé's "Pure/Honey," Dylan starts waxing nostalgic about the ballroom scene of the nineties, when he came up as a DJ in the House of Aviance. I egg him on, and soon he's in a confessional mood. He tells me about Shatter, the gay bar whose monthly goth parties he frequented as a gaunt college dropout in Columbia, Missouri; about the loneliness that drove him back to school to study psychology in New York; about moving to LA for his master's degree, then simultaneously dealing with both the outbreak of the pandemic and the death of his father midway through his program; about how much he's come to dislike his forties, which have made him both more afraid of mortality and more wistful for the past, though he knows it's easy to romanticize his youth and forget how messy it could be; and about his first K-hole, in which he felt like he was dying for what seemed to be two hours, but it turned out to be only twenty excruciating minutes. ("If you ever experiment with club drugs," he adds with paternal earnestness, as if suddenly worried I might be either an extremely impressionable young man or a narc, "make sure to do them in a controlled environment with someone you trust.") I ask what parallels he sees between his two lives as a DJ and a therapist, and he says both require a similar balance of attunement and detachment, an instinctive ability to read the room without being a people-pleaser. He cites a maxim attributed to legendary DJ Larry Levan: "If I don't clear the dance floor at least once a night, I'm not doing my job."

Am I doing my job? I suppose my job tonight is, in theory, to find a stranger to flirt with, but now I can't recall why I wanted help with that in the first place or why we're going through so much trouble to accomplish that goal. After all, I already have a boyfriend I love, who also loves me, and while Tom doesn't enjoy coming to the Eagle nearly as much as I do, he enthusiastically supports whatever I've been doing here without him over the past year. ("Good luck!" he texted me earlier this evening. "Go get that exposure!") I'm not exactly lacking for pleasure or affection, nor do I feel plagued by pathologically lustful urges, but I do aspire to be the kind of person who isn't afraid of his own desires, who doesn't shy away from saying hi to the handsome man across the room—in other words, to be a little more like Bruce. Where to begin? Well, I see there's an empty billiard table under a poster for the Oedipus Motorcycle Club—a detail I can't wait to mention to my therapist. Then I remember he's right next to me, and I ask if he's up for a round of pool.

Dylan is game, but the universe clearly has other plans. As soon as we step away from our drinks, a barback whisks away our unattended mugs, ignoring our efforts to get his attention, and dumps our half-finished gin and tonics down the drain. Then I remember we need quarters to play pool, but when I go to the bar for change, a burly older man—probably the same one who elbowed me out of the way when I was still a novice here—cuts in front of me for the same purpose. By the time I return to the table, someone else has already claimed it. While waiting for me, Dylan has started chatting with a goateed young man, and he beckons me over. I'm too flustered to be sociable right now, but I'm moved by Dylan's obvious eagerness to help, and it's oddly heartwarming to hear him introduce me as "my friend Steven." Dylan offers to get another round of drinks, gives me an encouraging pat on the shoulder, and leaves us to our devices. The boy asks if Dylan and I are together, and I laugh—perhaps too hard, judging from the awkward silence that follows. He asks what I do, and I try not to roll my eyes at this boring icebreaker, but I don't exactly have a better one in mind. After a bit of small talk about my writing and his interior design work, the boy tells me he's going to find his friend and gives me a lukewarm but sweet "nice to meet you" as he walks away.

I turn back to the bar, where Dylan is waiting in line and chatting with a guy closer to his own age. He tries again to make introductions, but this time his acquaintance just nods dismissively and turns around, and Dylan's long face makes me wonder if I've just cock-blocked my own therapist. I try to defuse the tension by remarking that the bartender looks like a famous gay porn star, but Dylan claims not to know who I mean and drops the subject. By now I feel too anxious to flirt with anyone, but this second gin and tonic is strong enough that I could change my mind any minute. And all my ballooning adrenaline deflates when Dylan tells me, unprompted, "You're doing great."

"What do you mean?"

"I mean you did what we came here to do."

I guess he's right, though I don't know if it technically counts as flirting with a total stranger when your therapist is facilitating the encounter. The Eagle's getting fuller and barstools scarcer, so I suggest we step outside. As I follow Dylan to the patio, it occurs to me that this is the closest I may get to visiting the Eagle with Bruce by my side, and I try to hide my dopey smile. But Dylan isn't my uncle, and he isn't cheering me on purely out of friendliness or familial duty, no matter how convincing we are at playing fellow scouts.

"And how am I doing?" he asks.

Is this a trick question? Maybe I'm a guinea pig in some field experiment. Maybe he's deliberately turning the tables as some kind of sneaky mind game. Or maybe this is a moment to be radically honest, to throw out all the artificial codes and structures of our relationship. But I don't think I want to break the fourth wall; I don't want to know whether Dylan would have chosen to accompany me to the Eagle if I weren't paying him to be here tonight. So I just mumble something vaguely affirmative, since I can tell he's genuinely concerned, and I can tell he also shares my fear of being left in the lurch. We're both exposing ourselves to this dicey situation where the boundaries could easily get blurry or unstable, and we're both trying to keep each other safe. But while Dylan is required to maintain total confidentiality, he surely knows how much I want to document this experience—the occupational hazard of working with a nonfiction writer. Where do you put that kind of exposure on a distress scale?

Nine o'clock approaches, which means the party's just getting started, but our time is almost up. I don't want Dylan to feel obligated to stay, but I don't want to cut this night short, and he doesn't seem to be in a rush. He gestures toward a guy to my left and hints that I'm being cruised; I catch a glimpse and shake my head at Dylan, who laughs and agrees that this twink is a little too "WeHo actor" for me. He asks me who I find cute here, and I take pains to avoid pointing out anyone who looks vaguely like Dylan, but that rules out a significant percentage of the crowd. I offer a few examples, and Dylan says, "Oh, so you're into otters your age." Before I get a chance to question whatever diagnosis he's forming, Dylan tells me he's going to the restroom. Somehow this is the first time my therapist has explicitly disclosed that he is, in fact, a person with a bladder and therefore a whole flesh-and-blood body, and somehow nothing else we've shared with each other tonight seems more intimate than this revelation. To distract myself from picturing Dylan with the piss thief, I scan the burgeoning crowd. I recognize a number of Cub Scout regulars, but luckily they don't seem to recognize me or remember any of the numerous times I've made a fool of myself here. I used to think the Eagle would be the place where I would learn to outgrow my nephewhood, where I would begin a new life as—well, what? There's a heartbreaking moment near the end of the *Purgatorio* when Dante, having completed his education in vice and virtue, looks behind him and realizes Virgil is no longer there—a moment he's long anticipated, yet he's still devastated when his beloved mentor is suddenly gone. I think of this scene as I turn back inside and swear I see Bruce walking by the arcade machine, coming to congratulate me on passing my final exam. But no, it's Dylan returning from the toilet.

"Ready?"

I follow him out of the bar, ask if we can hug goodbye, and thank him for this night at the Eagle.

"Of course," he says. "You deserved a reparative experience after your last time here."

I want to ask which time he means and what kind of repair he thinks I "deserved," but I don't want to spoil a sweet moment, and we'll have a chance to debrief all this during our usual session on Tuesday afternoon. We part ways, and as I climb up Manzanita Street toward my parking spot, I mentally rehearse what I'll tell Tom when I get home. I search for some big epiphany to share about the purpose of this night with Dylan, the meaning of this bar, the changes I've undergone after weeks and weeks of repeatedly loitering at the Eagle; I want a scrap of definitive proof that I've been remade, renewed, purified. But I find no such thing by the time I reach my car at the top of the hill. At least there's a pretty good view of the stars.

Boy

Call me "good boy." Some years ago, I never would have expected to be making such a request, but here we are. It all began, as many gay stories do, with a harness. My friend Roger bought his first one on a whim and invited me, a fellow bondage novice, to be his guinea pig. Roger is nine years my senior, and we've both had fun with this relatively small but noticeable age gap in our sexual rapport: I don't like the label *friend with benefits* (too transactional) or *fuck buddy* (too crude) or *lover* (too romantic), but I like when each of us teasingly addresses the other as "young man." And I liked the new and formidable severity he radiated when he first buckled those straps on his chest.

After flipping over on all fours, I asked, "What should I call you when you wear this?"

"Whatever feels good to you," Roger said.

"Daddy?" I don't know why this was the first nickname to come to mind; I'd never before uttered this word, since its hokeyness used to embarrass me, but now *daddy* sounded right.

I couldn't see Roger's face, but I could hear him sniff some poppers behind me, and I could feel the rush of excitement coursing through both of our bodies when he rested his hands on my hips and nuzzled his furry crotch against my rear and answered, "Good boy."

This was my initiation into a popular subset of gay sexual role-play: daddy/boy. Unlike many forms of power exchange, such as sadism/masochism and dominance/submission, this one is defined by an exchange of care between a strong, protective "daddy" and his eager, obedient "boy," who is usually but not always the younger of the two. Not all May–December sexual relationships between men operate in the daddy/boy framework, and even when they do, the attraction might have nothing to do with a disparity in years. The key appeal of this dyad, according to psychotherapist and pleasure activist Don Shewey, is that it offers a sense of both mutual affection and hierarchical imbalance, an opportunity for mentorship in which the "rewards of mentoring go both ways": the boy gets "to receive the particular masculine love that a tender and nurturing daddy can offer," and for the daddy, "receiving attention from younger men by modeling the virtues of stability, caring, and perseverance gives new value to the experience of aging." Shewey concludes that the daddy/boy scenario can be therapeutic, but "the healing comes not just in, say, getting from your partner what you didn't get from your biological father but also in developing inside yourself whatever qualities you need to achieve your full potential as a human being. And—as daddy/boy enthusiasts know—not just because it's good for you, but because it's hot."

I'm no psychologist, but based on what I've observed, Shewey's diagnosis rings true, though I have no idea what my "full potential as a human being" is, and I don't know if recreational sex is how I'll achieve it. I still don't even understand how and why I fell down this rabbit hole in the first place. For a long time I was aware of daddy/boy but didn't get what was "hot" or "healing" about it, mostly because I had little experience in the worlds of kink, fetish, and BDSM. And so far, the majority of my romantic and sexual partners—including Tom—have been close to my own age, so I've come to enjoy being treated as an equal rather than a subordinate. But then Tom and I started watching the first season of *The White Lotus*, and I developed an enormous crush on Armond, the show's debonair, devilish hotel manager, played by silver fox Murray Bartlett. I had just turned thirty, and it occurred to me that more and more of the men in my orbit were versions of this character, and it was getting harder and harder to pick a number at the upper limit of "too old for me." Tom and I joked that I should refer to this widening circle of Bartlett-esque figures—including Roger, my first hookup-app acquaintance in LA and now my closest friend in the city—as "my Armonds." An attraction to this type of man may be unoriginal, but it was new to me, so this wave of Armonds seemed to herald a sea change. In my daydreams, I wanted these Armonds to take good care of me, and I wanted to take their orders. What I wanted, as I eventually realized, was to be a daddy's boy.

One is not born but rather becomes a boy. I feel a little silly finally learning this lesson in my thirties, but before now, I don't think I ever allowed myself to take *pleasure* in being a boy. I spent most of my childhood waiting to grow up, since I associated being little and looking young with feeling helpless and misunderstood. What changed? Maybe I'm embracing my receding youth while I still can, though the magnetism between a daddy and his boy goes much deeper than one's perceived age. Maybe I'm owning my fondness for being doted on, though I wouldn't dare to reveal this soft spot to someone who isn't fond of doting on a boy like me. Maybe I'm craving more of the kind of mentorship that Shewey describes, but fortunately I've already had plenty of gay mentors, so this isn't my first chance to enjoy the privilege of being a protégé. Or maybe the steady support of a loving boyfriend and a smart therapist and a reliable friend like Roger is what's allowed me to start taking these risks. Whatever the reasons may be, I know that something gets rewired in my brain whenever a daddy calls me a good boy—not just because it's gratifying to receive positive feedback for, say, skillfully sucking a man's dick, but because it's surprisingly rare to be told in such straightforward terms, "I see what kind of boy you are and what you can do, and what I see is good."

I wish I could point to a specific moment in my past that would explain my hunger for this kind of praise. For many gay men, daddies seem to scratch a unique itch for validation—in part because internalized homophobia can leave a boy feeling that he's fundamentally bad, but also because many gay boys don't receive such unequivocal support from their families of origin. This may be why the uninitiated tend to assume, as I once did, that this fetish is a symptom of "daddy issues," which may be true for certain boys. But that's not the whole story, as Shewey acknowledges: "While some gay men have memories or fantasies (happy or unhappy) about sex with their biological fathers, most daddy/boy play has nothing whatsoever to do with real-life incestuous desires." I for one am not among the men who have such memories or fantasies or desires, and I'm grateful to have a healthy, uncomplicated relationship with my biological father; I'm not thinking of him—and I would prefer not to think of him—when I'm in bed with other men I know, most of whom seem to be on the same page. But even when you maintain a clear boundary between erotic fantasy and "real-life" family, I don't think you can take the *dad* out of *daddy* altogether.

Something shifted the first time Roger addressed me, in the middle of our smutty banter, as "son." At first I felt a tinge of squeamishness, but I soon discovered that there's a big difference between being a good boy and being a good *son*. When a man asks me to get on my knees and I answer, "Yes, Dad," I feel a profound sense of belonging and security, and I can tell that we're tapping into something much more visceral and emotionally intense than the titillating thrill of forbidden desire. I'm reminded of a favorite passage from *The Faggots & Their Friends Between Revolutions*, Larry Mitchell's 1977 book of subversive, speculative, and delightfully slutty fables and manifestos about a utopian community of queer men known as "the faggots":

> The faggots created a rite of cleansing. The faggots sit in a circle. The first faggot enters into a father's head while the second faggot becomes a son. Then they enact a part of that endless story. With a blink,

> the second faggot enters the father and the third faggot is born into a son. And another part of the endless story is revealed. Like a wind over sand, faggots are transformed from father to son to father to son. A father's hatred and a son's anger; a father's ambitions and a son's failures; a father's fantasies and a son's rebellion reenacted until the spell of dead generations is broken. With a scream of laughter the faggots see, and for a moment they love each other freely, fathers making love to sons, and sons making love to fathers.

This fantastical "rite of cleansing" may seem gratuitously profane, yet I also sense a sacred conviction in the faggots' wish to break "the spell of dead generations." Mitchell doesn't explain what kind of "endless story is revealed" through this circular game, but by playing as "freely" as possible with the archetypal roles of fathers and sons, the faggots manage to alchemize their hatred and anger and ambitions and failures and fantasies and rebellions into something joyful. The boy next door might not have such lofty goals in mind when he checks the "son" box in his Sniffies profile—but why shouldn't he, and why stop there? What other heads are there to enter, endless stories to enact and reveal, and generational spells to break with a scream of laughter?

—

Call me "nephew." This is the challenge I present Douglas when he picks me up for a trip to the Tom of Finland Art &

Culture Festival, where queer and leather-friendly artists and merchants from around the world gather to show off their work and sell their wares. Douglas is a new friend in LA, a teacher and musician with whom I initially bonded over our shared love of Beyoncé, and on each leg he's tattooed the words *if you want to*—a nod to one of Ms. Knowles-Carter's songs addressed to a "daddy." It's an apt phrase he's chosen to emblazon on his skin—facing upward on the left thigh, facing downward on the right, so you can read it from either above or below, depending on your position—and not just because Douglas, a bearded and bespectacled bear in his forties, has undeniable daddy energy. It also reflects one of his most distinctive virtues: permissiveness. As a vocal coach, Douglas is well-practiced in coaxing younger performers to feel safe, open, and at ease in their bodies. And as one of my most erotically omnivorous friends, Douglas has a rare talent for taking care of younger queer men and satisfying their most deviant desires. So when we first met a few months ago, I immediately felt comfortable talking with Douglas all about our astrological signs, our relationship histories, our recent sexual explorations, our forays into kink, my writing about uncles, and the overlaps between these topics. Right away, I wanted to be vulnerable with him, and I was curious to try things with him that I hadn't yet done with anyone else. I wanted to call him Uncle Douglas, and he graciously granted my wish to be his nephew.

Now that we've spent some time rehearsing this dynamic in our private exchanges, I feel an urge to experiment with it in public, to see what happens when

Uncle Douglas introduces me as his nephew to all the porn purveyors and fetish gear vendors. I imagine Uncle Douglas spinning a whole yarn about initiating his innocent nephew into this smutty, grown-up world; I'm even wearing a pastel-pink shirt and baby-blue neckerchief to accentuate my position as the doe-eyed, guileless rookie. But to my surprise—and, I admit, to my disappointment—nobody blinks when Uncle Douglas asks a clerk for help with picking out a jockstrap or harness or cock ring for his nephew. I suppose this festival's attendees are well-versed in role-play, so maybe everyone sees right through our charade. But as far as I can tell, most folks don't care whether we're playing make-believe; in fact, I gather some are excited by the possibility that we're not pretending at all.

Between a gay uncle and a gay nephew, no matter what's actually happening behind closed doors, sexual tension seems to be a given. At least that's what many of my acquaintances have tended to assume: when I tell them the kind of book I've been writing, even when I say nothing about my angle or my own story, they often ask with a knowing glance if I "go there." What they want to know, I understand, is whether I'm writing about "the handsy uncle," "the pervy uncle," "the lecherous uncle." If you browse pop culture wiki pages like fandom.com or allthetropes.org, you'll find many permutations of this figure, who occupies the center of the Venn diagram where "the wicked uncle" overlaps with "the dirty old man." I once dismissed this stereotype as just a symptom of gay panic among homophobic parents, to whom the gay uncle embodies the specter of sexual corruption, but now I'm struck by its persistence among queer men of my age, who've made a running joke of the gay uncle's reputation as a sexual libertine. (Consider one of the most memeified moments from the second season of *The White Lotus*, when Tanya McQuoid reveals that she saw a young man who "was kind of fucking his uncle"—a line that lands, thanks to Jennifer Coolidge's blasé delivery, as an offhand punch line rather than a dramatic bombshell.) What is the lineage of this filthy gay uncle, and why does he loom so large in the lives of his nephews?

I sought an origin story in classical myth, which features many relationships between older and younger men—some interpreted as instances of pederastic mentorship (Socrates and Alcibiades), some as primarily emotional attachments (Achilles and Patroclus), and some as rape (Zeus and Ganymede). Daedalus, better known as the father of Icarus, was also the uncle and teacher of Perdix, a fellow inventor; when Perdix became more successful, Daedalus attempted to murder him, but he seemed to feel nothing but professional envy toward his nephew. There's nothing overtly gay about Heracles's uncle Hades, who abducted his niece Persephone and made her his queen consort in the underworld. But according to Plutarch, one of Heracles's many lovers was his nephew Iolaus, whose tomb became a destination for couples to "make reciprocal vows of their affection"; one ancient sculptor even carved a relief of Iolaus and his uncle flanking the god Eros, who appears to be giving the two men his blessing. As with many myths, though, it's hard to tell from the extant sources how Heracles and Iolaus themselves would have defined what they meant to each other. In Egyptian lore, there's Set—the god of storms, earthquakes, eclipses, and general chaos—who tries and fails to assert his preeminence among the gods by sexually dominating his nephew Horus. But most scholars seem to interpret the discord between Horus and Set as an allegory for the earliest political conflicts in Egypt, not as a commentary on the nature of uncles; intrafamilial sex was relatively common among ancient deities—after all, Horus is already the child of a brother and sister, Osiris and Isis—so Set's avuncular status isn't the crux of this story.

I've yet to find an ancient narrative that would explain the provenance of the queer uncle as an erotic archetype, and accounts of uncle–nephew intimacy are relatively rare in modern literature. As far as I know, one of the first authors to explore this subject at length was the twentieth-century English writer Jocelyn Brooke. In Brooke's 1948 novel *The Scapegoat*, Duncan is a delinquent orphan who moves in with his late mother's brother Gerald, a lonely bachelor who's fallen on hard times at his failing farm in the countryside. At first, Duncan is intimidated by the "dark and minatory power" he perceives in his new warden, yet once he glimpses the "beefy youthfulness" of the forty-five-year-old war veteran's muscular body, he can't hide his admiration for his hunky uncle. Flattered to be admired and grateful for the companionship, Gerald is happy to grant his sensitive nephew's wish for a strong, masculine role model. Brooke doesn't shy away from the homoerotic in describing the bond between Duncan and Gerald, who strip naked for calisthenic workouts in the bathroom each morning and sneak a furtive kiss under the mistletoe at Christmas. And in one pivotal scene, Brooke implies that the two of them share some kind of physical contact in bed: "The boy moaned in his sleep, and turned over, pressing himself unconsciously against Gerald's body. Gerald shifted to the edge of the bed, turned over, and tried to sleep. But sleep would not come. At last, after an hour or so, he climbed gently out of bed, put on his slippers and dressing-gown, and stole guiltily downstairs." (Note the telling elision of that "hour or so" before Gerald "guiltily" flees.)

But shame and self-loathing get the best of these closeted outcasts, who begin acting out in increasingly evasive, deceitful ways: as Gerald spends more and more time away from his nephew, carousing—and probably cruising—at the taverns in the nearby village, Duncan becomes a petty thief, stealing food and money from his uncle to curry favor with the handsome soldiers camping in the woods. Gerald takes this kleptomaniac streak as a symptom of a deeper and more difficult degeneracy, and he tries to discipline the "profoundly abnormal" boy, but his attempts backfire, since Duncan seems to enjoy submitting to "a damned good thrashing" from his uncle. Their love–hate relationship fills the two of them with "a queer sense of hopelessness," and their conflicts escalate until Gerald feels he has no choice but to murder Duncan. The novel closes with Gerald shifting Duncan's body "into a more decent position," gently kissing the dead boy's face, and hearing from afar "the faint nostalgic note of a bugle, sounding reveille. Gerald turned away, seeing everything clearly at last: knowing that the long initiation was over; the rites observed, the cycle completed."

Throughout the novel, Brooke repeatedly characterizes Duncan as the titular scapegoat, whom Gerald unjustly blames for his own misfortunes, but it's not clear what killing the boy will accomplish. Duncan and Gerald seem to be impelled by forces beyond their control, but Brooke doesn't specify what kind of "cycle" is "completed" here, so this abrupt finale leaves me wondering how to interpret Gerald's actions. Do I choose to view him as a "bad uncle" who's failed to restrain his mixed feelings of attraction and resentment toward his nephew, ultimately leading him to neglect his familial duties and commit a crime of passion? Or do I view him and Duncan both as victims, doomed by the destructive forces of sexual repression? In other words, is this a horror story about the perversity of uncle–nephew desire, or is it a tragedy about the perversely restrictive society that has poisoned both Duncan and Gerald with "a queer sense of hopelessness"? In some ways, Brooke is radically open-minded for leaving these questions unanswered, inviting readers to imagine how *The Scapegoat* could have ended differently, though he doesn't go so far as to suggest that Duncan and Gerald might have lived happily ever after. Yet in other ways, the novel joins a long, ongoing tradition of morality tales that equate taboo eroticism with villainy and violence, illustrating the worst-case scenario that could unfold when a boy like Duncan is entrusted to a man like Gerald.

I don't know what the best-case scenario would be, but I'm intrigued by the proliferation of more recent novels that navigate the messy middle. As critic Alan Sinfield writes in his book *On Sexuality and Power*, there is often "an ominous though unspecified overlap between sexual and filial emotions" in literary portrayals of queer uncles and their nephews. In Paul Monette's *Halfway Home*, the narrator longs to form a strong—and purely nonsexual—bond with his brother's seven-year-old son, yet he fears getting too close to his nephew, lest the boy's parents perceive the narrator as a predator. In Jack Dickson's *Oddfellows*, a young man falls in love with his uncle, but the possibility of a romantic relationship remains "an ideal, a fantasy [. . .] not made for the real world, a world in which [the nephew] had to learn to function." And in Larry Kramer's *Faggots*, a man is horrified to see his nephew at a gay sex club called The Toilet Bowl, but even once the two of them agree to "join each other in family togetherness" (i.e., suck each other off), the uncle immediately deems this encounter the most "abnormal, immoral, illegal, dirty, shameful, wretched" thing he's ever done, a sign that he's brought "upon himself the onslaught of doom."

Why so many stories of hand-wringing over the sex lives of gay uncles and nephews? Perhaps because many of us don't know what to do with the unavoidable but troublesome presence of eros in family dynamics, and an easy target for projecting that anxiety is the gay uncle, a big bad wolf who threatens to tear down the nuclear family with his unseemly desires, even when he has no real intention of exposing his nephews to harm or danger. But as queer authors like Brooke, Monette, Dickson, and Kramer surely know, the big bad wolf would hold no power over anyone if there weren't a part of us that kind of likes him. So when acquaintances ask whether I "go there," I sense they recognize that it's worth exploring not just the shadow side of the gay uncle's sexuality but also its allure. As I've tried to understand what makes the gay uncle such a seductive figure, I've learned the most from a narrative genre that dares to go all the way there, one that follows this line of inquiry to many possible conclusions—namely, porn.

Soon after my twenty-ninth birthday, I was catching up with my friend M, who said his business had been picking up since the recent onset of the COVID pandemic. I asked what he meant, since I knew M primarily as a portrait photographer, and face-to-face shoots seemed risky. "You mean I haven't told you," he said, "my day job is running SayUncle.com?" I pretended to be a longtime devotee of this beloved gay studio and half-facetiously offered to audition for the role of a nephew, but when I first browsed the site, I sensed I was already at least as old as some of the actors playing uncles. SayUncle describes itself as a "gay cinematic universe for serious porn lovers," and it offers a wide range of channels that cater to specific tastes, including "Missionary Boys," "Young Perps," "Boys at Camp," "Doctor Tapes," and "Twink Trade." But the best-known channel might be "Family Dick," which features several hundred videos of diverse sexual scenarios between actors pretending to be relatives. For complicated contractual reasons, SayUncle is now required to emphasize that these characters are stepfamily members, not blood kin, but these overtly fictional videos have always opened with the same caveat: PORN IS FANTASY.

I'm fascinated by the nature of this fantasy. What

drives a porn consumer to choose an uncle–nephew narrative over, say, dad–son, and what qualities make an actor especially well-suited to playing an uncle or a nephew? I'm tempted to ask M, but I sense that mining for a deeper meaning might be a fool's errand, since it's not easy to intellectualize what makes someone or something "hot," and most people don't spend much time drafting academic thesis statements on their own porn preferences and erotic inclinations. So I've decided to come to my own conclusions.

I've watched dozens of SayUncle clips and other canonical films, from the Falcon Studios classic *Spring Break* to Joe Gage's *Uncle Pruitt Taught Me How to Do It*. I've collected a handful of pulpy novels with titles like *Uncles & Lovers*, *His Willing Nephew*, *Hard Like Uncle*, *Horny Chicken Nephew*, and *Good Head, Uncle!* I've even browsed FetLife, the kinky social network that looks like a Y2K-era message board, and scrolled through the hundreds of uncle-related fetishes that users have tagged in their profiles, from the vanilla to the perplexing, including "bathtime with uncle," "being an uncle to all and everywhere," "Being spanked by Uncle David," "cuddles with Uncle Peter," "Daddy shares me with 'special' uncles," "dirty uncle," "Driving Uncle Louie to drink :P," "DUMPING GLITTER ALL OVER UNCLE GARYS WALL," "Financial support from loving Uncle," "funny uncles," "gay uncles," "Going to StarBucks with My Uncle," "HAVEING THE MOST AMAZING UNCLES EVER," "Having a Daddy and an Uncle," "hearing my uncle unzip his pants," "making Uncle smile," "naughty pictures for uncle," "obedience to my Uncle," "older 'uncles,'" "Peeing while sitting on My

Uncle's lap," "Story time with Uncle Dragon," "Story time with Uncle Ogre," "teasing Uncle Travis," "the weight and size of Uncle Louie's liver," "uncle bob's magic shovel," "Uncle Eric's thick, black leather belt," "Uncle Fester is looking for you," "'Uncle' is not a safe word," "'Uncle' should be considered a safe word," "Uncle Jesse from Full House," "Uncle Jimmy's pony rides," "uncle Leigh is a very nice man," "Uncle luke is my hero . . . ," "Uncle Max's grilling and BBQ," "uncle moist," "Uncle Otter," "Uncle Sam the Bald Eagle of Justice," "Uncle Sinful," "Uncle Ted Talks," "uncle touchy's naked puzzle basement," "Uncle with Benefits," "uncle with the candy," and "uncle's bdsm magazine i never got to finish." (Fellow nephew, I hope you eventually got to finish that magazine.) I'll spare you most of the sordid details, but I will share with you, based on what I've gleaned from these artifacts, a working theory I've formulated. Roland Barthes once wrote that the writer is someone who plays with his mother's body, and I don't know if that's true, but I do have some hypotheses on the appeal of playing with the uncle's body:

(1) "I can teach you a few things," says Uncle Chad to his twinky nephew in *Spring Break*, which seems to get to the core of this fantasy. An uncle is a man who can teach you what your father can't, particularly if you're a boy with straight parents who don't know what your uncle knows about the ins and outs of gay sex, in which case your uncle is the authority figure you're more likely to seek out when it's time for "the talk," a talk that will inevitably involve bonding over a shared

experience of queer sexuality. Acting out this fantasy, whether as a porn entertainer or as an off-camera role-player, is a chance to ferret out the latent eros that is always already present in all kinds of mentor–protégé bonds between older and younger queer men—no matter how deeply that erotic charge is sublimated in otherwise respectable family ties—and to explore as freely as possible the "few things" that an uncle is ready and willing to teach his nephew.

(2) "Don't tell Mom and Dad" is another common line in uncle–nephew dialogues, a reminder that both parties are skirting around the gravitational center of this solar system: the parents. Even though the uncle is *above* the nephew, by virtue of either his age or his rank in the hierarchy of generations, he is also *to the side*, a sibling of the nephew's parents and therefore a sibling-adjacent figure to the nephew, a coconspirator in stretching the rules that structure the nuclear family. No matter what "Mom and Dad" actually think or whether they even exist in the world-building of this fantasy, their spectral, offstage presence allows uncle and nephew to enjoy the furtive thrill of being accomplices and fellow outlaws.

(3) "Uncle's fun because he can be a mess," according to adult performer Jonah Wheeler, who's played a few uncles. "He can be selfish. He can be needy. Dad should be grounded and solid. Uncle cares about you but ultimately isn't responsible for you." But even when the dad isn't part

> of the equation, Wheeler says, part of the uncle's appeal is his "scattered and sleazy vibe," a mercurial trickster energy that can keep his nephews on their toes. "Trickster is a boundary-crosser," writes critic Lewis Hyde in his book *Trickster Makes This World*. "We constantly distinguish—right and wrong, sacred and profane, clean and dirty, male and female, young and old, living and dead—and in every case trickster will cross the line and confuse the distinction. [. . .] Trickster is the mythic embodiment of ambiguity and ambivalence, doubleness and duplicity, contradiction and paradox." One could say the same of the ambiguous, paradoxical bond between uncles and nephews, who are both close and distant kin, both emotionally intimate and vaguely foreign to each other. No matter how loyal they are, an uncle and his nephew know the tables can always turn, they can always walk away from each other, and this potential mutability heightens the intensity and redoubles the fun.

This is what I might tell a man who agrees to play my uncle and asks why I want to play his nephew. But the *why* is often less interesting than the *how* of a scene. In her writing on erotic fantasy, psychoanalyst Avgi Saketopoulou argues that "the sexual [. . .] is not meaningful but precisely that which cannot be organized through meaning." Saketopoulou recalls the "incomprehensible fragments of experience" that "leapt forward" in a patient's account of a fraught encounter with a stranger at a bathhouse: "These were not objects to be dissected for meaning. Rather than vivisect, to cut them open in the hope of discovering some hidden truth, and thus killing off their vitality, we followed their intensities." I'm interested in what happens when we dare to follow those intensities without hoping to discover some hidden truth. Do you want to join me?

—

Let me call you "uncle." Let's say I'm eighteen, though I look younger. (My costume: Chuck Taylor low-tops, cutoff shorts, old Little League T-shirt, dirty-blond curls, clean-shaven face with dimples you could hide a dime in.) Say I've just graduated high school, I'm about to move to the big city and begin my first semester of college, and I'm feeling on top of the world. I'm too much of a bratty know-it-all to admit how nervous I am about what the future holds, and I would certainly never admit that to *you*, the uncle I've looked up to ever since I was a baby gay, when you were the first person I came out to, and I don't know just how much I still don't know about the ways of the world. Say I'm spending a weekend at your place, where I've come to celebrate your seventy-first birthday, and now we're chatting and joking and laughing and swapping stories in the living room, as we often do late at night, after everyone else has gone to bed.

Have a seat. (Your costume: bare feet, khaki shorts, white A-shirt, silver chain necklace and bracelet, wire-framed glasses, graying but still relatively thick comb-over, stubbly jawline, Tom Selleck mustache.) Ease into your favorite armchair and tell me stories from your youth while I, sitting across the room on the couch where I always sleep when I visit you, watch and listen and take notes. Let the enthusiastic attention of your captive audience embolden you to impress me with taller and taller tales of your gay exploits. Pour yourself another vodka and Pepsi to loosen your lips as the stories range wider, the facts get slipperier, the jokes get dirtier. I'll still be sipping the glass of chardonnay you offered me with a wink earlier in the evening, when I was too pleased by this conspiratorial gesture to refuse and too proud to tell you that I haven't yet acquired a taste for wine, which I like less and less as it gets warmer in my sweaty hands. When you're ready, ask me very casually, as if we're two old pals catching up at a leather bar, "So how's your sex life?"

I'll look down at the floor, probably blushing, since you've never before posed such a question. Somehow we've hardly talked about sex, even though we've discussed practically everything else about being gay. I could answer candidly and say, for example, "Well, my first boyfriend and I fooled around in his basement a few years ago, and I've since dabbled in some light hand and mouth stuff, but that's about it." But instead I'll dodge the question and say, "I don't really have one." Still studying the floorboards, I should by now be able to catch a glimpse of you grinning. Wait a beat to leave me wondering what you're getting at. Then sit beside me on the couch, close enough that your bare knee grazes mine, retrieve a photo album from the stack of books below the coffee table, and fan it open on our laps. Turn the pages and point to old pictures of you—maybe wearing an elegant suit at your brother's wedding, before I was born, when you were slimmer and darker-haired and thicker-mustached—and say, not as a question but as a statement of fact, "Wasn't I handsome." I'll smile and nod, not wanting to disagree, but also not sure how openly I should agree, since you've never remarked so bluntly on your looks. Wait another beat to see if I can do the math and figure out where this is going. Then sit a little closer, take my right hand in your left and lace your fingers between mine and start twiddling, as if in one, two, three, four, you'll declare a thumb war.

Finally I'll face you head-on and ask, "What are you doing?"

Lock eyes with me and lick your lips and don't blink as you slowly bring my hand toward your mouth.

A little louder this time, I'll ask, "What are you doing?"

Freeze. Keep holding my outstretched hand near the tip of your tongue, close enough that I can feel your hot breath against my fingers, and stare agape at me as if you've forgotten who I am. I'll silently stare back until you register that I really don't know what you're doing, nothing has prepared me for this, and whatever you intend to do next, whether or not I might want or even enjoy it, a line has been crossed, and now there's no going back. Pause long enough to form your own answer to my question, but keep it to yourself. Then abruptly drop my hand, rise from the couch, head to the kitchen, and approach the sink, out of my field of vision but still within earshot. I should be able to hear you open your fly, take a piss down the drain, and mutter, "Never mind—I'm just your dirty drunk uncle." Once you've expelled all the Pepsi and vodka from your bladder, zip up and return to the living room, where I'll have turned off the lights and burrowed under a blanket on the couch. I'll tilt back my head on the armrest and watch the upside-down silhouette of your body looming over me and looking down at my own upturned, illegible face. Hold still. It'll be too dark to determine the winner of this staring contest, so just linger there until the silence shifts from awkward to vaguely ominous, until you can feel in the air that each of us has tensed up to brace himself for whatever's about to happen. Then say good night and head to your room and go to bed. Don't close the door, or at least shut it quietly enough that you leave me wondering if you're waiting up for me. But I won't move; I'll just curl up and try to get some sleep.

In the morning, rise early. When I wake, I want to see you back in your armchair, sipping your coffee and reading your paper and humming a show tune as if it's just another day. I could choose to ask you again what you were doing or planning to do on the couch last night; I could shrug it off and accept that you were probably too drunk to realize what was happening and move on; I could assume that you knew exactly what you were doing but were too embarrassed or ashamed to own it, and I could get on my knees or on your lap to finish what you seemed to be starting; or I could just do nothing and leave without knowing what to think. When I return home and my parents ask about my weekend with my uncle, I could tell them the whole truth, at the risk of misrepresenting your intentions and losing control of the narrative; or I could refuse to bring it up at all, not even in my own private diary, at the risk of bottling up this uneventful event until its significance blows out of proportion in my mind. Whenever I overhear a friend or classmate making a lewd joke about an uncle, I could speak up, lest someone else reduce you to a punch line, to just another dirty drunk uncle; or I could keep my mouth shut, recalling the stories I've read about other uncles doing much worse things to their nephews, since I can't really say you've even *done* anything, I can only speculate on what you *could* have done or *might* have done, though I can't tell whether living with that partial knowledge is easier or harder than having concrete evidence of something one's uncle actually *has* done. Whenever another older man or authority figure greets me with a flirty wink, I could accept his proposition by telling him all about you, in case that context makes things even hotter; I could flee before I give him any reason to think of me as a boy who's too fixated on a single memory to distinguish the past from the present, a boy who has one weird experience and makes it his whole personality and projects it onto every man he meets; or I could simply make a move without explaining myself, without confirming or denying anyone's guesses about what's going on here. Whenever I see you in the future, I could be more afraid of you, now that I know what you're capable of, but I also could be even more endeared to you, now that I've had a chance to see the flawed and vulnerable man behind the curtain. I could clear the air, or I could wait for you to take the lead and help me make sense of all this, even if that means I'll still be waiting for closure long after you're gone, maybe even after someone else joins me in reenacting the scene I'm now enacting with you. Once you and I have played out this whole story, before it comes to an end, tell me what you think of the choices I've made. Have I been a good boy?

Uncle

What kind of uncle can't remember his own nephew's name? Not long ago, I was in my apartment on the top floor of an old, haunted house, where a young man was rearranging my tiny kitchen. He looked just like a twenty-something twink I had been DMing, but he also could have easily passed as my long-lost little brother. I wasn't sure why he was there or what had compelled him to tidy up my belongings, but I was so moved by his meticulous efforts to organize all my cookware by color and shape that I kissed him. We took off our shirts and held each other close in the morning sunlight, and I felt giddy and carefree in a way I hadn't felt since I was a kid; I couldn't tell if I was falling in love with this young man or just getting excited about our budding bond, but I kept those feelings to myself. Now the two of us are at a party, sitting with a group of strangers who are passing around my baby photos and my parents' wedding photos, and I keep spilling rosé everywhere as I try to refill all our wine glasses. The young man remarks on what a cute baby I was, how beautiful my mother was in her bridal gown, but when I start to introduce him to the other guests at the dinner table, I realize I've forgotten his name. It's Nick, he says, clearly hurt and disappointed. Nick then puts on the silver necklace and matching bracelet and wristwatch I offered him to wear to the party, a set of heirlooms I inherited from my uncle Bruce. As I admire him admiring himself in a mirror, I get a flash of recognition, and I start to wonder if Nick might be not just any young man but my nephew.

—

I don't remember most of my dreams this vividly, so it seems fitting that this one culminates in a lapse of memory—and especially apt that it came to me when I was figuring out how to finish writing this book. I'd been ruminating on this question for a while, but I hadn't worked through the issue with other people until a few nights before this dream, when Tom and I shared a curious experience. We decided to attend a "queer community salon," hosted by a friend of a good friend and described in the invitation as "a community conversation inspired by the salons of old. It's time for us to gather and feed each other's souls and nurture each other's hearts." This month's theme would be "biggest fears," a topic we could look forward to discussing "with incredibly smart, insightful, compassionate, intuitive, and thoughtful queers (and some allies)." But first there would be a vegan potluck dinner followed by a round of icebreakers, for which we should be prepared to tell a joke. Everything about this RSVP email, from the gushy salutation ("Hello, beautiful people!") to the presumptuous signoff ("I love you all!"), indicated that this salon would be my idea of hell. Naturally, I said yes.

I arrived with few expectations, but as soon as Tom and I stepped in the door, I immediately felt a visceral reaction, a resounding "nope" in my gut. Maybe my body was responding to the cats (I'm mildly allergic) or to the crowd (roughly thirty people were packed into our host's cozy Silverlake apartment) or to the overwhelming décor (as much as I love Dolly Parton, there were so many portraits of her displayed on the pink and green walls that her smile began to look vaguely sinister). As everyone settled into a circle around the living room, I brought my plate of pasta salad to a corner where I could steer clear of making any small talk that would betray my discomfort.

An otter around my age with a quirky pair of asymmetrical glasses, a caterpillar mustache, and an impressively hirsute chest framed by a sheer lace blouse ("made by my beautiful husband!"), our host rose to address the room as if about to deliver a sermon or a TED Talk. "All pronouns are fine," they told us, with the nonchalant confidence of someone who seldom worries about getting misgendered in a way that *isn't* fine. "And this house is your house," they added. "What's mine is yours. Nothing is off-limits. I love you." I was beginning to feel love-bombed, as if this near-stranger were importuning me to reciprocate their unreserved trust and affection; I was tempted to vandalize their furniture or steal one of the Dolly Parton photos on the walls, just to test their professed limitlessness. Then our host read us a Mary Oliver poem, reread it, and asked the audience what it might say about fear.

"The point is that you don't need to be a social justice warrior."

"When you don't know what to do, just sing."

"It's about queer joy."

I glanced around to see if anyone found the evangelical vibes of this situation as cringe as I did, but most of the circle looked riveted. Had they been brainwashed, or was I being a snarky and cynical spoilsport? Or does everyone else just have a better poker face than I do? In any case, soon it was time for jokes, and I sensed I might be taking things too seriously when nobody laughed at my contribution, an elliptical head-scratcher that always tickles me: "There are two types of people in the world: those who need closure . . ." (Cue a dramatic pause, prolonged until those who *don't* need closure realize this is the whole joke.) So I made an earnest effort to lighten up and keep an open mind once we split into triads to discuss our biggest fears.

The first to speak in my group was Pato, one of our host's neighbors, a sheepish boy who seemed not entirely sure what was going on. He muttered something about his fear of loneliness; I asked him to elaborate, but I was embarrassed to admit I still couldn't hear his explanation over the much louder voices around us. Next was Crystal, who was brought to this salon by a friend she had just met, and who made sure we understood that she wouldn't otherwise have chosen to be here. She mentioned fearing her mother's death, but since she had already processed that in therapy, she felt no need to discuss it further with Pato and me. Then it was my turn. I was going to talk about my fear of losing my memory, but that seemed too obvious. Instead, I shared my fear of never becoming an uncle—at least the kind of gay uncle that Bruce once was for me. Pato and Crystal stared at me; clearly they found this disclosure even more baffling than my joke.

"Can't you just babysit your friends' kids?" Crystal asked. "Or get a dog? Or a houseplant?"

No, I wanted to tell her, *you don't understand, it's not about babysitting a kid or walking a dog or watering a plant, it's so much deeper than that.* But Pato and Crystal kept watching me warily as though I were playing a cruel prank on them, and I began to wonder if it really might not be that deep, if this might not be such a big fear, if I've deluded myself into wanting something without understanding why I want it in the first place. For so many years I've told myself that unclehood should be the end goal of my nephewhood, that I should pay forward what I've received from Bruce and my other gay mentors. But I should know by now that I'm not in full control of this narrative; I can't expect this plotline to unfold on its own, without my deliberate effort to cultivate a relationship with a potential nephew, but I also can't force along my avunculescence without seeming creepy or desperate. Maybe I should have told Pato and Crystal that I was really afraid of never *meaning* something, never attaining a degree of significance that might compel a younger man to write about me in the ways I've written about Bruce. As I watched our host working the room of this salon, I still suspected they might be a small-time cult leader, yet I couldn't deny that their insistent craving for adoration wasn't so different from the narcissistic desires underlying my fear of never becoming an uncle—the kind of solipsism that might drive someone to tell a stranger, "I love you."

So a few nights later, when I envisioned bequeathing my uncle's jewelry to a boy named Nick—perhaps to thank him for decluttering my kitchen, perhaps because I had a crush on him, perhaps because he really was my nephew—I questioned the wish fulfillment offered by this dream. On one hand, this oneiric scene is the closest I've ever come to feeling like a "real uncle," picking up where I left off with Bruce and passing along a piece of my queer avuncular lineage; on the other, my unconscious seemed to be warning me not to get too big for my britches, too confident in my ability to provide something useful to a younger man when I don't even know what his name is, let alone what he might need from me. I woke before finding out what Nick would have done after putting on that necklace and bracelet and wristwatch, but I wouldn't have faulted him for simply taking these gifts and walking away. After all, I would've assured him, my house is his house, what's mine is his, and nothing here is off-limits.

—

A month later, I get a surprising text from Tom:

Right away I reply in all caps, “PICTURE,” and Tom sends a photo of his friend Alexandria holding a puppy they saw running aimlessly around the neighborhood near USC’s campus: a brindle mutt with velvety rose ears, a long snout, and a brow that appears to be permanently furrowed above his chestnut-brown eyes. He’s probably no more than a year old, but it’s hard to pinpoint his exact age: he has the mature features and concerned expression of a wizened man, but with that little body and that pair of big, floppy ears on his head, he also looks like Oliver Twist in his newsboy cap. He could be a mix of so many breeds one tends to see roaming around LA—chihuahua, pit bull, shepherd, terrier, maybe even a bit of dachshund—yet his smooth coat and long claws suggest he hasn’t been living on the street, and he looks so trusting and affectionate that I imagine he must belong to a loving family. But he doesn’t have a collar, and Tom confirms with a vet on his way home that there’s no microchip. Where did this dog come from, I wonder, and who is he? An hour earlier, Tom says, he and Alexandria were trying to remember the name of a European boy they’d recently met. Alexandria asked if it was Laszlo, and Tom said no, but wouldn’t that be a good name for a dog? Then they crossed paths with this one, who ran right into their arms and didn’t hesitate to get in Tom’s car, and so it was decided: his name is Laszlo.

My heart feels both buoyant and heavy as I process this bittersweet news. On one hand, I hope we can reunite this poor stray with his rightful owners; on the other, I selfishly hope no one is looking for him so we can keep this adorable puppy. On one hand, how lucky that

Laszlo found Tom, who knows how much I've craved a hound's love, and who happened to be with his friend Alexandria, a seasoned dog owner with plenty of advice and spare supplies to offer us; on the other, this is not how I've dreamed of a dog coming into my life. I didn't choose this dog, nor did he choose me; by the time I meet him, he will have already cemented a formative bond with Tom, his original rescuer, and he will have already begun to think of himself as a Laszlo—not the name I would have chosen. I would have called him Rocco.

Saint Rocco—aka Roch, Rollox, or Roque—was born in Majorca in the mid-fourteenth century. A deeply religious child with a distinctive, cross-shaped birthmark on his chest, he was the only son of the city governor, who died when Rocco was twenty years old. Uninterested in public life, Rocco donated his inheritance, let his uncle take the helm of the city, and embarked on a spiritual pilgrimage to Rome. Along the way, Rocco witnessed the Black Death spreading across Europe. He began to care for the sick, despite the risk of exposure, and earned a reputation as a miraculous healer, making sure all were cured in every town he passed through. Midway on his journey, an angel visited Rocco in a dream and announced that he would be struck down by the plague. Soon Rocco developed a painful lesion near his groin, and he retreated to the woods on the edge of town, where he could avoid imperiling anyone else. As he waited for death in a remote, abandoned hut, Rocco was discovered and befriended by a local nobleman's dog. Day after day, the dog returned, bringing loaves of bread and licking Rocco's wounds. Once Rocco fully regained his strength, the dog guided him back to town, and the grateful villagers helped him return home. Rocco found the city at war, but having renounced his former life, he refused to disclose his identity so he could remain a private citizen. But the locals were suspicious of this mysterious stranger; they accused Rocco of being a spy disguised as a missionary, and they demanded his arrest. Unyielding in his devotion to serving the poor and the sick, Rocco didn't protest, not even when he was put on trial and sentenced to life in prison by the governor. Rocco died in jail five years later, and only then did the governor realize, upon seeing the telltale birthmark, that he had failed to recognize his own nephew.

I was unfamiliar with this story until my early twenties, when I first visited the Cloisters, the museum of medieval art in Upper Manhattan. My date led me to a wooden sculpture of a doleful man lifting the hem of his extremely short tunic and pointing to his swollen thigh while a little dog offers him a loaf of bread. "Showing off a bit of leg," my date joked, and I agreed that this figure's pose did seem pretty swishy and flirtatious. I'm no Catholic, so I don't know if any saints have been as widely embraced by the gays as Sebastian, but ever since I learned about Rocco—officially the patron of invalids, bachelors, pilgrims, the falsely accused, and dogs—he's held a special place in my heart as the unofficial saint of gay nephews, particularly those who have fraught relationships with their uncles. There's nothing overtly sexual about Rocco's iconography, apart from those impractical short shorts that barely protect his crotch from contagion, and his familial role may be inconsequential. But having spent the majority of my life thinking about the affinities between gay uncles and nephews, I'm irresistibly drawn to these details in Rocco's story.

This is the longer, more honest answer I'm tempted to give when people ask why Rocco has topped my list of "boy names" for a dog; instead, I usually explain that I've never had a chance to live with a canine companion, and it must be good luck to invoke the "heavenly protector" of the species. But now my recent conversation with Crystal and my subsequent dream about Nick have me questioning my attachment to Rocco. Maybe I want to be seen as the saint suffering in the woods, the good-hearted martyr waiting to be deemed worthy of love and care and attention. Maybe I also want to be the loyal, compassionate dog, sniffing my way toward a stranger who needs me to lick his wounds and save the day. But maybe I'm really more like Rocco's uncle, so myopic and self-involved that I might not recognize my own nephew when he shows up at my door.

As soon as Tom introduces me to our new houseguest in the backyard, I can't imagine calling him Rocco—a much too weighty name to give this delicate creature, who's even smaller and frailer and more nervous than I expected. Laszlo approaches me with a tentatively wagging tail and gives the back of my hand a polite lick, and then Tom passes me the temporary leash he got from the vet so he can call LA Animal Services. As we watch Tom disappear inside our apartment building, I can't tell if Laszlo looks even more worried than before or if that's just his resting face. Then he starts whimpering and fidgeting, and I have no idea what to do. I sit beside Laszlo in a sunny patch on the lawn, and he presses his skinny body against the side of my leg as he basks in the warmth and takes in his unfamiliar surroundings. Soon he closes his eyes and starts nodding off, and I don't blame him, he's had a stressful and disorienting day. I loosen my grip on the leash and hold him closer, gently caressing the ribs and spine on his scrawny torso—then Tom opens the door, and Laszlo darts toward him, yelping with relief, tugging so hard on the leash that he almost topples me on the turf and drags me along for the ride. *Great,* I think, *he already perceives Tom as his mommy, and I'm just the second-rate stepdad who showed up late to the party.* But this isn't the time for my own petty resentments. Perhaps this little dog cares whether we call him Rocco or Laszlo or whatever name he used to be called, but he certainly doesn't care who I am, as long as I give him food and water and somewhere to poop.

For someone with no firsthand experience in this domain, I've come to harbor surprisingly strong feelings about the language of dog guardianship. I've always disliked the words *owner* and *master*, since I have no interest in treating a living animal as my private property; *handler* and *minder* seem not much better, since they still foreground physical or mental control. Thanks to the Instagram algorithm, which figured out long ago that I mainly want to see thirst traps and puppies, I've seen many poignant posts about the Hawaiian term *kahu*, meaning an animal's honored attendant or beloved steward—but I fear assigning myself this lofty label would be pretty self-important, not to mention appropriative. If you call yourself a dog dad—or a plant dad, or really any kind of dad—congratulations, consider me ready to swipe right; I like a man who takes sincere pride in his paternal responsibilities. But for some reason referring to myself as an animal's "dad" feels even weirder than letting a hot acquaintance address me as "son."

Something strikes me as perversely unqueer about relating to a nonhuman foundling in terms of human parenthood. In "Training in the Contact Zone," an essay on entering agility competitions with her dog Cayenne, scholar Donna J. Haraway notes that "it is essential for a human being to understand that one's partner is an adult (or puppy) member of another species, with his or her own exacting species interests and individual quirks, and not a furry child, a character in *Call of the Wild*, or an extension of one's intentions or fantasies. People fail this recognition test depressingly often." Haraway writes that she prefers to think of herself as Cayenne's "companion" rather than "mom" because this relationship exists "outside reproductive teleology and off-category—that is, off-topic, out of *topos* (proper place), into *tropos* (swerving and so making meaning new)." Haraway posits that this may be why interspecies kinship appeals to so many queer people: it can be an opportunity to take on a caregiving role that has nothing to do with breeding or child-rearing. "The coming into being of something unexpected," Haraway adds, "something new and free, something outside the rules of function and calculation, something not ruled by the logic of the reproduction of the same, *is* what training with each other is all about."

Poet Eileen Myles puts the point more bluntly in their dog memoir, *Afterglow*:

> Humans are always looking for . . . the obvious. Very low, very base, very banal kinds of puppetry. They can't imagine their own animation ending. [. . .] They decide their children will be their future puppets. They build institutions and write books to carry on their names. Quack, quack, quack. Everything will speak their name while they are alive, and especially when they are gone. The pathetic thing about humans is they think that everything is in their hands, and their hands are in or on everything. Pat, pat, rubbing behind the ears, looking in your eyes for years.

These words are attributed to Myles's late pit bull, Rosie, in a chapter structured as a transcript from an imaginary talk show hosted by one of Myles's childhood toys, a rag doll named Oscar—in other words, the writer has turned their own dead dog into a fictional interview subject to critique the human impulse to write the kind of book we're in the middle of reading. Oscar replies that Rosie seems to be getting the last laugh on this subject ("So you had your say. First in the book [. . .] and now here. I would kill for that experience"), but at the end of this tongue-in-cheek "interview," Rosie emphasizes the seriousness of her contributions to *Afterglow*: "We've written a book, this very sad book about trying to listen."

If Rosie were still alive and able to talk, who knows what she would say, but I appreciate Myles's willingness to attune to Rosie's desires, independent of the heteronormative ideals that humans tend to impose on dogs.

Throughout *Afterglow*, Myles celebrates Rosie as a kind of queer muse, a creative collaborator and nonprocreative partner. “It’s not that I don’t like kids,” Myles says. “It’s just I don’t need them and they don’t need me. [. . .] For me it makes a lot more sense to have a dog.” But Rosie is no substitute for a child, nor is she especially interested in having kids of her own. Another chapter details Rosie’s unsuccessful “date” with a stud named Buster—a messy encounter that fills Myles with shame, regret, and fear, but also excitement. “It probably was a biological time clock thing that I never felt about my body,” Myles explained at a public reading from *Afterglow*:

> But somehow I just had this displaced thing where I thought, “She’s such a beautiful dog, she’s so perfect, she’s so great, everybody loves this dog so much, why can’t we breed and make more Rosies?” It was kind of a narcissism projected onto my dog, and I guess I just wanted to go through that whole process. [. . .] At a certain point I realized I was just being cruel to a city dog. I went to the vet, the vet checked her out, because I was sure I spent a summer dedicated to her having puppies, and she wasn’t even pregnant, and so when the vet felt her stomach, he just looked at me and said, “You know, some dogs just don’t want to have puppies.” I was like, “Oh, yeah, okay, this is like the two of us.”

Going through this process teaches Myles to reframe their partnership with Rosie as an alternative to the nuclear family unit—a chance to cocreate something unexpected, something new and free, something outside the rules of function and calculation, something not ruled by the logic of reproduction. Putting these sentiments in a dog's mouth might seem like a bizarre gesture of anthropomorphism, but *Afterglow* is of a piece with Myles's many other experiments in autofiction, which play with perspective to challenge received ideas about gender, sexuality, class, family, and—in this case—species. I want to believe that queer writers like Myles have taught me to resist internalizing and perpetuating outworn social scripts—but if even Myles is guilty of projecting those very scripts onto their own beloved dog, then what low, base, banal puppetry could I end up foisting onto Laszlo?

I can tell he can tell I'm dwelling on him as we face each other on the couch, which Laszlo has claimed as his comfort zone. He watches me intently with those mournful eyes of his while gnawing on a yellow, sausage-sized key attached by a short rope to a pink, heart-shaped locket—the first plush toy Tom could find near the vet's office. It's getting close to dinnertime, no one has responded to our lost-and-found posts, and by now it's clear that Laszlo will be staying with us for the night, if not longer. Tom steps out to pick up some kibble and assures us he'll be right back, but Laszlo looks horrified. After running to the window, standing on his hind legs, and resting his front paws on the sill to watch Tom drive away—looking more and more like a forlorn Victorian waif—Laszlo begins to wail as though this is the worst thing that's happened to him all day, if not all his life. He starts pacing the house, shaking and crying so hard that he's almost dry-heaving; I worry he's going to choke or throw up, so

I sit on the floor and hold him on my lap and tell him not to worry, Tom's only a mile away, he's just at Vons, but Laszlo doesn't know a thing about Vons, for better or worse, and nothing I do or say could possibly console this poor animal. If he misses his family of origin, whoever and wherever they are, I can't imagine returning Laszlo to them in good conscience unless they're as grief-stricken as he is now. As Laszlo's shaking and squirming gradually subside, I wonder if Crystal was right, if taking care of this dog could be my chance to become a kind of uncle, the role I've been practicing for my whole life. After all, dogs are social animals who appreciate well-defined hierarchies and identifiable authority figures, so why not try to lead this little pack in the way I know best? Yet I don't need to put Laszlo on an imaginary talk show to recognize, as Eileen Myles does, the hubris of getting too attached to a certain relational dynamic that means nothing to this creature with his own unknowable mind. Unless he takes a page out of Rosie's book and learns to write or speak, I'll never fully understand what Laszlo wants or needs from me, but I'll try to listen anyway.

Laszlo quiets down, looks up, and gazes directly into my eyes. It's the kind of pleading expression I imagine on Saint Rocco's face as he awaited his uncle's verdict, though Laszlo seems to be the one forming a judgment of my trustworthiness. I tear off a piece of turkey from the cold cuts in the fridge and let Laszlo nibble it out of my hand, and he thanks me by hugging my leg—okay, no, wait, he's *humping* my leg. For the first time I register the disproportionately large balls between his little hind legs and realize we'll have to do something about those if Laszlo sticks around, though I know I'm getting ahead of myself, and it's too soon to start weighing the ethical pros and cons of taking this animal's future into my hands. I pick him up, cradle him against my chest, and improvise a lullaby, setting Rosie's words to an ad-lib melody: *Pat, pat, rubbing behind the ears, looking in your eyes for years*. Finally Laszlo starts to relax, and it seems like he might hold still, but then he hears a noise in the driveway and tries to wriggle out of my arms, so I let him go to roam freely. "Good boy."

—

I wake on the top floor of my uncles' house, in a sewing room stocked with spools of thread in every color imaginable. I recall my uncles telling me this room doesn't exist, I must have dreamed it up, neither of them can sew anyway, and now I know I didn't just imagine it, this place is real. I lower the attic ladder and hurry downstairs so I can share the news and prove I've been telling the truth, but the house is empty. Everything is where I remember it, nothing seems to have changed since yesterday, yet nothing seems to welcome my presence here; the shaving mirror mocks my boyish face, the bathtub has no intention of filling itself, and the piano shrinks from my touch. So I cross the road, wade through the wild carrot to the riverbank, and lie on the lichen-spotted dock. It's a humid August morning, warm enough to skinny-dip, so I didn't think twice about leaving the house without getting dressed, but now it occurs to me how exposed I am in the broad daylight. Soon the neighbors start sailing by on their rowboats and calling my uncle's name; I shake my head and try to answer but my voice cracks, and no one can hear me over the din of the singing cicadas, so the neighbors just smile and nod and wave and sail onward. Shards of my uncles' blue china plates keep washing ashore. I begin to see my body drift in and out of context, as if I'm the ghost haunting this house. As if I'm the last nephew on Earth.

—

When I try to summon my earliest memories of my uncles' house, I picture this scene, which has replayed in my brain so many times that I now can't tell which parts I dreamed and which actually happened. It's a bit like the phenomenon Elisa Gabbert describes in her essay "The Little Room (or, The Unreality of Memory)," in which she vividly recalls a room she saw long ago in her grandmother's house in Vermont, though she hasn't visited that house since she was a young girl, and her parents claim to know nothing about this room. Yet when Gabbert, as an adult, later mentions the house, her mother describes a different room that no one else can picture, until Gabbert conjures a "flimsy" memory, "like a memory of a dream," of entering that room as a child. "You could say," Gabbert concludes, "the story is about unreliable memory, the ultimate unknowability of the past, the impossibility of securing a single version of the truth. But [. . .] it feels like the house in Vermont belongs to two realities. You don't know which reality you're in until you open the door."

You could also say, I suppose, that my recurring dream is rooted in anxieties about reopening the door of my uncles' house, which I've mythologized as the site of my Gay Nephew Origin Story. I've kept a copy of their key as a kind of good-luck charm, and I've never taken it off my chain, though I managed to visit only a handful of times between Bruce's death and my cross-country move for grad school. Then COVID happened, then Will took in his friend Drew, who was going through a messy divorce, and who moved into Bruce's old room with his two dogs, and the cats withdrew to the attic—Bruce always had a cat or two, he was never what I would call a "dog person"—and then the neighbors grew suspicious of Will's new housemate, one of the only Black people living in this increasingly conservative town in rural Connecticut, and they accused Drew of littering needles on the riverbank and threatened to call the police whenever they saw him sunbathing on the dock where I used to swim with Bruce, though of course there were no needles, so Will installed a security camera on the porch and changed all the locks, and now seven years have passed since I last crossed their threshold, and this key is just a useless artifact. The nephew in me still wants to think of this place as my home, a place where I can always feel free to invite myself inside without knocking, as I often did when Bruce was here. Perhaps I avoided returning sooner because I wasn't ready to burst that bubble, but now I've come back with unfinished business, a task with which I've been promising for far too long to help Will.

I should have remembered how warm this house can get on a muggy August evening—and anticipated how crowded it would feel with the dogs around. At this point I'm accustomed to sharing space with furry familiars, since Laszlo has been living with Tom and me for seven months now, but Jack (an energetic pit bull mix with shaggy white fur and a missing eye) and Friday (a sweet, elderly black Lab whose paunch seems to constitute half of his body mass) are more rambunctious and assertively friendly than my cuddly softboi puppy. It saddens me that Laszlo will never meet Bruce, but it's even sadder to realize upon stepping inside that no dog would be able to smell a trace of my late uncle, since the scent of Jack and Friday—though not unpleasant—has overwritten the musty, smoky, greasy, slightly sweaty aroma I've always associated with Bruce's presence in this house. (Perhaps that sounds even less pleasant, but I used to detect a vaguely similar fragrance in the stairwell of an apartment I once rented on top of a dive bar, and every time I got a whiff, it would stop me in my tracks and bring me to tears. Now I know why Laszlo finds my dirty socks so comforting.) So I've proposed that we get some fresh air and catch up on the lawn, where we circle up some Adirondack chairs to watch the sunset.

"All set," Drew says—partly so the dogs will mind their own business and quit begging for attention, partly to get them away from the fire pit, where Will has assembled and ignited some kindling. Jack and Friday heed this release command and dutifully return inside, and I marvel at how the tables have turned: once upon a time, *I* was the bratty boy banished into the house for a timeout while the grown-ups enjoyed themselves al fresco. Drew squirts some lighter fluid into the fire, shooting a jet of flames in my direction; I'm tempted to ask if this is his way of warming up to me, since we met just a few hours ago, but we haven't yet established enough of a rapport that I could get away with such a bad joke. And the mood swiftly shifts when Will asks whether they'll have enough logs for the winter, when this drafty house's cast-iron stove is the main source of heat. I'm surprised that Will, ever the wise woodsman, hasn't already assembled his trademark cord of lumber—the stray stumps and branches he gathers on the roadside and splits with his own maul and stacks in an elaborate assemblage throughout the summer and fall—but I suppose that labor's no longer easy on his seventy-five-year-old hips. Will posits that they could cut down one of the aging trees in the yard, and I try to hide my grimace. *Just don't kill the Japanese maple,* I think, since that's the one I used to climb as a boy, when Bruce would pretend I was Tarzan swinging from the branches, or when I would pretend to be Dorothy arriving in Oz, since the golden-hour sunlight filtered through the bright red late-summer leaves could give the whole house a Technicolor glow. Drew widens his eyes at Will and gasps in indignation.

"You can't touch that Japanese maple," Drew says. "I love that tree." I smile, pleased that he read my mind, and Will catches my reaction.

"You're awfully quiet," he tells me. "Bruce always wondered what you were thinking about and what you were scribbling in those journals of yours." News to me, since Bruce seemed to enjoy holding forth while I took notes—why didn't I realize he was waiting for me to speak up? As a cheeky icebreaker, Drew proposes grilling me with a mock interview. Sitting upright, clearing his throat, and putting on his own caricature of "NPR voice," he asks what I would wish for if I could have any magical power (the ability to tell all my crushes exactly how I feel without making things awkward); he asks which three living artists I would want to invite to a dinner party (Fiona Apple, Annie Ernaux, Keke Palmer). These answers seem to please Drew, who nods in agreement and pours me some more wine. Soon I'm interviewing him about his sci-fi writing and his favorite PlayStation games, and Will looks pleasantly surprised by how well we're hitting it off. But once I start tipsily muttering the ninety-word title of Fiona's second album, I know it's time to call it a night.

Will hinted before I arrived that there might be "no room at the inn," so a gracious neighbor has agreed to put me up. But before escorting me to my quarters, Will retrieves two heavy file boxes from the attic and asks me to bring them along. My hosts have already gone to sleep, so I sneak inside, tiptoe upstairs to the guest room, set the boxes on the bedspread, and gently inspect the contents—some mementos Will has been setting aside for me, including a blue china plate depicting a peacock surrounded by blossoms, a first edition of Edmund White's *Nocturnes for the King of Naples*, and Bruce's yearbook from Whitehaven High School. Reading his classmates' autographs, I can't tell which boys were just chummy with Bruce and which were secretly horny for my uncle, who was an undeniably handsome teenager in 1955:

Best of luck to the best friend a guy could have (when he has him). —Gary

We'll be buddies until "death do us part." Write me sometime this summer. —Dickey

Lots of luck to one of the most versatile boys I know, and believe me you are just as good as the word says you are. —J.D.

What exactly *was* "the word" about Bruce? There's also a trove of mail he received as a young man, among them an anguished dispatch from someone named Wendy:

> *Thanks for those notes, your recent letter & your lingering brotherly affection. It's wonderful for me to know that you weren't really a dream of mine & that you do love me. I want to have you know how I feel, or more basically, feel how I feel, but I don't want to write it, because then I'd have let myself go all to you, & there would be nothing ever to fill up that empty space except dirt & filth & on & on. That probably won't make sense. It's a feeling I know myself well enough at the moment (& in the future if things go the way I hope) to know that I can't marry someone who has the kinds of problems you have, & that is exactly what I want to do. And even if I were still irrational enough to really think that I could be happy in such a situation, I have been told quite plainly by you that you could never be interested in me, and would never want me as your wife. Getting letters from you sends me into a tumble, & I start*

> *making impossible plans & schemes. If any of them came about, I'd be more miserable than I am now. So please, dear Bruce, leave me to my obscure fantasies & the hope that they'll vanish soon.*

There are many, similarly effusive love notes from Sal, a man my uncle must have met when he ran away to Mexico, but I don't know Spanish well enough to read his missives, except this one:

> *Daddy, am sorry but not write you before, but I hope your letters for to cant aswer you. Baby, I am very sad here in Tampico, am working one convention of tourist mans, also but you say me in your letter, that I have a other person in my life, baby don't be silly I allways am waiting for you. ¡Am sorry baby for to write you in english! Is my first time that I write in this idiom, so you sorry me my falts. ¿Yes?*

Then there is a stern letter signed with love from "Daddy," and it takes me a surprisingly long time to figure out that this is my grandfather, who died before I was born:

> *Bruce, don't indulge yourself with excuses or be self-condemning like saying your thoughts are immature or pick up phrases from my letters to dwell on. Anything I have said to you was with the hope that sometime I would strike the right chord to shake you loose and make you want to be just yourself. That is good enough for me and should be very pleasing to other people.*

It's tempting to keep reading these one-sided conversations, seeing the sides of Bruce he never showed me: the heartbreaker whose "problems" made him an impossible dream to Wendy, the jealous fuckboy who kept sweet Sal on his toes, the insecure son who aired his excuses and wallowed in his anxieties instead of trusting his father's acceptance. I can relate to that heartbreaker, that fuckboy, that son—being annoying must run in the family—yet it's also tempting to reply with everything I've ever written about Bruce, to vindicate the uncle I knew and loved and still love, even though many of these correspondents are dead or untraceable. Once again, though, I question this territorial reflex, this proprietary urge to have the last word on *my* uncle, especially now that I'll never get to ask whether my depiction of Bruce is "good enough" for him, let alone "very pleasing."

I'm reminded of a letter Bruce sent me roughly fifteen years ago, one I still carry with me and often reread:

> *Dear Steven—*
>
> *Thanks for the card—and thanks for the interesting idea. It makes my brain buzz.*
>
> *I just devoured the 2009 biography of John Cheever. You know him? Pulizer and National Book Award winner and ~~every~~ recipient of every other literary award known to man. 119 short stories in the New Yorker over decades and four novels. A brilliant, successful life—a tormented tri-sexual alcoholic—a charmer, a fake, a nasty drunk, a father, a seducer of*

> *men, a hater of homosexuals. In other words, a fully rounded individual.*
>
> *When I read, I'm also comparing the story, the ideas, the philosophy to my own. Don't you? What I took away from this book (in part) was: we all are multi-faceted individuals and it illuminated for me my own modest but odd, crazed history and persona. And right now I'm in a mood to examine that.*
>
> *So your idea sort of appeals to me. Let's talk.*
>
> *Real love,*
> *Bruce*

I forget what I wrote in the card that prompted this note, but the "interesting idea" he mentions must have been one of my many pleas to write a book about Bruce. Usually he balked at being committed to paper, but this is the closest he ever came to giving me a green light. I don't know how I replied, if I replied at all, but clearly we both avoided following through—perhaps because we hoped in vain that he would live forever, perhaps because we tacitly feared that enshrining his life in a traditional biography would be a death knell. Now I've tried to pay a posthumous tribute to his modest but odd, crazed history and persona, but have I done justice to the fully rounded individual who was Bruce? As I read these letters, part of me wonders if Bruce used to yearn for the kind of avuncular mentor he would become for me, but then I have to remember the many kinds of people who looked after him: Wendy, Sal, his father, and eventually Will, to name just a few, not to mention his own resourceful self. And if I should live at least seventy-eight years, as Bruce did, who knows what queer boys will need from their uncles by then, or what kinds of uncles they might want in the first place; if the planet hasn't imploded by 2069, I may have to think less avunculocentrically about what I have to offer and how I can be of service. Maybe everybody has a gay uncle these days, as my acquaintances keep telling me, but the *idea* of the gay uncle is still a historically contingent phenomenon, and *my* idea of the gay uncle may be obsolete by the time I fully step into that role. I may not be the last nephew on Earth, but someday, when all the uncles I've known are extinct, I may not recognize the generation of queer neophytes who cross my path. At one point that discontinuity might have frightened me, but now it doesn't scare me at all.

I sleep without dreaming and wake just in time for Will to pick me up. But once I buckle up in the passenger seat, he seems in no rush to get on the road. "I'm not ready for this," he says. Neither am I, though my eyes are drier and hands are steadier than his; I half-consider offering to drive, but I don't want to micromanage. We stop at the plant nursery, where I pick up a pot of white crape myrtle for the occasion—the sweet florist rightly noted that it would be suitable for a Southern queen like Bruce. When we return to the house, Drew is still wrapping up a job interview, so we remain outside to avoid rousing the dogs and disturbing his Zoom call. Will offers me a root beer and invites me to sit with him at the patio table, which he's covered with an indigo cloth and adorned with a framed photo of Bruce's face in profile, a sprig of red cedar, a pack of nag champa incense, a shoebox-sized carton, and the crape myrtle. I haven't prepared anything, so I borrow a pen and some paper from Will and start taking notes.

"All set?" Startling me from behind—my jumpiness will be the death of me—Drew opens the gate he's built to keep Jack and Friday out of this section of the backyard. The dogs are nowhere in sight, so it takes me a beat to understand he's addressing Will and me. No, I'm not all set, I've barely managed to write anything, but I grab a trowel and kneel on the grass anyway. Once I've helped Will dig a shallow hole, he opens the carton on the table, unseals the bag inside, and heaps some fistfuls of gray powder in the ground. As Will rises to his feet, Drew and I instinctively flank him, as if we've agreed to be his phalanx of bodyguards. The humid afternoon has all three of us sweating through our T-shirts; if any passersby ask what's going on, we'll say we're fertilizing the soil for the crape myrtle, which isn't entirely untrue. Will asks me to light some incense and then, without further ado, unfolds the paper in his pocket and starts to read.

"You were my guide, my guardian, a mentor and a mensch. That said, I fear I took your presence—and that you would always be here—for granted. It was a happy, vibrant relationship. We were able to legally wed long before you left. It was twenty-five years together, but somehow too short a time together. I'm fortunate to still have your nephew and other family to share my memories. You were much beloved by many too.

"You were a lifeline to me. Kind and compassionate

and grand, with much to teach, even though I wasn't that good a learner. I remember the night you left. Called as I was leaving work. I'd made meat sauce the day before and you told me, 'If we don't have spaghetti tonight we're getting divorced.' When I arrived home, heard the TV on, blaring. I figured you'd dozed off as you would sometimes do. Went in the kitchen, you'd put the sauce on the stove and the pasta was already done. So I headed in to wake you. I found you leaning, slumped against the fireplace mantel in front of Grandmother Zola's picture of you and her. Your face was already slightly blue. I thought three things simultaneously. One: 'Oh God, Bruce is dead.' Two: 'I have to do CPR.' Three: 'How'd he get into that position?'

"I lowered you to the floor and began compressions, with one hand dialed 911. The dispatcher began asking questions and I responded, 'For Christ's sake, man, get with it!'

"'Oh, you are alone.'

"'Yup.' And he began coaching me until the EMTs arrived, twenty minutes later. They revived you but you never came back. Two days later, you left your physical frame. And you were gone. Now we place your ashes where you wanted, in our yard, at your house. I still miss you. Though I'm told you are still here."

Will pauses, perhaps for a moment of silent remembrance, but I'm disturbing the peace with my ongoing struggle to strike a match, so I give up on lighting the incense. "Anything you want to say?" he asks. I shake my head and squat down to secure the sapling. Once I've made sure the crape myrtle is firmly rooted among the ashes, I thumb an indentation to enclose what I've written in the dirt. It may be an unfinished elegy, but at least that will keep this impromptu ceremony from feeling like the end of anything—and if Bruce still wants to know what I've been scribbling all this time, now at least I've given him a little something to read. Will suggests we all go out for lunch, which sounds like a great idea, but first I'd like to stay behind and linger a bit longer with Bruce.

Are you still here? I'll choose to believe you are, sitting on the patio where my father took that photograph of us almost thirty years ago, when this whole story began. You look just the same but better, as you liked to say; as for me, I'll let you be the judge. I would apologize for not giving you a more ceremonious burial, but I know you would've hated something so maudlin. When I try to imagine how you would respond, I remember the best thing you ever told me, a pearl I may have a chance to pass along someday. Once upon a time, I was a sullen boy, a lonely teenager engulfed in such a deep depression that I often felt half-asleep. I was visiting for your birthday, and all I wanted to do was celebrate you, but I could hardly muster the energy to stay awake, let alone summon words that would adequately convey how it felt to call you my uncle. "Sorry to be so boring," I said, and you just scoffed. Your roundabout answer snapped me out of my doldrums but also left me puzzled; I still can't tell whether you meant to tickle my ego or your own, but I suspect the circularity of it all may have been the whole point.

"You're not boring," you said. "You're my nephew."

Acknowledgments

Bruce Pfau and Will Brady, thank you for being my uncles. This book exists because of you.

Catherine Marenghi and Tom Pfau, thank you for being such loving and supportive parents. And deep thanks to the teachers, mentors, role models, and figurative uncles and aunties who encouraged me early on, including Kelli Auerbach, Jay Austin, Teodolinda Barolini, TT Baum, Benaifer Bhadha, Liz Brown, Collomia Charles, Daniel Chiarilli, Julie Crawford, Courtney D'Alessio, Nicholas Dames, Rob Flaggert, Helene Foley, Lydia Goehr, Max Hekler, Matt Hutton, Hannah Jones, Philip Kitcher, Elisabeth Ladenson, Ken Lundberg, Jerry Marenghi, Joseph Marino, Karen McCalley, Leila Merl, Jessica Netishen, Lynn Pfau, Susan Pier, Laura Pinsky, Cathy Popkin, Deborah Schneebeli, Jeff Seroy, James Shapiro, Pamela Stransky, Zoë Sundra, Rich Tennant, Bonnie Weiss, Jenny Williams, Shireen Yadollahpour, and Mariko Zapf.

Brian Blanchfield, thank you for saying yes to this project from the beginning. Jessica DuLong and Rachel Syme, thank you for showing me how to get started and motivating me to keep going. Tal Nadan, thank you for your invaluable help with archival research. Anna Banks,

Kim Barnes, Stephan Flores, Michael McGriff, Alexandra Teague, Zachary Turpin, Tobias Wray, and all my teachers, colleagues, and students at the University of Idaho, thank you for reading, thinking, and talking through this work with me. Rebecca Brown, Jennifer Clement, Maggie Nelson, and Kate Zambreno, thank you for your guidance and feedback; your insights were lifelines at some of the most difficult stages of the writing process.

I'm grateful to the editors of *DIAGRAM*, *Guernica*, *The Iowa Review*, *The Offing*, and *Passages North* for publishing earlier versions, respectively, of "Ghost," "Guest," "Reader," "Nephew," and "Amateur."

Will Lippincott, thank you for believing in this book's potential and being such a thoughtful, passionate advocate. Alicia Kroell, thank you for editing the manuscript with such great care, and Rob Shapiro, thank you for beautifully shepherding this book into the world. Alli Armijo, Barrett Briske, Nicole Caputo, Wah-Ming Chang, Andrea Córdova, tracy danes, Rachel Fershleiser, Megan Fishmann, Alyson Forbes, Dan Goff, Olivia Hammerman, Ashley Kiedrowski, Victoria Maxfield, Elizabeth Pankova, Lily Philpott, Kendall Storey, Skye Tarshis, Miriam Vance, Eric Wilder, and everyone at Catapult, thank you all for your hard work on publishing *Say Nephew*.

Chani Nicholas and Sonya Passi, thank you for your kindness and generosity. Thea Anderson, thank you for making me feel at home. And Jen Curran, Nic Davis, Kacie McGeary, Grace Mungovan, Eliza Robertson, Sarina Romero, and Stephanie Warner, thank you for making me a better editor.

Many friends, companions, correspondents, and interlocutors played significant roles in the making of this book. Thank you, Mounia Abousaid, Larry Arrington, Jeremy Atherton Lin, Juno Barbosa, Norma Barksdale, Jeremy Bertsche, John Birtle, Travis Black, Stacy Boe Miller, Celia Cooper, Avi Edelman, Joely Fitch, Katie Frank, Max Freeman, Lia Friedman, Court Fund, Christopher Gollmar, Kevin Graves, Dewayne Green, Ryan Grubbs, Alexandria Hall, Steven Holt, Brandon Jackson, Derrick Jefferies, Patrick Kellogg, Wayne Koestenbaum, Drew John Ladd, Marc La Pointe, Rony Lenis, Evelynn Maas, Amanda Malcolm, Jack Manning, Cameron Martin, Paul McAdory, Theodore McCombs, Maya Meredith, Ross Middleton, Billy Miller, José Gabriel Montelongo-Mendez, Janell Moon, Milo Muise, Patrick Nathan, Emmy Newman, Gwen Niekamp, Alexis Nowicki, Alejandra Oliva, Kurt Ostrow, Jonathan Parks-Ramage, Jacob Parsons, Lizzy Paul, Douglas Peck, Eli Petzold, Betty Jean Pinkston, Spencer Quong, Christopher Richards, Brigid Ronan, Arya Roshanian, Joe Shaskus, Clare Shearer, Robert Siegelman, Matthew Stadler, Thor Stockman, Ed Thereault, Justin Torres, Steffan Triplett, Claire Tuna, Stephen van Dyck, Sarah VanGundy, Leo Walker, Lauren Westerfield, and Adam Wilson.

Tom Renjilian, the best reader and writer I know, I adore you. Thank you.

Laszlo, I may never know who I am to you, but you will always be my favorite nephew.

Sources

Nephew

Allers, Roger, and Rob Minkoff, directors. *The Lion King*. Buena Vista Pictures, 1994.

Baldwin, James. *The Fire Next Time*. Dial Press, 1963.

Baldwin, James. *Giovanni's Room*. Dial Press, 1956.

Barthes, Roland. *Roland Barthes*. Translated by Richard Howard. Farrar, Straus and Giroux, 1977.

Bechdel, Alison. *Fun Home: A Family Tragicomic*. Houghton Mifflin, 2006.

Blanchfield, Brian. *Proxies: Essays Near Knowing*. Nightboat, 2016.

DaCosta, Morton, director. *Auntie Mame*. Warner Bros., 1958.

Dayton, Jonathan, and Valerie Faris, directors. *Little Miss Sunshine*. Fox Searchlight Pictures, 2006.

Dennis, Patrick. *Auntie Mame: An Irreverent Escapade*. Vanguard, 1955.

Dorfman, Ariel, and Armand Mattelart. "Uncle, Buy Me a Contraceptive . . ." In *How to Read Donald Duck: Imperialist Ideology in the Disney Comic*. Translated by David Kunzle. International General, 1975.

Edelman, Lee. *No Future: Queer Theory and the Death Drive*. Duke University Press, 2004.

Halperin, David M. *How to Be Gay*. Belknap Press, 2012.

Hitchcock, Alfred, director. *Shadow of a Doubt*. Universal Pictures, 1943.

Koestenbaum, Wayne. *The Queen's Throat: Opera, Homosexuality, and the Mystery of Desire*. Poseidon Press, 1993.

Mankiewicz, Joseph L., director. *All About Eve*. 20th Century Fox, 1950.

Marenghi, Catherine. "A Letter to My Son in Brooklyn." In *Breaking Bread*. Finishing Line Press, 2020.

Nelson, Maggie. *The Argonauts*. Graywolf Press, 2015.

Nichols, Mike, director. *The Birdcage*. MGM, 1996.

Proust, Marcel. *In Search of Lost Time, Volume IV: Sodom and Gomorrah*. Translated by C. K. Scott Moncrieff, Terence Kilmartin, and D. J. Enright. Modern Library, 1992.

Salamon, Gayle. *The Life and Death of Latisha King: A Critical Phenomenology of Transphobia*. New York University Press, 2018.

Sedgwick, Eve Kosofsky. "Tales of the Avunculate." In *Tendencies*. Duke University Press, 1993.

Shakespeare, William. *The Second Part of King Henry the Fourth*, edited by Claire McEachern. Penguin Books, 2000.

Sondheim, Stephen. *Finishing the Hat: Collected Lyrics (1954–1981) with Attendant Comments, Principles, Heresies, Grudges, Whines and Anecdotes*. Alfred A. Knopf, 2010.

Stockton, Kathryn Bond. *The Queer Child, or Growing Sideways in the Twentieth Century*. Duke University Press, 2009.

Thompson, Stith. *Motif-Index of Folk-Literature: A Classification of Narrative Elements in Folktales, Ballads, Myths, Fables, Medieval Romances, Exempla, Fabliaux, Jest-Books, and Local Legends*. Indiana University Press, 1955.

Van Sant, Gus, director. *My Own Private Idaho*. Fine Line Features, 1991.

Reader

Andrews, Terry. *The Story of Harold*. Holt, Rinehart and Winston, 1974.

Bartlett, Neil. *Who Was That Man? A Present for Mr Oscar Wilde*. Serpent's Tail, 1988.

Brickner, Richard P. "An Adult in a Child's World." *The New York Times*, May 12, 1974.

Greenwell, Garth. *What Belongs to You*. Farrar, Straus and Giroux, 2016.

Holleran, Andrew. *Dancer from the Dance*. William Morrow, 1978.

Keller, Karl. "The Story of *The Story of Harold*." *The Advocate*, October 18, 1979.

Kirkus Reviews. "*The Story of Harold*." April 1, 1974.

Lange, Maggie. "Maggie Nelson Writes Books Like She's Hosting a Party." *The Cut*, March 31, 2017.

Livingston, Jennie, director. *Paris Is Burning*. Off White Productions, 1990.

Maupin, Armistead. *Tales of the City*. Harper and Row, 1978.

Salinger, J. D. "Uncle Wiggily in Connecticut." In *Nine Stories*. Little, Brown and Company, 1953.

Selden, George. *The Cricket in Times Square*. Farrar, Straus and Giroux, 1960.

Selden, George. Personal letters. Farrar, Straus and Giroux, Inc. records. Manuscripts and Archives Division. The New York Public Library. Astor, Lenox, and Tilden Foundations.

Soller, Kurt. "The 25 Most Influential Works of Postwar Queer Literature." *The New York Times*, June 22, 2023.

Summers, Claude J. "Andrews, Terry (1929–1989)." *The GLBTQ Encyclopedia Project*, archived 2002. www.glbtqarchive.com/literatureindex.html.

White, Edmund. "Edmund White Thinks Most People Misread *Lolita*." *The New York Times*, August 6, 2020.

White, Edmund. "*The Story of Harold*." In *Lost Classics: Writers on Books Loved and Lost, Overlooked, Under-read, Unavailable, Stolen, Extinct, or Otherwise Out of Commission*, edited by Michael Ondaatje, Michael Redhill, Esta Spalding, and Linda Spalding. Bloomsbury, 2000.

Friend

Andrews, Terry. *The Story of Harold*. Illustrated by Edward Gorey. Avon Books, 1975.

Clarke, Shirley, director. *Portrait of Jason*. Film-Makers' Distribution Center, 1967.

Crowley, Mart. *The Boys in the Band*. Farrar, Straus and Giroux, 1968.

D'Arcangelo, Angelo. *The Homosexual Handbook*. Ophelia Press, 1969.

Foucault, Michel. "Friendship as a Way of Life." In *The Essential Works of Michel Foucault, 1954–1984, Volume One: Ethics*. Translated by John Johnston. New Press, 1997.

Grahn, Judy. *Another Mother Tongue: Gay Words, Gay Worlds*. Beacon Press, 1984.

Greyson, John, director. *Pissoir*. Greyson Productions, 1988.

Jay, Karla, and Allen Young, editors. *After You're Out*. Pyramid, 1977.

Mekas, Jonas. "Conversation with Jason Holliday." In *Conversations with Filmmakers*. Spector Books, 2018.

Mekas, Jonas. "Shirley Clarke on *Portrait of Jason*." In *Conversations with Filmmakers*. Spector Books, 2018.

Millhauser, Steven. *Edwin Mullhouse: The Life and Death of an American Writer 1943–1954, by Jeffrey Cartwright*. Alfred A. Knopf, 1972.

Mordden, Ethan. *Buddies*. St. Martin's Griffin, 1986.

Muniz, Vik. *Perfect Strangers*. 72 St. Q Station, New York, NY, 2017.

O'Hara, Frank. *The Collected Poems*, edited by Donald Allen. Alfred A. Knopf, 1971.

Purdy, James. *Malcolm*. Farrar, Straus and Company, 1959.

Schulman, Sarah. *The Gentrification of the Mind: Witness to a Lost Imagination*. University of California Press, 2013.

Spring, Justin. *Secret Historian: The Life and Times of Samuel Steward, Professor, Tattoo Artist, and Sexual Renegade*. Farrar, Straus and Giroux, 2010.

White, Edmund. *States of Desire: Travels in Gay America*. Dutton, 1980.

Ghost

Barthes, Roland. *Camera Lucida*. Translated by Richard Howard. Farrar, Straus and Giroux, 1981.

Bersani, Leo. *Is the Rectum a Grave? and Other Essays*. University of Chicago Press, 2009.

Bianchi, Tom. *Fire Island Pines, Polaroids 1975–1983*. Damiani, 2013.

Crimp, Douglas. *Melancholia and Moralism: Essays on AIDS and Queer Politics*. MIT Press, 2004.

Dean, Tim, Steven Ruszczycky, and David Squires, editors. *Porn Archives*. Duke University Press, 2014.

Guadagnino, Luca, director. *Call Me by Your Name*. Sony Pictures Classics, 2017.

Guibert, Hervé. *Ghost Image*. Translated by Robert Bononno. University of Chicago Press, 2014.

Howard, Billy. *Epitaphs for the Living: Words and Images in the Time of AIDS*. Southern Methodist University Press, 1989.

Humphreys, Laud. *Tearoom Trade: Impersonal Sex in Public Places*. Duckworth, 1970.

Koestenbaum, Wayne. "The Porn Punctum." In *Figure It Out: Essays*. Soft Skull Press, 2020.

Love, Heather. *Feeling Backward: Loss and the Politics of Queer History*. Harvard University Press, 2007.

Manseau, Peter. "How We Find Our Way to the Dead." *The New York Times*, October 28, 2017.

Muñoz, José Esteban. *Cruising Utopia: The Then and There of Queer Futurity*. New York University Press, 2009.

Nealon, Christopher. *Foundlings: Lesbian and Gay Historical Emotion Before Stonewall*. Duke University Press, 2001.

Powell, Jessica. "The Problem with Banning Pornography on Tumblr." *The New York Times*, December 6, 2018.

Reynolds, Daniel. "Tumblr's Ban on Adult Content Alarms LGBTQ Twitter." *The Advocate*, December 3, 2018.

Rosenberg, Eli. "Tumblr's Nudity Ban Removes One of the Last Major Refuges for Pornography on Social Media." *The Washington Post*, December 3, 2018.

Sontag, Susan. *On Photography*. Farrar, Straus and Giroux, 1977.

Amateur

Alloway, Lawrence. "Rauschenberg's Development." In *Robert Rauschenberg*, edited by Walter Hopps. National Collection of Fine Arts, 1976.

Barthes, Roland. *A Lover's Discourse: Fragments*. Translated by Richard Howard. Farrar, Straus and Giroux, 1978.

CAConrad. *While Standing in Line for Death*. Wave Books, 2017.

Cage, John. "On Robert Rauschenberg, Artist, and His Work." In *Silence: Lectures and Writings*. Wesleyan University Press, 1961.

Cage, John, and Merce Cunningham. *Love, Icebox: Letters from John Cage to Merce Cunningham*. John Cage Trust, 2019.

Dickerman, Leah, and Achim Borchardt-Hume, editors. *Robert Rauschenberg*. Museum of Modern Art, 2016.

Giorno, John. *Great Demon Kings: A Memoir of Poetry, Sex, Art, Death, and Enlightenment*. Farrar, Straus and Giroux, 2020.

Glück, Robert. "Writers Are Liars." In *Communal Nude: Collected Essays*. Semiotext(e), 2016.

Goldberg, Ariel. *The Estrangement Principle*. Nightboat, 2016.

Katz, Jonathan. "The Art of Code: Jasper Johns & Robert Rauschenberg." In *Significant Others: Creativity and Intimate Partnership*. Thames and Hudson, 1993.

Katz, Jonathan, and David C. Ward. *Hide/Seek: Difference and Desire in American Portraiture*. Smithsonian Books, 2010.

LeSueur, Joe. *Digressions on Some Poems by Frank O'Hara*. Farrar, Straus and Giroux, 2003.

McDowell, Tara. *The Householders: Robert Duncan and Jess*. MIT Press, 2019.

Miller, D. A. *Bringing Out Roland Barthes*. University of California Press, 1992.

Molesworth, Helen. *Leap Before You Look: Black Mountain College 1933–1957*. Yale University Press, 2015.

Nelson, Maggie. *Women, the New York School, and Other True Abstractions*. University of Iowa Press, 2007.

O'Hara, Frank. *In Memory of My Feelings*. Museum of Modern Art, 1967.

Rauschenberg, Robert. *Thirty-Four Illustrations for Dante's* Inferno. Museum of Modern Art, 2017.

Rivkin, Joshua. *Chalk: The Art and Erasure of Cy Twombly*. Melville House, 2017.

Schimmel, Paul, editor. *Robert Rauschenberg: Combines*. Museum of Contemporary Art, 2005.

Sedgwick, Eve Kosofsky. *Epistemology of the Closet*. University of California Press, 1990.

Small, Zachary. "Why Can't the Art World Embrace Robert Rauschenberg's Queer Community?" *Artsy*, May 19, 2017.

Solomon, Deborah. "Jasper Johns Still Doesn't Want to Explain His Art." *The New York Times*, February 7, 2018.

Tomkins, Calvin. *Off the Wall: A Portrait of Robert Rauschenberg*. Doubleday, 1980.

Guest

Dean, Tim. *Unlimited Intimacy: Reflections on the Culture of Barebacking*. University of Chicago Press, 2009.

Delany, Samuel R. *Times Square Red, Times Square Blue*. New York University Press, 1999.

Derrida, Jacques. *Of Hospitality: Anne Dufourmantelle Invites Jacques Derrida to Respond*. Translated by Rachel Bowlby. Stanford University Press, 2000.

Elliott, Stephan, director. *The Adventures of Priscilla, Queen of the Desert*. Gramercy Pictures, 1994.

Grimm, Jacob, and Wilhelm Grimm. *The Original Folk and Fairy Tales of the Brothers Grimm: The Complete First Edition*, edited and translated by Jack Zipes. Princeton University Press, 2014.

Hyde, Lewis. *The Gift: Imagination and the Erotic Life of Property*. Random House, 1983.

López, Matthew. *The Inheritance*. Faber and Faber, 2018.

Mirkin, David, director. *Romy and Michele's High School Reunion*. Touchstone Pictures, 1997.

Perrault, Charles. *The Complete Fairy Tales*. Translated by Christopher Betts. Oxford University Press, 2009.

Peacock

Earnest, Jarrett, editor. *The Young and Evil: Queer Modernism in New York, 1930–1955*. David Zwirner Books, 2019.

Ellenzweig, Allen. *George Platt Lynes: The Daring Eye*. Oxford University Press, 2021.

Ellenzweig, Allen. *The Homosexual Photograph: Male Images*

from Durieu/Delacroix to Mapplethorpe. Columbia University Press, 2012.

Gabbert, Elisa. "A Complicating Energy: Notes on a Year Without Strangers." *Harper's Magazine*, July 2021.

Haas, Steven, editor. *George Platt Lynes: The Male Nudes*. Rizzoli, 2011.

Harder, Matthias, and Max Scheler, editors. *The Essential Herbert List: Photographs 1930–1972*. Schirmer/Mosel, 2008.

Jones, William E. *True Homosexual Experiences: Boyd McDonald and* Straight to Hell. We Heard You Like Books, 2016.

Leddick, David. *Naked Men: Pioneering Male Nudes 1935–1955*. Universe Publishing, 1997.

Mack, David. "It's Your Birthday. Bring on the Nudes." *The New York Times*, August 18, 2023.

Malanga, Gerard, editor. *Scopophilia: The Love of Looking*. St. James Press, 1985.

Mann, Thomas. *Death in Venice*. Translated by Michael Henry Heim. Ecco, 2004.

McDonald, Boyd, editor. *Meat: How Men Look, Act, Walk, Talk, Dress, Undress, Taste & Smell. True Homosexual Experiences from S.T.H. Vol 1*. Gay Sunshine Press, 1981.

Merrill, James. *The Changing Light at Sandover*. Atheneum, 1982.

Mishima, Yukio. "The Peacocks." In *Voices of the Fallen Heroes and Other Stories*, edited by Stephen Dodd. Translated by Juliet Winters Carpenter. Vintage, 2025.

Morrison, Toni. *Song of Solomon*. Alfred A. Knopf, 1977.

Nabokov, Vladimir. *The Annotated Lolita*, edited by Alfred Appel, Jr. McGraw-Hill, 1970.

Nathan, Patrick. *Image Control: Art, Fascism, and the Right to Resist*. Counterpoint, 2021.

Ruszczycky, Steven. *Vulgar Genres: Gay Pornographic Writing and Contemporary Fiction*. University of Chicago Press, 2021.

Ryan, Michael J. *A Taste for the Beautiful: The Evolution of Attraction*. Princeton University Press, 2018.

Sawyer, Drew, and Laurie Simmons, editors. *Jimmy DeSana: Submission*. DelMonico Books, 2022.

Sedgwick, Eve Kosofsky. "Shame, Theatricality, and Queer

Performativity: Henry James's *The Art of the Novel*." In *Touching Feeling: Affect, Pedagogy, Performativity*. Duke University Press, 2002.

Stadler, Matthew. *Allan Stein*. Grove Press, 1999.

Stadler, Matthew. "Keeping Secrets: NAMBLA, the Idealization of Children, and the Contradictions of Gay Politics." *The Stranger*, March 20, 1997.

Stadler, Matthew. *The Sex Offender*. HarperCollins, 1994.

Steward, Samuel M. *Bad Boys and Tough Tattoos: A Social History of the Tattoo with Gangs, Sailors, and Street-Corner Punks, 1950–1965*. Routledge, 1990.

Wilde, Oscar. *Salome: A Tragedy in One Act*. Translated by Lord Alfred Douglas. Dover, 1967.

Wilde, Oscar. *The Uncensored Picture of Dorian Gray*, edited by Nicholas Frankel. Belknap Press, 2011.

Scout

Alighieri, Dante. *Purgatorio*. Translated by Mary Jo Bang. Graywolf Press, 2021.

Amin, Kadji. *Disturbing Attachments: Genet, Modern Pederasty, and Queer History*. Duke University Press, 2017.

Aster, Ari, director. *Hereditary*. A24, 2018.

Atherton Lin, Jeremy. *Gay Bar: Why We Went Out*. Little, Brown, 2021.

Barolini, Teodolinda. *Digital Dante: Commento Baroliniano*. Columbia University Libraries, 2019.

Bollas, Christopher. "Cruising in the Homosexual Arena." In *Becoming a Character: Psychoanalysis and Self Experience*. Hill and Wang, 1992.

Bradway, Tyler, and Elizabeth Freeman, editors. *Queer Kinship: Race, Sex, Belonging, Form*. Duke University Press, 2022.

Chauncey, William. *Gay New York: Gender, Urban Culture, and the Making of the Gay Male World 1890–1940*. Basic Books, 1994.

Coel, Michaela, director. "Ego Death." *I May Destroy You*, episode 12. HBO, 2020.

Earnest, Jarrett. "Tom's Men." *The New York Review of Books*, May 9, 2024.

Fassbinder, Rainer Werner, director. *Querelle*. Gaumont, 1982.
Fischer, Hal. *Gay Semiotics: A Photographic Study of Visual Coding Among Homosexual Men*. NFS Press, 1977.
Friedkin, William, director. *Cruising*. United Artists, 1980.
Garnett, Jean. "There I Almost Am: On Envy and Twinship." *The Yale Review*, May 19, 2021.
Genet, Jean. *Querelle*. Translated by Anselm Hollo. Grove Press, 1974.
Greenwell, Garth. "A Moral Education." *The Yale Review*, March 20, 2023.
Greig, James. "Everyone Needs to Grow Up." *Dazed*, March 10, 2023.
Handler, Rachel. "Allow Fiona Apple to Reintroduce Herself." *Vulture*, April 17, 2020.
Kantrowitz, Arnie. "Swastika Toys." In *Leatherfolk: Radical Sex, People, Politics, and Practice*, edited by Mark Thompson. Daedalus, 1991.
Kierkegaard, Søren. *The Sickness unto Death*. Translated by Alastair Hannay. Penguin Books, 1989.
Lorde, Audre. "The Uses of Anger: Women Responding to Racism." In *Sister Outsider: Essays and Speeches*. Crossing Press, 1984.
Marenghi, Catherine. *Glad Farm*. Tate, 2016.
Milton, Adrian. *Lavender Light: Daily Meditations for Gay Men in Recovery*. Perigee, 1995.
Ngai, Sianne. *Ugly Feelings*. Harvard University Press, 2005.
Rapper, Irving, director. *Now, Voyager*. Warner Bros., 1942.
Stein, David. "S/M's Copernican Revolution: From a Closed World to the Infinite Universe." In *Leatherfolk: Radical Sex, People, Politics, and Practice*, edited by Mark Thompson. Daedalus, 1991.
Steward, Samuel M. "Dr. Kinsey Takes a Peek at S/M: A Reminiscence." In *Leatherfolk: Radical Sex, People, Politics, and Practice*, edited by Mark Thompson. Daedalus, 1991.
Thompson, Mark. Introduction to *Leatherfolk: Radical Sex, People, Politics, and Practice*, edited by Mark Thompson. Daedalus, 1991.

Tilsen, Julie. "Is That Unethical or Just Queer? An Ethical Stance for a Queered Practice." In *Queering Your Therapy Practice: Queer Theory, Narrative Therapy, and Imagining New Identities*. Routledge, 2021.

Tucker, Scott. "The Hanged Man." In *Leatherfolk: Radical Sex, People, Politics, and Practice*, edited by Mark Thompson. Daedalus, 1991.

von Praunheim, Rosa, director. *It Is Not the Homosexual Who Is Perverse, but the Society in Which He Lives*. Bavaria Film, 1971.

White, Edmund. "Los Angeles: A Haven for Hedonists." In *States of Desire: Travels in Gay America*. Dutton, 1980.

Boy

All the Tropes. "Creepy Uncle." www.allthetropes.org/wiki/Creepy_Uncle. Accessed November 18, 2024.

All the Tropes. "Evil Uncle." www.allthetropes.org/wiki/Evil_Uncle. Accessed November 18, 2024.

All the Tropes. "Nephewism." www.allthetropes.org/wiki/Nephewism. Accessed November 18, 2024.

Barry, Rick. *His Willing Nephew*. Hardboy Series, 1975.

Barthes, Roland. *The Pleasure of the Text*. Translated by Richard Miller. Farrar, Straus and Giroux, 1975.

Bartlett, Neil. *Ready to Catch Him Should He Fall*. Serpent's Tail, 1990.

Berns, Mike. *His Uncle's Boy*. Wildboys Collection, 1975.

Bettelheim, Bruno. *The Uses of Enchantment: The Meaning and Importance of Fairy Tales*. Alfred A. Knopf, 1976.

Bronski, Michael. "A Dream Is a Wish Your Heart Makes: Notes on the Materialization of Sexual Fantasy." In *Leatherfolk: Radical Sex, People, Politics, and Practice*, edited by Mark Thompson. Daedalus, 1991.

Brooke, Jocelyn. *The Scapegoat*. Bodley Head, 1948.

Bulfinch, Thomas. *Myths of Greece and Rome*. Viking, 1979.

Carney, William. *The Real Thing*. G. P. Putnam's Sons, 1968.

Dickson, Jack. *Oddfellows*. Millivres Books, 1997.

Ellis, Cliff. *The Fist-Fits*. Numbers Paperback Library, 1978.

FetLife. "Fetishes with 'Uncle.'" www.fetlife.com/search/fetishes?q=uncle. Accessed November 18, 2024.

Greenberg, Arielle. *Superfreaks: Kink, Pleasure, and the Pursuit of Happiness*. Beacon Press, 2023.

Hammers, Corie. "Reworking Trauma Through BDSM." *Signs: Journal of Women in Culture and Society* 44, no. 2 (2019): 491–514.

Harris, Mark. "Yes, These Gays Are Trying to Murder You." *The New York Times*, August 17, 2023.

Hartley, John. *Uncles & Lovers*. Surey Books, 1982.

Hopcke, Robert H. "S/M and the Psychology of Gay Male Initiation: An Archetypal Perspective." In *Leatherfolk: Radical Sex, People, Politics, and Practice*, edited by Mark Thompson. Daedalus, 1991.

Hyde, Lewis. *Trickster Makes This World: Mischief, Myth, and Art*. Farrar, Straus and Giroux, 1998.

Kincaid, Tim, director. *Joe Gage's Sex Files Vol #2: Uncle Pruitt Taught Me How to Do It*. MSR Blue Label, 2003.

Kramer, Larry. *Faggots*. Random House, 1978.

Lennox, Michael. *Llewellyn's Complete Dictionary of Dreams*. Llewellyn, 2015.

Mars-Jones, Adam. *Box Hill*. Fitzcarraldo Editions, 2020.

Melville, Herman. *Moby-Dick; or, The Whale*. Harper, 1851.

Mitchell, Larry. *The Faggots & Their Friends Between Revolutions*. Calamus Books, 1977.

Monette, Paul. *Halfway Home*. Crown, 1991.

Pepper, Peter. *Good Head, Uncle!* Surree Stud Series, 1975.

Plato. *Plato's Erotic Dialogues: The* Symposium *and the* Phaedrus. Translated by William S. Cobb. State University of New York Press, 1993.

Plutarch. *Moralia, Volume I*. Translated by Frank Cole Babbitt. Harvard University Press, 1927.

Ross, Johnny. *Horny Chicken Nephew*. Greenleaf Classics, 1985.

Saketopoulou, Avgi. *Sexuality Beyond Consent: Risk, Race, Traumatophilia*. New York University Press, 2023.

SayUncle. "Family Dick." www.sayuncle.com/series/familydick. Accessed November 18, 2024.

Shewey, Don. “Daddy/Boy: Love, Power, and Masculinity.” www.donshewey.com/sex_articles/daddy-boy.html. Accessed November 18, 2024.

Silva, Tony. *Daddies of a Different Kind: Sex and Romance Between Older and Younger Adult Gay Men*. New York University Press, 2023.

Simpson, William Kelly, editor. *The Literature of Ancient Egypt: An Anthology of Stories, Instructions, Stelae, Autobiographies, and Poetry*. 3rd edition. Yale University Press, 2003.

Sinfield, Alan. *On Sexuality and Power*. Columbia University Press, 2004.

Sterling, Matt, director. *Spring Break*. Falcon Studios, 1986.

Townsend, Larry. *Run, Little Leather Boy*. The Other Traveller, 1971.

Wheeler, Jonah. Text message to author, March 26, 2025.

White, Edmund. *The Farewell Symphony*. Alfred A. Knopf, 1997.

White, Mike, director. “Arrivederci.” *The White Lotus*, season 2, episode 7. HBO, 2022.

White, Mike, director. “Recentering.” *The White Lotus*, season 1, episode 4. HBO, 2021.

Whitmore, George. *Nebraska*. Grove Press, 1987.

Wilson, George. *Hard Like Uncle*. Wildboys Collection, 1976.

Uncle

Cleary, Gregory. “St. Roch.” *The Catholic Encyclopedia*, volume 13. Robert Appleton Company, 1912.

Gabbert, Elisa. “The Little Room (or, The Unreality of Memory).” In *The Unreality of Memory*. Farrar, Straus and Giroux, 2020.

Haraway, Donna J. “Training in the Contact Zone: Power, Play, and Invention in the Sport of Agility.” In *When Species Meet*. University of Minnesota Press, 2007.

Ladd, Drew John. *Wolfsong Beloved*. Self-published, 2021.

Myles, Eileen. *Afterglow (a dog memoir)*. Grove, 2017.

Strand Book Store. “Eileen Myles | Afterglow.” YouTube, September 15, 2017. www.youtube.com/watch?v=WqN6seTLU48.

White, Edmund. *Nocturnes for the King of Naples*. St. Martin’s, 1978.

© Jack Manning

Steven Pfau is a writer and editor based in Los Angeles. He graduated from the University of Idaho's MFA program, and his work has appeared in *DIAGRAM*, *Guernica*, *The Iowa Review*, *The Offing*, *Passages North*, and other publications.